THE
PAUL HAMLYN
LIBRARY

DONATED BY
THE PAUL HAMLYN
FOUNDATION
TO THE
BRITISH MUSEUM

opened December 2000

THE STRINGS ARE FALSE

Books by Louis MacNeice

COLLECTED POEMS
Edited by E. R. Dodds

SELECTED POEMS
Edited by Michael Longley

THE STRINGS ARE FALSE
An Unfinished Autobiography

LETTERS FROM ICELAND
With W. H. Auden

Of related interest

LOUIS MACNEICE
A biography
by Jon Stallworhy

LOUIS MACNEICE
A critical study
by Edna Longley

THE STRINGS ARE FALSE

An Unfinished Autobiography

by

LOUIS MacNEICE

faber and faber

LONDON · BOSTON

First published in Great Britain in 1965
by Faber and Faber Limited
3 Queen Square London WCIN 3AU
Paperback edition first published in 1982
Reissued in 1996

Printed in England by Clays Ltd, St Ives plc

All rights reserved

© 1965 by the executors of Louis MacNeice

*This book is sold subject to the condition that it shall not, by way of trade
or otherwise, be lent, resold, hired out or otherwise circulated without the
publisher's prior consent in any form of binding or cover other than that
in which it is published and without a similar condition including
this condition being imposed on the subsequent purchaser*

A CIP record for this book
is available from the British Library

ISBN 0–571–11832–1

2 4 6 8 10 9 7 5 3 1

CONTENTS

EDITOR'S PREFACE

I think it was in 1941, at a time when London was under bombardment, that Louis MacNeice, who was working there, came down to Oxford to see me and gave me a manuscript, which I was to put away in a safe place without reading it. It was, he said, a piece of autobiographical writing which he could not publish at present but hoped to use at some later date. I obeyed his injunction. Louis never mentioned the manuscript again, and as the years passed I forgot about it. It was only after his sudden death in September 1963 that I fished it out of its drawer and examined it. It proved to contain chapters i to xxxii of the present book. The first three chapters are in the abbreviated script, with many head-and-tail contractions, which Louis habitually used for his rough drafts and private notes; the rest is in clear and easily legible longhand, except for some typed paragraphs in the Oxford chapters which seem to be taken from the text of a lecture given in 1939 or 1940 to an American audience. This manuscript I shall call B. It carries no title, but it was accompanied by a typescript of chapter xxxii, evidently designed for separate publication in some journal, which bears the superscription 'A Visit to Spain: Easter 1936 (excerpted from a book, now in preparation, entitled *The Strings are False*)'. I have adopted this title, which is the only one known to me.

Subsequently another manuscript version of the same book came into my hands as Literary Executor. It is physically in two parts. The first part, A¹, is a folio notebook containing a mutilated fragment of a draft introduction, not reproduced in B, and drafts (in a different sequence) for what appears in B and in the present volume as chapters iv to ix. It also contains a variant draft for B's chapter i, with a pencil note '? Beginning'; this seems from internal evidence to have been written at Cornell in February or March 1940. The second part, A², is a continuation of A¹, written–often in abbreviated script–on loose sheets, not numbered, one or two of which appear to be missing; it contains rough drafts of the present chapters x to xxxviii. Marginal notes by Louis indicate possible addenda, some of which are introduced in B. For chapters xxxiii to xxxviii A² is my sole source.

The order of composition of these various drafts is fairly clear: first A¹ (written in part early in 1940) and A² as far as the end of the present chapter xxxii; then B (of which the first three chapters were written on shipboard in December 1940); finally chapters xxxiii to xxxviii in A². These last chapters, which cover the gap between 1936 and 1940, would seem to have been composed as an after-thought. Manuscript B is designed to be self-complete without them; moreover, A² has at the end of chapter xxxii a note 'Link up', and at the end of chapter xxxviii a similar note 'Link up – Samaria¹ – Cornell – Airlines etc. etc., ending in Other Man in hospital.' This suggests that Louis's final intention may have been to transfer the substance of chapters i and ii (which were still in rough draft) from the beginning of the book to their chronological place at the end, either omitting chapter iii or perhaps using part of it as an introduc-tion. But that plan would have involved considerable rewriting, which was never done. I have accordingly left chapters i to iii where they stand in B. They introduce Louis at a pause in his life, isolated in a temporary limbo between two worlds, looking back over his past and forward to a future which for him as for all British subjects was in 1940 dark and uncertain.

Comparison of manuscript B with the earlier draft reveals how much trouble Louis took over the writing of this book. Almost every paragraph has been retouched if not completely rewritten: super-fluous words have been eliminated, epigrams sharpened to a finer point, the imagery made more concrete and more vivid. Much new material has been added and some of the old has been left out. The omissions are for the most part no great loss, but there are excep-tions to this. Here and there, especially in the Birmingham chapters, B omits a revealing incident or comment which there is now no reason to suppress, or shortens an amusing description to its detri-ment. I have with some hesitation included a few such passages in the present text rather than lose them altogether, placing them in square brackets to distinguish them from the text of B. Otherwise I have reproduced B as it stands, save for the silent correction of a few

¹ The ship on which Louis sailed both to and from America in 1940.

trivial factual errors and the very occasional omission of a phrase or a sentence which might cause unintended pain to humble persons still living;[1] for advice on these matters, and for footnotes signed 'E.N.', I am indebted to Louis's sister, Lady Nicholson.

Chapters i to iii and xxxiii to xxxviii presented problems of a different nature. In the first place, they are hard to read (the contractions are often ambiguous). But with the help of Louis's secretary, Miss Jenny Sheppard (Mrs. Clement), of Lady Nicholson, and of the specially skilled typist placed at my disposal by Messrs. Faber and Faber, I have (I think) made out almost everything: only a very few words have had to be abandoned as undecipherable; in a few others the reading is uncertain. Secondly, these parts of the book are unrevised. Had Louis subjected them to the same drastic revision as the rest, he would have polished the style; he would have made additions (a few of which are indicated by marginal scribbles in A[2]); and he would probably have eliminated some of the 'reportage', e.g. in the American chapters and in the disproportionately long account of his visit to Barcelona during the Spanish Civil War. As it is, these chapters must be accepted for what they are, an unpruned first draft. The only liberty I have taken with them is the omission of a couple of irrelevant paragraphs, of no autobiographical interest, which obviously fail to 'come off'; I feel pretty sure that Louis, always a severe critic of his own writing, would not have let them stand.

I shall be asked why Louis never published, or even completed, a book which he had contracted to write[2] and on which he had expended so much pains. I do not know the full answer, but from my recollection of what he told me in 1941 it seems to me likely that he decided against publication during the lifetimes of his father and stepmother.[3] His father died in 1942; but his stepmother survived until 1956, and it appears that by then he had plans for a different

[1] In order to avoid such offence Louis used pseudonyms (which I have retained) for certain of the characters in his story. His treatment of public figures is another matter: being public, they were fair game; he did not provide them with masks, and I have not attempted to soften his comments on them.
[2] In a contract dated November 15th, 1939, he undertook to deliver to Messrs. Faber and Faber by August 1st, 1940, the manuscript of 'an autobiographical work'.
[3] The real strength and warmth of Louis's feeling for his father, deeper than all

sort of autobiography constructed on different lines. In 1957 he contracted with Messrs. Faber and Faber to write a book provisionally entitled *Countries in the Air*. This was to be at once a new kind of autobiography and a new kind of travel book: it was to reflect the interaction between what the landscape brings to the traveller and what the traveller brings to the landscape. 'My purpose in this book', said Louis, 'is to explore, in the light and shade of my own experience, the corroborations and refutals of my myths, the frustrations and illuminations I have found in various travels.'

This ambitious project never got far. All that remains of it is a pencil draft–full of the usual contractions–of the first two chapters, which carry the story of Louis's travels down to his first visit to Paris in 1927. I have transcribed this fragment and printed it as an appendix under the title 'Landscapes of Childhood and Youth', omitting only some preliminary remarks about travel in general. The amount of overlap with *The Strings are False* is less than might have been expected; and where it occurs I have thought that some readers may be interested in observing the changed light under which certain experiences are presented, with less in the way of verbal fireworks but sometimes, perhaps, in a truer perspective and with a better eye to the balance of the picture.

It remains to add that despite (or rather, because of?) his failure to complete either *The Strings are False* or *Countries in the Air* Louis's childhood and youth continued to haunt him. In a paper entitled 'When I was Twenty-one', published in *The Saturday Book* (1961), Louis described once again the Oxford of his undergraduate days; and the subject of his last broadcast talk, delivered only a few weeks before his death, was his recollections of life in the rectory at Carrickfergus. Neither of these adds anything substantial to what appears in the present book, but they illustrate his continu-

surface irritations, comes out less clearly in *The Strings are False* than in the moving poem on his father's funeral, published as section vii of 'The Kingdom' (*Springboard*, p. 52), where he celebrates him as

> courteous
> And lyrical and strong and kind and truthful,
> A generous puritan, above whose dust
> About this time of year the spendthrift plants
> Will toss their trumpets heralding a life
> That shows itself in time but remains timeless
> As is the heart of music.

Cf. also 'Landscapes of Childhood and Youth', p. 233.

ing preoccupation with his own past, with memories that 'flitter and champ in a dark cupboard';[1] this emerges repeatedly in his poems,[2] and amounted almost to an obsession. As he expressed it in one of the rough drafts in manuscript A, 'I trail too many of these barren facts behind me. One must either forget them or arrange them in some kind of order.' He never succeeded in forgetting them. How far he succeeded in giving them what he meant by 'order'—which is more than sequence—I must leave the reader of this book to judge.

One thing, however, needs to be said. Whether because he had not yet come to terms with his past or because he was performing a necessary act of catharsis, in *The Strings are False* Louis did less than justice to his own personality: he has conveyed far too little of the rich flow of fun and fantasy, the mercurial gaiety, the warm vitality and love of life which endeared him to the friends of his early days. For the sake of righting the balance, as well as for their intrinsic charm, I am grateful for permission to include as an appendix the memories of one such friend, Mr. John Hilton, which are buttressed by the secure evidence of contemporary letters.

January 1965   E. R. DODDS

[1] *Ten Burnt Offerings*, p. 67.
[2] Incidents, images and motifs drawn from his early experience recur in his poems from first to last. I have called attention in footnotes to some of the more obvious examples.

I

So what? This modern equivalent of Pilate's 'What is truth?' comes often now to our lips and only too patly, we too being much of the time cynical and with as good reason as any old procurator, tired, bored with the details of Roman bureaucracy, and the graft of Greek officials, a vista of desert studded to the horizon with pyramids of privilege apart from which there are only nomads who have little in their packs, next to nothing in their eyes. Thus here I am now on a boat going back to a war and my feelings are too mixt to disentangle. The passengers' faces are settled in gloom and I have plenty of reason to be gloomy too, being a mere nomad who has lost his tent.

Yet I am not so gloomy as I might be. I am going back to a past which is not there (that England—or Europe for that matter—will never be the same again is already a cliché) but, though that past had its charm, I am glad to see it evaporate. Leaving America, which for me is mythical future, I am going over to somewhere without tenses ('Time,' a Scotsman is saying at my elbow, 'doesn't mean a thing to me'; 'There's no hurry,' they are saying, thinking of this voyage's uncertainty), returning somewhere I belong but have not, as it now is, been. The world for me has become inverted; America is the known and England the unknown.

And now, only a little later, the passengers' faces are no longer gloomy because they are different passengers. The boat is suddenly swarming with seamen and Canadian airmen, queuing up for beers, laughing, the airmen terribly young. Who have come on board for nowhere for, as time has no more tenses, so places have no longer names. But where are the people of the day before yesterday, the Americans with whom I felt at home, who are not at war, whose present tense is a continent wide, who can live and let live for a few months longer? They are back there just as they were. Just as they were the day before yesterday. But for me the day before yesterday is smoke gone up the chimney and even the chimney is gone. There is no more fireplace and no more fuel, and finally there's no hurry.

It was on this same boat I came over in January. Now that there is no hurry I can look back on it as if it were mounted under glass; although at the time I was tense, anxious, muddled, expecting the moon, guilty of the war, so full and so empty of myself. The Mersey had been mined which held us up two days. Freighters dingy in their war paint dozed on the river, factory chimneys were camouflaged in sombre harlequin patterns, the sun was fuzzy in the mist, a crowd of Jewish refugees ran after their oddments of baggage like hens running after ducklings. But the baggage had a will of its own, what was meant for the cabins dived into the hold leaving its owners leaning over railings, shrill at this new evidence of the great anti-Jewish conspiracy. And all of us shuffled our feet, took a few turns on the deck, plucked at our lips or our noses, thought 'Why don't we start?' and some of us said it. 'Let the passengers take her out,' said the crew who were nonchalantly leaning on the railings of the deck.

I shared a cabin with a young man from Winnipeg who had rosy cheeks (he was a farmer) but had a nervousness, an anxiety to make friends, a general frailty which were not a farmer's at all. When I first met him in the cabin he showed me his collection of coins, stammering badly, then went on to do card-tricks. (Now in a different cabin but in the same small portion of the same boat I am being interrupted in my writing by a drunken old Irishman with a bogtrotter's face—he has got through two bottles of whisky—who leans over me, spittle falling from his mouth, which has only teeth on one side of it, on to his chin and from his bristly chin on to the paper, and runs his finger down a paragraph; 'Ye're a decent young man,' he says to me, 'ye're deep as hell's gates but grammar is grammar. Where is your full stops? Where is your apostrophe s's? I'm an old dumb Irishman bedamn but I know me apostrophe s's.')

Winnipeg and I shared a table for meals with a middleaged Catalan couple from Barcelona, travelling on diplomatic passports and bound for Columbia, and a young German Jewish refugee whose wife was Swiss; above our table was a print of Whistler's mother. The young German Jew was lean, had thick rather sensual

18

lips and anxious prominent eyes which twinkled—perhaps sadisti-cally, perhaps in self-defence – when he talked about his time in the concentration camp; his wife who was plump and blonde, with vermilion nails, always waited for him to speak, usually expostulated afterwards. The Spanish couple had left Barcelona the night before the Fascists entered, had lost all their property and were without word of their friends but remained groomed and ebullient, flirting with each other the whole way over the Atlantic. The husband who had friendly pea-soupy eyes was like a rather puffy but efficient schoolboy, the kind who wears two or three pens and pencils clipped on the upper outside pocket of his coat; the wife had dyed blonde hair, rouge, ear-rings, a carillon of laughter. Both of them made jokes to the Scottish waiter about seasickness, women and torpedoes, Winnipeg timidly throwing in his chestnut on the first subject—'Six meals a day, three up and three down'; the German Jew and his wife always had to have these jokes explained to them. The waiter, who was tall, debonair and very un-Scottish in manner, responded to the Spanish charm, told us that his little girl was learning ballet dancing, that his wife was six foot one and had been a swimming instructress on board the Queen Mary, and that on this boat he slept next to the ammunition store; 'Life is very sweet,' he said.

There were on board about one hundred refugees from Central Europe. Most of them had spent a year in England. England was fine, they said, but the girls cost too much. They were mostly optimistic about their prospects in America, kept asking me if such and such a city was *good*, i.e. good for their particular line of business. The butt of this group was called Butcher by the others. Because he was a butcher and could not conceivably have been anything else. He had a solid, loud body, a blunt red face, coarse hair, thick lips, enormous hands, the charm of brute self-confidence. His English was very bad—never tried to learn anything from books, he proudly explained—but he could say 'Blimey' in perfect cockney. He had been in London a year, working in a big butcher's shop in Whitechapel from 4.15 in the morning till 6.00 in the evening for £2 10s. a week; had had a room in Aldgate for ten shillings, spent a pound a week on food, had enough left over to watch football matches and take a girl to the pictures. Every match Arsenal plays, he told me, is an international. He and I played pingpong together but he was indignant that I did not know the difference between Irish sausage and English sausage. I found him fascinating like some archaic Rip Van Winkle god who has just woken up and goes shuffling, snuffling for his burnt offerings and thighbones to an altar which has long been a ruin. He was sure he would make good in the States as a butcher; kept showing his biceps.

An Atlantic crossing is always an interregnum and this one in January 1940 was more so than most. I walked up and down the deck with the Spaniard, enjoying the submersion of myself and my problems, listening with pleasure to him generalising just as I expected, on politics or racial characteristics; he could not, he told me, understand the Englishman's attitude to sex–the Englishman prefers a cup of whisky. So we walked up and down making believe to be friends and I was sillily flattered towards the end of the voyage when, 'I hope you don't mind,' he said with a smile of apology, 'I think you are perhaps a little red.'

In the evenings they played Keno in the lounge, directed by the purser, who like all ship's pursers had to be facetious. (And the magazine *Punch* too still goes on the same.) *Kelly's Eye, Number One.* And the tipsy refugees join in–*Shake-a the bag.* The boat was a babel of people addressing each other in the wrong languages. Thus one evening in a silence, a tall Russian ballet dancer with a *fin de siècle* air, suddenly announced portentously '*Ich muss essen viel Fleisch*'. I did not like the look of him but I liked his remark; it carried the same deeprooted faith as Butcher's remarks, the ultimate faith that oneself is of ultimate importance and it was all the more impressive for being bad German. Like an illiterate making his mark on some finally binding document.

In such an interregnum it is easier to like people without an ulterior motive. I found myself even liking them because, as far as I was concerned, they would cease to exist once the voyage was over, and because conversation remained casual. Only one day the Catalan lady flared up, said to me, 'Do you know what they say now in Spain? *A bajo la inteligencia*', and at once I thought to myself–that goes for more than Spain. Knowing the temptations inside me to abandon reason because of the failures and follies of rationalists, and because of the political chaos to give up the quest for political or social faith. Or, in other words, to have an interregnum for ever.

For five months I had been tormented by the ethical problems of the war. In Ireland most people said to me 'What is it to you?' while many of my friends in England took the line it was just power politics. Why Poland of all places? And then there was India. I had decided, however, that any choice now was a choice of evils and that it was clear which was the lesser. But it is hard to risk your life for a Lesser Evil on the off-chance of some entirely problematical betterment for most likely a mere minority in a dubious and dirty future. I felt that I was not justified in supporting the war verbally unless I were prepared to suffer from it in the way that the un-privileged must suffer. But I was not yet prepared to do this, so I had made use of certain of my privileges to escape for a little to America. I had an especial reason for wanting to return to America,[1] but apart from that I thought I could think things out there, get myself clear before I went back into the maelstrom. Clarification—it may be too much to demand of most people but a writer must demand it of himself.

On the day we landed in New York Winnipeg had put an extra load of brilliantine on his hair and the refugees were crowding the deck to watch the towers of Manhattan—a cluster of mad aspirations, a weight of concrete plumped on the lid of Europe to keep the bad dreams down. Only the Catalan said to me: 'That is not my idea of a city.' There was ice around the quays, the air was sharp on the nose, the sky was a candid blue like the eyes of a frigid woman. I went down the gangway to meet a nine months' longing.

Our life being so episodic we are always wanting to hitch our wagons to stars. Which cannot be done. This romantic self-indulgence is in fact a self-abdication, and the Christian paradox—Whoso saveth his life shall lose it—still holds good, in politics and social life, in art, in personal relationships. Born in the epoch of the crooked Gods—*al tempo degli Dei falsi e bugiardi*—our logical con-clusion, if we thought those gods supreme, would be nihilism. And many of us admit that they are supreme but, the flesh being too weak for nihilism, we try to isolate something in our lives and blow it up to become the whole. Which cannot again be done. But anyhow it need not be done, for those gods are not supreme.

My second night on shore I found myself again on a steamer. Who

[1] See p. 204.

had enjoyed so much and believed in so little, who with pinpricks of malice and minutiae of wit and spasms of song had manœuvred my way to a certain reputation and a comfortable income, I found myself riding to my doom on a steamer that was running amok. Among other steamers that were running amok—the machines at last taking over, the skippers and pilots and engineers ignored—in a boiling yellow incredible sea out of which great pylons stood up like hazards. The steamers were all converging, bound to collide, but it looked as if first we should strike on a pylon. At the last split second our boat swerved clear but I was flung high in the air, caught an upper bar of the pylon, hung there like an ape above the cauldron, was still hanging on when I woke; and I woke exhilarated, happy.

II

I had been in America before, so took for granted many of the things which are strange to newcomers—the *sine qua non* of the nickel in the slot, the odd combinations of foods, a quarter of five instead of a quarter to five, or the way Americans use their knives and forks. I had also come already to distrust the generalisations which the English make about America—that Americans are tough, efficient, quickmoving, that American women are fast, that America has no culture. I was almost inclined—though that would be going too far—to make the opposite generalisations. Look at the typical hardboiled American novel. Is it really hard or is it pulpy, sentimental, at the core? And American efficiency? Look at some of the railways or consider the ratio in so many instances between noise and result, between bustle and actual speed. (For bustle in some quarters is an end in itself, just as the skyscrapers are not so much functional, a saving of good space, as concrete fantasies of power; thus half the offices in the Empire State building have never been rented.) As for the women of New York, they are more outspoken perhaps, but they appear on the whole when it comes to practice less sexy than the women of London, while the college girls are Vestal Virgins compared with their counterparts in England. The English like to think of America in terms of Hollywood, a fairyland of chromium and tricklighting inhabited by beautiful fools whom they can envy for their eroticism and despise for their lack of education. This is nonsense. Intellectually Americans of the top stratum may be less well educated than their counterparts in England, but education pervades further strata than in England; and American students, and ex-students for that matter, have, far more than the English, something which is a prerequisite of education, a keen curiosity about the world.

I spent the Easter semester of 1940 teaching at Cornell University. I was supposed to be teaching Poetry which is in fact unteachable;

for this reason I told them to suspect everything I said. I had too many students—about sixty in each course—and too young; but their saving grace was their lack of selfconsciousness.

'Have you ever written poetry?'

'Oh yes, I wrote a lot of poetry when I was about 16.'

'Why did you do that?'

'Because I was in love with a young lady and I wanted to please my mother.'

'You showed your poems to your mother?'

'Yes, I showed them all to my mother. I wanted her to tell me I would be a great poet.'

The Cornell campus is on top of a steep hill, with a long thin ice-cold lake below it into which run streams through spectacular—or, as Americans say, scenic—gorges; these gorges are used by the students for suicide. The campus is dominated by a brick campanile out of which come chimes in the morning and evening—hymn tunes, Irish and English folksongs and college anthems. Woken by these chimes in the morning I used to feel 'It is like being back at school, though oh so much more comfortable, but the basic fact is the same—a closed community.' The Cornell students made out to be very much *au fait* with current affairs but those affairs were translated into Cornell, became the local business of the student societies and clubs.

I lived in an Institute founded by a millionaire, an engineer who had made his money in gold-mines. He wanted to provide an education free of cost for future engineers who could thus acquire a general culture which he knew himself to lack. So here we had a large house, luxuriously equipped and with an excellent cuisine, in which lived twenty-odd students (by now only about half were engineers) and two or three members of the Faculty; there were several spare rooms in which they put up most of Cornell's distinguished visitors. *What is the purpose of this Association? The purpose of this Association is to further the moral order of the Universe.* This had been the founder's first stipulation. The boys, who were self-governing, had a meeting once a week in which in the light of the cosmic purpose they discussed domestic problems, whether to buy a new electric toaster, whether to censure a boy who had got drunk, or whether to limit the time of telephone calls.

24

The boys came from all over the country and many of them in their vacations had worked on the roads or done other manual jobs. Though without the specialised learning of English students they struck me as having a surprising fund of general information and also a surprising *savoir-faire*. They were nearly all of them isolationist or indeed anti-British, thought of the British as crooks and of the war as an imperialist war. When Harriet Cohen, who was giving a piano recital, stayed in the house and, having told all the boys to call her Harriet, went on to talk British propaganda, the boys were wonderfully polite but I could see them writing her off as a phoney; they remarked afterwards that she could not play the piano.

There was staying in the house a Frenchman whom I shall call André. No one quite knew how he came there; he was doing some research work and giving one course in French. He was goodlooking, with a charming smile, his hair brushed back like Borotra's, in his late 30's, very self-centred. In his room he had placed a large chest of drawers flush along his bed like a rampart so that he slept in a cell; this chest of drawers was one great filing-cabinet; every day he made many cuttings from the newspapers, which he classified meticulously and filed. And he studied the American *Who's Who*, learning by heart little facts about prominent persons; some day he might meet them at a cocktail party and it would help his career if he could say to them, 'Oh yes, in 1932 you were doing so-and-so.' He usually went without a shirt, wearing a thick blue woollen scarf crossed neatly over his chest under a buttoned coat. From March on, though it was still freezing, he began to sunbathe on a balcony, getting his skin gamboge; he sat out there in bathing-drawers and dark glasses, studying his newspaper cuttings, acquiring his tan with a solemn religious ardour. None of this worried the boys, who thought he was very French.

Early in April I flew from New York to Chicago. Spring had not yet come and much of the eastern landscape, now that the snow had gone, was dull and dirty from the train. But from the air it was elegant. Enormous plains of beautifully inlaid rectangles, the grain running different ways, walnut, satinwood or oatcake, the whole of it tortoise-shelled with copses and shadows of clouds; here and there were little lakes nailed down on the top of the ground like strips of canvas; khaki or bile-green rivers; the cities a mere encrustation limpeted on to a sublimely indifferent continent. I ate my breakfast high among the clouds—scrambled eggs and strawberries and cream neatly arranged in rectangular dishes on a snow-white enamel tray—and thought that this is life, forgetting for a couple of hours that the sliding map below me was infested with human beings and that life for human beings has always death at its elbow.

At last spring came—which I had not believed in—and upper New York State went green as England. While the *débâcle* began in Europe. Norway, Holland, Belgium, France. Early in June the students began leaving. Some of the boys and Viktor, a German professor who lived in the house, and André and I went down to Ithaca's Chinese restaurant for a farewell meal. André scrutinised the waitress sadly. 'She has no *seins*,' he said. 'No what?' 'No *seins*,' André explained it with his hands. 'No American women have *seins*. Why is that?' No one could tell him. André held his chopsticks in the air as if he were hypnotised; this question, it seemed, was one of enormous importance.

Then came the College Reunion, swarms of boisterous middle-aged businessmen, wearing the costume of their class, nightshirts or shorts, pierrots or what-have-you, and with babies' hats on their heads that bore the date of their class—Class of 1925, Class of 1911, Class of 1066. As our house had ceased to serve meals, André and Viktor and I used to have breakfast together on a terrace outside a great cafeteria which was thronged with these class reunionists. 'What is this?' André said angrily. 'Have these people no sense? In this hour of France's tragedy . . . they are like children.' It was a time of cantaloupes but André tried a cereal for breakfast. 'What *is* this?' he said. 'It is dog-soup.' And at that moment a dog appeared beside him, a white long-haired long-faced pink-eyed dog of no known breed. 'Yes,' André said. 'It is dog-soup. Soup for degenerate dogs. Look at that dog. He is degenerate.' And so he was.

From the terrace which was lined with geraniums we could see across the lake to the far side of the valley; on some days it looked like Ireland, gave me just enough nostalgia to blend with my mood of abandon. France was collapsing and we could not take it in; why bother? But André bothered, spent his time sending cables to ladies all over Europe—'All is not lost. Courage!' He did not attend

26

to Viktor and me as we gossiped, would abruptly interrupt, look at me piercingly and say in a manner less than half whimsical, more than half pathetic: '*Poète*, why are you doing nothing? You must show us a course, it is your business. *Poète, prends ton luth . . .*' Viktor said to me: 'André is taking it well. He has some kind of humorous philosophy.' '*La fin du monde!*' said André, but still with a sparkle in his eyes. '*La fin du monde! Merde!* There is nothing to be done now,' he went on, 'but to form a new society, an *anarchiste* society. It will be called Les Merdistes. *Poète, prends ton luth.*'

I left Ithaca for New York and next week was joined by Viktor who told me that André had gone off his head. Yes, really, I'm being serious. It began over the sealing-wax. André and he were almost alone in the house and André wanted sealing-wax. Viktor had none and André burst into tears; it was a matter of life and death, he must have sealing-wax. But why? Because he had a letter that could not go unsealed, a letter to Princess Juliana of Holland telling her how to stop the war. Viktor thought that André was a little hysterical but nothing to be wondered at; the Third Republic did not come to an end every day. André turned on all the lights in the house and played Debussy over and over on the Victrola. He could not be left alone, followed Viktor like a dog, asked for protection. Viktor lent him a book for the night. In the morning André came in in tears, said that he knew he was no longer any good because of Viktor's '*Ex Libris*' plate which he had found in the book; Viktor, who was only an amateur, had designed it himself whereas André, who was by profession a designer, could never do anything so good. I know now, André said, that it is not for me to have initiative; all I can do is obey. He must have someone to obey, Viktor must give him orders. Tell him to do something at once, the harder the better; André would be his slave. Then André got worse and worse, confessed how he was troubled by devils, and they took him away.

In July I received orders to return to the U.K., was about to snatch what of idyll or glamour I could in the two or three weeks before my boat when I got appendicitis in Portsmouth, New Hampshire. A ruptured appendix and peritonitis – streptococcal infection – they thought I would die. But I had no thought of dying, enjoyed my morphine, another interregnum. For the first week in hospital I was puzzled by something which I was too tired to look

27

into. Who was the man who had got into me? There was some man who had been slid into my body like a hand into a glove; otherwise I could not have had an operation. This man therefore was doing me a service and it was odd in such an intimate relationship not to know his name or what he did in life.[1]

The doctor who had operated on me was a breezy little man, bald (except for short white hair at the sides) with small piggy eyes that tunnelled behind octagonal rimless glasses and under no eyebrows. He visited me daily and every day he brought out some new story about murder, sudden death or disease. He was violently anti-German. Europeans were no good, he said, with the exception of the English, the Irish and the Scotch. If the Germans came over here, we'd blow them out of the sea. Then he would breeze off and leave me and I would lie alone in my private room with hygienic cream walls and a glass doorhandle. There was an oriental woman with an early Picasso profile and a robe without sleeves; her arm from elbow to wrist was a series of copper bracelets and whenever she held her arm out and pointed at the floor, I had to be sick. She never said anything, I never said anything back, I just was sick.

During the first week I also had diarrhoea. There was one night when I kept calling for the bedpan and suddenly I realised that using the bedpan was casting a vote. Then I became very indignant because it dawned on me how the hospital was subtly exploiting me. The hospital authorities were all pro-Willkie but, to show their broadmindedness and so do propaganda by bluff, they had had inserted in the gossip column of the Portsmouth daily paper that with their permission one of their patients had cast thirteen votes for Roosevelt in a night.

Then one day Wystan Auden was to come and see me, and the night before I lay on my back with the bed raised a little looking out of the window towards the Maternity Ward opposite where there was a window that periodically lit up brightly. Lit up, went dark, lit up, went dark. It was some time before I guessed what it was. It was a surgeon smelting metals. But oh so much more than a surgeon. He had wholly new methods of operating but he had also a new scheme of life, he held the panacea of history, Wystan knew

[1] Cf. L.M.'s poem 'Jigsaws', iv (*Visitations*, p. 39).

all about him. I did not always trust Wystan's taste but this time there was no mistake; this surgeon of his was more than a mere great man: he was a human being but raised to the power of n, had had a mutation of some sort, could act as a midwife to others—a new mutation for all. But he had one drawback; a Central European refugee, he was somehow without a surname; whenever he was introduced to anyone he had to hiccough. A hiccough was his substitute for a name; I could hear him hiccoughing now, all the way over from the other building. Out of sympathy I got the hiccoughs too and the nightnurse came in, asked me what was wrong.[1]

I had little to read during the long days, went over and over copies of *Life*, *The New Yorker* and *Time*. One issue of *Life* featured Charles McNary, the Vice-Presidential Republican candidate, and that night McNary himself came to me and talked politics. 'Undivarioustautiability,' he said. 'There's no such word,' I said. McNary drew himself up. 'Yes, there is,' he said, 'it means you can't lie on your side.'

When, after various dangerous complications, I was allowed to get up, I met the other patients in the sunparlor, a room with vitaglass walls and chairs in green and yellow. Hospital patients are like passengers on a ship, during their interregnum they can afford to be contemplative or sentimental, to let their thoughts wander, to relapse into children in a green and yellow nursery. Mr. Cavalcanti for instance who was here as a result of a car smash and whose face was covered with plasters, the skin in between all bristles. Mr. Cavalcanti was in insurance, a heavily built man in his fifties and probably a devil for business but now he was taking time off; you could not mention babies or women to him without his one good eye watering. Last year, he told me, he had seen the finest picture in the world, it was at the World's Fair, King George's Coronation and you might have been there yourself. Yes, he went on, his voice lyrical with nostalgia, and at the same time he had seen Malcolm Campbell's racing car and Magna Charta.

I went to Connecticut to convalesce, a beautiful September noisy with katydids,[2] and then on to New York. In October I went down for a weekend to stay in southern New Jersey with Mariette and

[1] Cf. 'The Messiah' (*Solstices*, p. 22).   [2] An American insect.

Tsalic. The train for Jersey City was called the Blue Comet and I sat in a luxury Pullman car that was all windows and beyond the windows a reel of autumn madness, the maple trees gone drunk with colour. Tigers and wine, pimento, copper, coral, the bells of St. Clement's jangling and fanfaronade of trumpets, fireworks out of the ground, Giorgione, Veronese, the tents of all the Sultans. People had told me about the American Fall, and this was it. On the way to Mariette's nothing could be more fitting. She had always been mad for colour and never found it cloying. Just as she could play the same records over and over again. I remember her dressed like a gypsy in a room like a gypsy's caravan bending over the gramophone, saying 'I must have it again.' But that was in Birmingham, England.

I slept in a room with the paper peeling from the walls and rats running in the roof. It was tidier, however, than the other rooms, where everything lay pellmell; Mariette had stopped doing housework when a fortune-teller told her it was bad for her, and now paid attention only to the poultry, whose houses were of the very latest pattern and everything Just So. From nine hundred laying hens they produced 3600 eggs a week. Not that the farm paid; like the other farmers they subsisted on Government loans.

On the Saturday afternoon Mariette and Tsalic and I went to Atlantic City. Which was meant to be a spree but it is hard to have a spree when you are walking with your past. We walked along the Board Walk, the long wide wooden esplanade that runs by the sea, and on our right was a wide grey beach with a dead grey sea beyond it and on our left was a series of monster hotels, towering up into pyramids or mosques or factories, with glassed-in balconies inside which the guests sat on deck chairs looking outwards, or they would have been looking outwards if they had not been asleep. It was a Jewish holiday, and besides the season was over; very few people were about, the funshows and booths were idle. On the grey sand were long rows of empty garish deck chairs and there were Negroes waiting with ponies and one or two gulls walking far out near the waves. Beneath the railings at the edge of the esplanade a man was displaying bas-reliefs in coloured sand – pirates, parrots and rum.

Mariette and Tsalic and I went on and on, meeting one or two Negroes pushing old ladies in two-seater wicker chairs, looking into shops that were closed, and every so often Mariette would say 'Isn't this fun?' There was a white shredded moon pinned up on the sky and everything was thin and without any back to it. No one can see the other side of the moon—Well, what of it? Tsalic and I weighed ourselves on a machine outside a drug-store. He touched 230, looked displeased. Mariette, who refused to weigh herself, hooted with laughter. 'What did I tell you?' she said. She and Tsalic bickered about each other's weight, then we had a drink through sanitary drinking straws, went back to the farm. Mariette broke twelve eggs and scrambled them for supper. Afterwards, while Tsalic was sizing eggs in the cellar, she talked to me alone about the world situation, told me how she *hated people*. 'I have always,' she said (and this was news to me), 'hated everyone I did not know.' And if she had her way, she would cut off the vitamins, feed them on muck, take away their energy, then there'd be no wars.

Tsalic was not so bitter about the world, would have preferred to move around in it. When he could get a word in he talked to me about writing; he wanted to write short stories, had bought whole quires of paper and sheaves of pens, but he never had time to start—what with the farm and working out the taxes on the roads and driving the truck to market—and Mariette besides did not believe in it. I remembered now how angry she used to get if anyone called me a poet; that, she would say, was something you became when you were dead.

The radio kept going all day long in the kitchen, the rats kept thumping behind the boards, and I sat up late, wondering if it made any sense, with Tsalic who had once been a star American footballer and Mariette who had been the best dancer in Oxford.

III

On board we have just had gas-masks issued and it occurs to me that it is time to readjust the Virgilian conception of the Gates of Horn and the Gates of Ivory; according to Virgil true dreams come through the former and false through the latter, truth as usual being thought of as correspondence to fact, and fact being limited to the waking world of the senses. But that will not do any more. My waking eyes show me human beings in gas-masks, archaic monsters but not, like the seahorse, beautiful, and why should I call that truth? It is worse than any dream that the Ivory Gates ever opened on. You can chop and change the words; if the world of gas-masks is x, you can call x Appearance or Fact or the Given or the Real or the Actual or Truth, but you have to suppose another world y which according to your phraseology may not be more factual or even more actual or even more true or even more real but, if not given, at least is *made*, which is better. So gas-masks are made too? In a sense of course you are right, but that is the paradox of technology. It begins with sheer creative imagination and it ends—at least that is how it looks in 1940—in a brute and random necessity, negation of human freedom.

Like the paradox of the Will. One supposes the Will to be the great instrument of individuality, of freedom, and one lets it rip, then cannot put the drag on, the Will runs away with the lot of us, we have no more choice in the matter than a falling stone. Hence Schopenhauer's view of the Will as determinist tyranny and his opposition to it of *Vorstellung*, the freedom which is freedom from the Will and from narrow personality, the presentation to the mind's eye in a crystal of entities which are not subordinate to any practical purpose, the death that remains visible and is not, as life is, the death of shape or pattern. Which is why long ago the Orphics put on their gravestones: 'I have flown out of the sorrowful weary wheel.' Which is why in despair today intelligent people who before the last war would have been rationalists are taking to yoga or maybe to

32

suicide. Which is why I, like many others, though wrongly, have lived a life of episodes, isolating incidents or people or aspects of people in the hope of finding something self-contained, having despaired of a self-contained world. But the masses, who are not intellectual, look for this in sport, recreation or the movies.

When Tsalic was staying with me in Birmingham, he and I, tired of going round in the circles of personal relationships, used often to go off at a tangent, indulge our common fancy for football. Tsalic had played a little rugby but did not know the finer points of it, and I would explain these while he in return would explain to me American football which sounded to me all wrong but I said I would like to see it. And soon after staying with him in New Jersey I had a chance to do so, when I went back to Cornell to collect my belongings.

Cornell, who had a very good team, were playing Syracuse. The players looked grotesque to me, padded and breeched, like deepsea divers in their helmets, and I did not like the arithmetical element, the counting of yards. Also I was uncomfortably conscious of the long row of substitutes sitting in their woollies on a bench; the rugby tradition makes two virtues supreme–individual endurance and the open game–and American football seems to require neither; if a man is tired or inefficient you can always bring on another, while the open game is precluded by the practice of the huddle, by individualist running and obstruction, by an excess of ratiocination. Technically, however, it has one great elegance–which is precisely what I expected to hate–and that is the forward pass. The Cornell team was famous for its passing and to see a man feint and then throw a long impertinent pass out of the palm of his hand into a space where no one is but someone suddenly appears and ball and man are wedded at the run, is exhilarating, almost a sacrament.

But half the joy of American football is the stage-management, the *choregia*. It is vulgar of course, like the water and fireworks display at the World's Fair, but, being on the grand scale, you have to give yourself up to it. Each side has half a dozen cheerleaders, supple young men, who bawl through megaphones, then toss them in the air and somersault, run through a repertory of antics and ritual cries. During the intermission the rival bands parade, Cornell covering the field with scarlet and three drum majors. They play the famous Cornell tune 'High above Cayuga's waters' while a Syracuse

33

representative walks before the crowd on stilts covered in long, long pants, chewing gum with a would-be nonchalance, and a little Jewish vendor with a Bronx accent pushes around the stands selling Hygeia Ice Cream (though the temperature is below freezing) and Hot Dog Deliriums. Or trying to sell them, for everyone is much too busy talking shop about the game or giving vent to sadistic instincts, 'That guy's only got two teeth left', 'Break his leg and have done with it.'

I met Viktor again at Cornell and he told me André had come out, had astonished all the experts and recovered. André had given him a detailed account of his time in the asylum, how first he had thought he was on the Riviera but a man had come up to him and said, 'I recognise you. You are an intellectual. I am a journalist. But hush,' he had said, putting his finger to his lips, 'I am preparing our escape.' After that André was careful not to say anything to the doctors in case he should give away the journalist and, whenever the other patients made gestures or grimaces, he took it for part of the code; they must all be conspirators.

André had also explained, precisely and in detail, how it was he had gone so queer in the first place. It was all a matter of signs. André had gone into a café in Ithaca and there was a waitress who was a peasant woman he had known in France. But when he spoke to her she was not that peasant woman. So he had walked back to the house and all the way a bird had flown above his head and when he sat down on the grass outside the house because he was tired, the bird sat down and looked at him. That was the second sign. Then that night he had seen Viktor's 'Ex Libris' and it made him think that he could not be one of the chosen; for at this darkest hour of France's history and the world's it was not just enough to be on the side of the good, you had to be one whom God would choose for His instrument. This 'Ex Libris' design contained the motif of a Greek cross and Viktor had the same cross on his cufflinks. The very next morning when Viktor came into the room the sun came in through the window and struck his cufflinks and that was the last sign; Viktor was one of the chosen and André was not.

The chimes chimed and I left Cornell, had more than a month left to fill in. Marking time but not killing it. Once I had wanted to kill time but not any more. Because I was in love and because I knew that, if I fell out of this love or if it fell away from under me, the vistas which it had opened would still be there and the wind which had come up would not die down.

I was staying now in a household on Brooklyn Heights, still being painted and without much furniture or carpets, but a warren of the arts, Auden writing in one room, a girl novelist writing–with a china cup of sherry–in another, a composer composing and a singer hitting a high note and holding it and Gipsy Rose Lee, the strip-tease queen, coming round for meals like a whirlwind of laughter and sex. It was the way the populace once liked to think of artists–ever so Bohemian, raiding the icebox at midnight and eating the cat-food by mistake. But it was very enjoyable and at least they were producing. The Left Wing movement in the thirties encouraged us to try to be normal, and all that affectation of the Normal only led to sterility. Because the Average Man today is either a myth or a dummy and the norms have got to be rediscovered, it is no good taking them over from people who have ceased to think and have no intention of acting.

I went into the country to dinner near the Hudson and the ice in my highball tinkled like a sheepbell and the boats on the night of the Hudson were like sheep on an endless moor and the lights of Tarrytown or Yonkers and the noises of trains called me to the further bank–*ripae ulterioris amore*–but it was more than the bank of the Hudson or even the east of the Atlantic, it was something such as Rilke meant by Death, something unknown but comprehensive where everything falls into place.

So I got on to this boat and here I am, fitted with a gas-mask, carrying my lifebelt from cabin to lounge to dining-room, watching the airmen who are more than young drink their pints of beer or listening to someone at the piano around the corner picking out with one finger *Land of Hope and Glory* or to a mouth-organ playing *The Rose of Tralee*. It is, as I said, the same boat that brought me over. That was in January 1940 and this is December 1940. But before all that? I am 33 years old and what can I have been doing that I still am in a muddle? But everyone else is too, maybe our muddles are concurrent. Maybe, if I look back, I shall find that my life is not just mine, that it mirrors the lives of the others–or shall I say the Life of the Other? Anyway I will look back. And return later to pick up the present, or rather to pick up the future.

IV

Hark the lying angels sing. Every man's birth might be a Messiah's but is it? All this nine months' trouble and forward-looking in order to produce, so the psycho-analysts tell us, a backward-looking child who longs again for the womb. Never to come out of the quarry to be made into a pillar of the temple or into more likely a paving-stone for pavement artists to draw on and blind beggars to spit. To be unpolluted, unused. But it can't be helped anyway, here we are and hail Pollution!

Memory cannot go back that far, fades into myth, I find myself walking down a long straight passage hung with bead curtains. Through one curtain after another, like sheets of coloured rain, but I notice very little in the passage, only at the end there is a staircase. I go up it several flights, at the last floor but one there is a small window of cheap stained glass which throws a stain on the floor mingling with the pattern of the worn-out linoleum. The last flight of the stairs is uncarpeted and the top is all but dark. The top is a blind alley, a small lobby without any doors and the roof sloping down as in an attic. It smells very fusty. Close in under the roof, but I can hardly see it, is a trunk, an old-fashioned trunk with metal studs on it. On the lid of the trunk there are initials but I cannot see if they are mine. Anyway the trunk is locked.

There were five of us in the family – my father and my mother and my sister and my brother and I – but there were many more people in the house. The red soldiers, for instance, who by day were tiny, you could knock them over with a finger, but by night they were ten foot high, came marching straight for you, drumming, and not the least change on their faces. There were people too in the cracks of the ceiling, in the mottling of the marble mantelpieces, in the shadows of the oil-lamps and the folds of the serge curtains.

The first house looked out on the harbour which was noisy and dirty, the salt pier on one side and the coal pier on the other, and beyond it there were sails on the lough and I never knew where they were going but I took it it was somewhere good. The nursery was at the back of the house and looked down on a coal-yard; there was a frayed red bell-rope swinging on the wall which went 'See-saw, Margery Daw' as it swung and my aunt was called Margery who hit my sister with a hair-brush.

The second house was in a garden, enormously large (an acre), with a long prairie of lawn and virgin shrubberies and fierce red hens among cauliflowers run to seed, and the other side of the hedge was the cemetery, you could hear the voice of the minister tucking people into the ground. The dining-room was sombre red and the drawing-room was faded yellow; in the dining-room there was a harmonium and in the drawing-room there was a piano and, if my mother drew up her chair to either, something would come out like a cloud–a Green Hill Far Away which was the same as the Fairy Mount, a round grass knoll near the yarn-mill, the mill where I could see through the windows the savage champing machines which would hunger and wait for me at night.

My mother was comfort and my father was somewhat alarm and my sister wore yellow shoes and a bow on her hair and my brother, who was a Mongolian imbecile, could not say many words but could mimic the gardener; the gardener, people would say, was touched in the head. I was the youngest. My mother made cakes in a big yellow bowl in the kitchen, the mixture was yellow and sticky and sweet, she would stir it around with a spoon and it came higher and higher up the inside of the bowl till a dollop would catch on the rim and then I was allowed to taste it.

There was always a sense of loss because things could never be replaced. There was a golliwog lost in the shrubbery and a teddy-bear who fell into the soot-heap and in the first house there was a spotted horse called Dan who failed to come with us when we left. Later I took my sister's doll, with a pink frilled dress and big blue eyes, and built her a house out of coloured bricks on the table but she was too heavy for the house, the walls fell down and over the edge of the table and she went with them and broke and was hollow inside. And my mother kept being ill and at last was ill all the time.

Before she got ill I used to get in her bed in the morning and there was only one thing I disliked in her room. That was a little

37

cone-shaped straw basket, trimmed with pink ribbon, which hung on the wall and in which she put the hairs that came out from her head in the comb. Whereas the little net pocket in the wall above the berth in the cabin on the boat that went to Wales was pleasant to look at, for in that she put her small gold watch.

I liked all ladies and they made me show off. Until I learnt the name for it. One day, when I was about four or five, I was telling two ladies to watch me spring-clean my pockets when my sister came in, very cross, and said '*You're showing off*.' After that Showing Off became something terrible and I kept myself to myself.

Pleasure was bright and terror had jagged edges. My father would seat me on his knee and imitate the train from our town to Belfast, chugging and whistling and stopping at all the stations – Troopers-lane, Greenisland, Jordanstown, Whiteabbey, Whitehouse, Green-castle, Belfast. And then the train back again – Greencastle, White-house, Whiteabbey, Jordanstown, Greenisland, Trooperslane, Carrickfergus. That was pleasant but what my father did by himself was frightening. When I was in bed I could hear his voice below in the study – and I knew he was alone – intoning away, communing with God. And because of his conspiracy with God I was afraid of him.

Things project other things, that was the trouble. The oil-lamp in the nursery made a brown stain on the ceiling which no one could get off; and when my mother put her hands together, made rabbits on the wall, how was I to know they would not stay when she took away her hands? I wished my mother would not encourage them but was too frightened to tell her I was frightened. And Annie the cook had a riddle which began 'What is it that goes round and round the house?' And the answer was the wind but, though I knew that was the answer in the riddle, I had a clammy suspicion that in fact it might be something else. Going round and round the house, evil, waiting to get me.[1]

Going to Wales was too far back – it was walking along white planks, they may have been deck or they may have been esplanade, there was hot buttered toast too and hooters and buckets – but Portstewart is the holiday I remember, we went there twice but the times have fused together. It is a little seaside resort on the north

[1] Cf. 'The Riddle' (*Solstices*, p. 15).

38

coast of County Antrim a few miles west of Portrush. On the train I was anguished because I had forgotten my toy boat but when we got out at the station a thrill came up in my stomach because I was really There. Outside the station there was a flowering bush of buddleia and my father produced a little bag of preserved ginger. The ginger was sweet too though it bit, brought tears to the eyes, but the buddleia was sweet only, sweet. Only where was the sea? I might have cried because the sea was not at the station but they said it would only be a little while now and I pattered along the road, my mouth full of ginger, and suddenly around a corner or over a crest came a strong salt breeze and a rich smell of herring and there down below us was blueness, lumbering up against the wall of the fishermen's quay, ever so or never so blue, exploding in white and in gulls.

We stayed in a house looking over the sea, there were tramcars running by the window and jellyfish melting on the beach and further along an enormous castle on a crag with a dangerous path going round it; one day we were climbing fearfully along this path with the sea boiling below us far among rocks when I saw to my horror two people in the boiling sea and curious pink bladders growing out from under their arms; I asked my mother what they were and she said they were wings. Wings! It was all too much to take in. Like the golf course along the river Bann. The turf there was crisp and buoyant to walk on but it had its queerness too. There were iron red things sticking up out of the Bann and my mother said they were waterworks but I caught my breath when we came near them, and there were also little red flags growing up out of the ground, flapping away to themselves and punctuating the distance.

On the roads we would come to signposts and my mother would read the name and say 'That goes to Coleraine.' I liked the name, translating it into cold rain, and, when I asked my mother what it was, she said 'Coleraine is a watering place', so I knew my translation was right. Everything nearly was joyful except when we went to watch the fishermen pull up their nets and caught in the nets there were several dead gulls. But I made myself forget them, collected shells with my sister. Then one day before we left I had a revelation of space. We were walking along a road between high walls and I could see nothing but the road and the air on the road

39

was quiet and self-contained. On the top of the walls, on the contrary, there were long grasses growing in the stonework and these were blown out, combed, by a wind which I could not see. I wondered what was over those walls and I thought that it must be space. Not fields or roads or houses but an endless stretch of a windblown something, something not I nor even my father and mother could ever, however we tried, walk to the end of.[1]

[1] Cf. 'Mutations' (*Springboard*, p. 13) and 'The Stygian Banks', iv (*Holes in The Sky*, p. 56).

V

The cook Annie, who was a buxom rosy girl from a farm in County Tyrone, was the only Catholic I knew and therefore my only proof that Catholics were human. She worked very well and fast and filled in her spare time doing Irish crochet work. We would watch the shamrocks and roses growing from her crochet hooks while in a gay warm voice she would tell us about Fivemiletown where she came from and the bansheees and fairies and cows of the Clogher valley. They had nice rhymes out there—Lisnaskea for drinking tea, Maguire's Bridge for whisky—and County Tyrone sounded like a land of content. Annie in fact was always contentful except when she had palpitations. And we were content with Annie.

One day, however, my mother engaged what was called a Mother's Help. My brother and I were busy laying pebbles along a little ledge outside the conservatory porch when the Mother's Help came up the drive. She was small and lean and scrawny, quite unlike Annie, her face was sour and die-hard Puritanical, she had a rasping Northern accent. The daughter of a farmer in County Armagh, she knew all there was to be known about bringing up children; keep them conscious of sin, learn them their sums, keep all the windows shut tight and don't let them run for it is bad for their hearts.

It was the end of *laissez-faire*. Miss Craig nearly pulled your ears off when she cleaned them and she always got the soap in your eyes. When she carried you off in disgrace your face would be scratched by the buckle on her thick leather belt. Though small she was strong as leather and we soon developed new reflexes when we saw the slaps coming. Believing in economy she made dresses for my sister out of the funeral scarves with which my father was presented at funerals. Obsessed by a righteous hatred of the Common Cold she loaded us down with perspiring layers of clothing. In spite of this my sister kept catching cold and Miss Craig would

41

jeer at her bitterly, say she would never live to grow up and they would write on her tombstone 'Here lies Old Snivelly'.

It was Miss Craig who brought Hell home to me.[1] Being one of a rector's family I had heard it mentioned before but it had never been cardinal; Miss Craig made it almost the Alpha and Omega, hell-flames embroidered her words like Victorian texts. I realised now that I was always doing wrong. Wrong was showing-off, being disobedient, being rude, telling stories, doing weekday things–or thinking weekday thoughts–on Sundays. I had done so much wrong I knew I must end in Hell and, what was worse, I could imagine it. Sometimes when Miss Craig had jerked me and thumped me into bed she would look at me grimly and say: 'Aye, you're here now but you don't know where you'll be when you wake up.'[2]

Miss Craig, however, had her glamour. County Armagh was not so romantic as County Tyrone but it was also somewhere unseen and Miss Craig told us of the will-o'-the-wisps that went skipping around in the bogs. Also she had a trunk which she would unpack for us sometimes for a treat; the contents were always the same but we always looked forward to seeing them. There was a photograph album–yellow snaps of gaitered and whiskered farmers–and a heavy Bible with a brown binding (always a novelty, for the Bibles we knew were all black) and at the bottom of all was a little parasol which took to pieces. We never even wondered what Miss Craig was doing with a parasol, Miss Craig who had hair on her face and whose style of dress was not only plain but repulsive.

My mother became steadily more ill and at last she went away; the last I can remember of her at home was her walking up and down the bottom path of the garden, the path under the hedge that was always in shadow, talking to my sister and weeping. I had no part in this, I did not know what it was all about.[3] Later I visited

[1] Louis's picture of Miss Craig is, I think, rather misleading. She was an eccentric person, and after our mother left she found herself in a position of responsibility for which she was perhaps unfitted. But in spite of her sharp tongue she had a kind heart and gave us many little pleasures. I am doubtful about the authenticity of the 'hell-fire' remarks attributed to her; I think that Louis may have heard or read these elsewhere and unconsciously projected them on to his memory of her. My father disapproved strongly of 'hell-fire religion', but it would have been hard for an imaginative child to escape some knowledge of it in the Ulster of fifty years ago. (E.N.)   [2] Cf. *Autumn Sequel*, canto xvii.
[3] In 1910 our mother developed a gynaecological complaint which occasioned intermittent attacks of illness, but these did not become frequent or serious

my mother in hospital and she offered me a box of chocolates. Something evil came up in me—I knew it to be evil, although it was quite different from the wrong-doings for which I was going to Hell—and I refused to take the box. I wanted the chocolates very much and also I wanted to be gracious to my mother, but something or other made me spite myself and her and stand there surly and refuse. When I got home the box was there (someone had brought it back furtively) and I was filled with remorse and remembered the other time with the poplar twigs. That had been a fresh spring morning and everyone well and gay and my father was perched on a ladder clipping the arbour which was made of little trees we called poplars. The long sprays fell on the ground with light green lively leaves and I gathered some of them up to arrange in a jam-jar. But one of my twigs was too long, whenever I put it in the jar the jar fell over. My mother came up smiling, folded the twig double, put it in the jar and the jar stayed upright. And I was outraged, went off in a sulk.

At the age of five, while my mother was away, I made my first rebellion. Thursday was Mrs. M'Quitty's Day and we always had

until late in 1912. In March 1913 she had an operation which completely cured her former malady, but at the same time she quite suddenly developed an agitated melancholia. Louis and I saw her change almost overnight from a mother who had always been the mainstay of the household—serene and comforting, apparently the very essence of stability—into someone who was deeply unhappy and no longer able to make decisions. Louis in particular, as the youngest, was greatly attached to his mother, and before her illness I remember him as being with her a very great deal. Through the early summer of 1913 she was still at home and Louis was still constantly with her. She always remained gentle and loving, but as she became more and more sad and restless Louis, who was only five and a half, must have been completely bewildered and greatly disturbed. His last memory-picture of her walking up and down the garden path in tears seems to have haunted him for the rest of his life.

In August 1913 she left the rectory for a nursing-home in Dublin. In the children's eyes (and I think this is important) she did not appear ill in the ordinary sense of the word, only inexplicably sad. Louis and I never saw her again (the chocolate-box episode took place on a visit paid to her by Louis after her operation six months earlier). For a long time after her departure both Louis and I waited for and expected her return; Louis has expressed his own feelings at this period in his poem 'Autobiography' (*Plant and Phantom*, p. 70). She died in December 1914 of tuberculosis, presumably contracted in the hospital where she then was.

I think that the shock of seeing the sudden change in the mother whom he loved so much, followed by the uncertainty of her return, may have been the chief factor which caused Louis's memories of childhood to be so sad and sometimes so bitter. He was too young to have any real understanding of what had happened. (E.N.)

stewed steak. Mrs. M'Quitty, the charwoman, was very stout and friendly, she had a son who was a fisherman and she had given us our cat but she had to have stewed steak. I could not bear stewed steak, I found it too tough to swallow, had to keep the pieces in my cheek till after dinner, then spit them out in the shrubbery. So one spring Thursday, as we were spending the morning with Annie raking up new-cut grass, I planned that, when the gong went, I would hang behind and hide and have no steak. So the gong went and I hung behind, crawled in under some laurel bushes at the side of the lawn. In a few minutes they came out and called for me but I did not answer. This was achievement, I felt, something entirely new, I had planned to do something outrageous and the outrage was working. The steak too must be getting cold.

There was a great hue and cry, Miss Craig and Annie and Mrs. M'Quitty screaming all over the garden but they never looked under the laurels; I was proud to be so clever. 'There he is now,' Miss Craig cried suddenly, 'I see the red cap on him in the cemetery.' So they all stampeded to the cemetery hedge but, whatever it was red, it was not my cap. I could feel ripples of delight going over my face as I lay snug under the laurels drawing patterns with my finger in the dried crumbly soil. Dinner-time—steak-time—was past but I was not in the least hungry, would lie there all afternoon; the experience was too precious not to exploit to the full. Mrs. M'Quitty and Annie brought out a carpet on to the lawn right in front of me and began to beat it, with great wicker bats; the thud of their strokes reiterated around me and the dust rose up in the sunshine. A terrible thing, Mrs. M'Quitty kept saying, me to be lost and my mother ill and away. Sure he may be killed on the roads; the master has the polis out looking for him.

I was a little scared to think that the polis were after me; maybe, I thought, I am in for a lot of trouble. I lay very quiet and left it to fate. I might not have come out for a long time had there not been a scratching and a blustering behind me in the nettles and there, broken out from the henyard, were the hens led by the rooster. The rooster looked like the Devil with his great scarlet wattles and crest and he was leading his hens straight into my hideout. It was too much for me, I scrambled out on to the lawn and was caught. Miss Craig told me I was bound for Hell and my father told me it was very wrong to make everyone so frightened and I ought to think of my mother.

Adventure did not pay and life settled into routine. In the morning I would have my lessons from Miss Craig in a small nursery with the window shut tight. On the walls there hung a multiplication table and a calendar with a picture of John Peel and a coloured picture from the *Sphere* of Queen Mary dressed for her Coronation; I liked Queen Mary very much because of her jewellery and I liked John Peel for the names of his dogs. Sometimes Miss Craig would put a new nail in the walls and the plaster would drop out. One day I picked up what looked like a piece of sugar and ate it and Miss Craig said at once it was plaster, I was a bad wicked child and would die. She was always talking of dying, and in winter, when the trees in between were not in leaf, would marshal us at the window to watch the funeral processions on their way to the cemetery next door.

In the afternoon when it was not raining too hard (which it often was) we would walk with Miss Craig up the road up the hill behind our house to a point called Mile Bush and back again. Always—or nearly always—the same walk because Miss Craig disliked going through the town; you never know what you might catch. We walked very slowly because of my brother and Miss Craig kept saying 'Don't drag.' My sister and I were agog to see something new, if only a horse drinking at the water-trough, but everything was usually just the same except that the hawthorn hedges which were flaming green in spring were jaded by autumn and in winter were barren black with raindrops ricocheting from twig to twig. Miss Craig, however, would tell us stories, always on the pattern of *Jungle Jinks*, the children's comic section in *Home Chat*; my brother was Jacko and I was Tiger Tim and my sister (Miss Craig's one original contribution) was Careless.

When we got home we would have tea in the nursery, strong tea thick with sugar, and sometimes before we went to bed Miss Craig, for a treat, would give us thick beef sandwiches with mustard or a cold drink made from cream of tartar. Possibly our diet, though it was not the cause, was one of the conditions of my dreams. These got worse and worse. Where earlier I had had dreams of being chased by mowing-machines or falling into machinery or arguing

45

with tigers who wanted to eat me I now was tormented by something much less definite, much more serious. There was a kind of a noise that I felt rather than heard, 'ah . . . ah . . . ah', a grey monotonous rhythm which drew me in towards a centre as if there were a spider at the centre drawing in his thread and everything else were unreal.

'Oh God, I do not want to have any dreams. If I am going to go to sleep, do not let me have any dreams. And if I am going to have dreams, do not let me go to sleep, God, please I will do anything if only You keep me awake.' But I always went to sleep all the same. One night I woke up and yelled, my father came up from downstairs, there was light and his voice, he told me nothing would hurt me.[1] I felt quite safe when he had gone but next morning Miss Craig was very angry; my father had forgotten to go down again to the study and had left the lamp burning there all night. I was a very wicked boy and might have burnt the house down.

There were also the terrors of Church. The church was cruciform, and the rectory pew, being the front pew of the nave, looked out on to the space where the chancel and the nave and the two transepts met. The transept on our left was on a higher level and was reached by a short flight of steps; the end wall of it was occupied by a huge Elizabethan monument to the Chichester family who had then been the power in the land. The father and mother, who were each very large, knelt each under an arch, opposite each other, praying; below them, much smaller, was a Chichester brother who had been beheaded by the rebels, and between them, like a roll of suet pudding, on a little marble cushion was a little marble baby. None of these marble people worried me at all; what I disliked were the things that hung high up on the wall on either side of the monument's narrower top. A decayed coat of mail, a couple of old weapons, a helmet. I could not see the coat of mail when I was sitting, thanks to the solid front of the first pew in the transept, but, whenever I had to get up, there it would be, older and older and deader and deader, yet somehow not quite dead enough.

On the other hand if I looked down the chancel there was a rich old widow who always wore black and whom therefore I took to be blind. And blindness was not a misfortune, blindness was evil

[1] Cf. 'Intimations of Mortality' (*Poems*, 1935, p. 39) and 'Autobiography' (*Plant and Phantom*, p. 70).

magic. When I was sitting down I could not see her either as she was hidden by the reading-desk, so the morning service became an alternation of agony and relief, but the relief itself shadowed with the knowledge that soon we should have to stand up again and there I should be, exposed to the blind old lady on the one hand and the coat-of-mail man on the other.

Our best antidote to these terrors and depressions was the gardener Archie,[1] in whose presence everything was merry. My father did not think of him in that way, as Archie, whose professional pride was easily wounded, would sometimes absent himself for weeks out of pique. But for us nothing that Archie could do was wrong and he cast a warm glow upon everything he touched. We would anxiously wait in the morning for him to appear–he rarely turned up before noon because of his rheumatism–and, whenever we could escape from Miss Craig, we would encircle him in the garden and listen to him, as my father called it, romancing.

Archie romanced largely about himself, always in the third person – 'Archie's the great fella now, aye, Archie's the queer fella for work, ye wouldn't find his like, I'm telling ye, not in the whole of Ireland. Sure he's the great fella.' His forte was cutting hedges; no one in the world could cut hedges the way he could. He would take a long heavy plank and rest it on one of the steps of a stepladder at one end and a wooden box or two at the other and he and I would stand up there as if we were on a captain's bridge and the hawthorn sprigs would leap from his shears as he rambled along in a voice that was half singing, going over and over again about the gentlemen's places he had worked on and his wife Maggie and his canary and King William and the Twelfth of July.

For Archie, though he could neither read nor write, was a great Orangeman and played a flute in the Twelfth of July procession. Until, that is, his rheumatism made him unable to march. The Orange Lily was his fitting emblem, for he took a childlike delight in the gaudy and was naturally histrionic, would sometimes turn up in the morning with a small Union Jack in his cap, level his blackthorn stick at a crow, sight along it and pull an imaginary trigger, then say 'I'm a Frenchman', and stand to attention and salute. He had snow-white hair and beautiful pure blue eyes and

[1] Cf. 'The Gardener' (*Plant and Phantom*, p. 49).

47

on his gnarled and abrased ring-finger he wore an imitation gold ring.

Even when we could not see him it assured us that life was good to hear him sharpening his scythe on the hone or mowing the lawn with the machine, mowing from a standing position because of his rheumatism, a shrill silver noise as he pulled it back and a deeper purring or snoring noise and a clack as he thrust it forward. Then we could imagine the emerald dance of the grass in the air which would afterwards be piled in heaps and become quite other than itself, no longer luminous and fresh but coagulated into lumps so that if you thrust your arm into the heap, you found inside it a perspiring animal warmth.

Archie preferred children (whom he called bairns) and cats and birds to grown-ups, but he would engage in badinage with Annie and Miss Craig, both of whom he called Maggie after his wife. With us his conversation was lyrical and interspersed with snatches of verse remembered from the kindergarten–'A bee met a wasp once runnin' by' or 'The cat sat by the barn-door spinnin''. Each spring when he cut the hedge between the garden and the cemetery a polished granite obelisk would reappear looking over at us. Then Archie would shake his fist, say 'Thon's a bad ould fella'; sometimes he would identify this obelisk with a blackleg gardener whom my father had employed once while Archie was privately on strike. He had also his moments of moralising, was a good Temperance man as well as an Orangeman, would speak with contempt of the whisky-drinking corner boys with their big stomachs and their great white faces. And sometimes he would point at the sky and say 'I believe in the Good Fella Up There', or point at the thin moon that appeared in the sky before twilight and say 'Thon's the Good Fella's lamp.'

If he did not have us for an audience he would do his romancing to the cats or else to the robins that waited around him for worms and his singsong voice would echo around the garden–'Archie's the great worker; ye wouldn't find his like in County Antrim.'

VI

Outside the house we knew very few people, whether gentry, working-people or children. When I was very little my mother had taken me to a children's party with big balloons and the wicked blue flames of a snapdragon, but after Miss Craig's time there were no more parties and you had to be careful whom you spoke to. Most of the world was untouchable.[1]

For instance there was a footpath near our house which ran along by the railway and led to the linen mill. We called it the Cinder Path because it was made of cinders, it put your teeth on edge to walk on it. If you went along there the wrong time of day you met the mill-girls—rude bold creatures, Miss Craig said—all with black shawls over their heads and the older ones haggard, dark under the eyes, their voices harsh and embittered and jeering. Or when we went through the town there were always men standing at the corners—standing there at least till the pubs opened—in shiny blue suits and dirty collarless shirts fastened with a collar-stud, and cloth caps pulled down over narrow leering eyes, and sour mouths which did not open when they spoke but which twisted sideways as they spat. The pavement around them was constellated with spittle and on the drab cement walls at their back there was chalked up 'To Hell with the Pope'.

Then there were the rude bold children who had no shoes and the cripples who swung along on crutches with a jaunty kind of insolence through the slum streets called the Irish Quarter. We rarely went into the Irish Quarter and I used to hold my breath till

[1] I don't think that Louis's childhood was in fact nearly so lonely and isolated as it appeared to him in retrospect. I remember our life before 1913 as happy and normal. My father and mother liked Carrickfergus and its inhabitants, and were on friendly terms with all kinds of people—Roman Catholics and Pro-testants, gentry and mill-girls. After our mother left, our father tried to keep life happy and social for us; but he was in poor health at this time and very sad, and this inevitably affected the whole household. (E.N.)

49

I got through it. There was a dense smell of poverty as of soot mixed with porter mixed with cheap fat frying mixed with festering scabs and rags that had never been washed. Many of the houses were mere cottages and you looked down over the half-door into a room below the level of the street, always dark but the glow of a grate might show up a mangy cat or a quizzical wrinkled face. The thatch on the roofs came down to within five feet of the street, was sometimes mottled with grass or moss, was usually dripping. And in Irish Quarter West there was a place which I knew was bad—a public house with great wide windows of opaque decorated glass out of which came randy voices and clinks and swear-words and a smell that was stronger than cheese and a mellow yellow light at night that fell on the gutter like a benison.

The Respectable People were few. One of them was Miss Smith, an old lady who lived in a home for indigent gentlewomen. Miss Smith who, being shaky in her grammar, was hardly by the ordinary assessment a gentlewoman, made up for this by her incontrovertible piety. Whenever we called on her she told us what she had been saying in her prayers; she prayed for all of us daily and this made me rather uncomfortable. She had aggressive white, white hair and sentimental grasping blue eyes and an over-prominent chin; all the time she talked her hand would waver out towards us, scutter like a mouse over our clothes, a contact I disliked but my sister enjoyed it for she thought Miss Smith was a saint. Miss Smith's little room was crowded with ornaments but specklessly clean. On the mantelpiece were daguerreotypes and china dogs and a photograph of my father. On the walls were a number of framed texts and a picture of a live stuffed dove perching on the finger of a live wax child.

In the dearth of contacts with children our own age my sister Elizabeth took refuge in a cult of the Old and I took refuge in fantasy; she shared her antiquarianism with me and I shared my fantasies with her. We were well off for oldnesses because both the church and the castle had been built by the Normans, and there was a lake two miles up the hill which had been a great city till someone put a curse on it, and even our own potato beds were full of pieces of flint which Elizabeth said people in the old days, the very old days, had used for knives and arrows. My father had a brand of writing-paper which came in boxes decorated with a

50

round tower and an ancient Irish wolfhound; whenever I looked at this trademark I felt a nostalgia, sweet and melting, for the world where that wolfhound belonged. All these things were old and being old were good. According to Elizabeth anything *modern* was evil. When a little house was put up down the road—something to do with filtering the water supply—she pronounced it especially evil, told me there was a bogy in it, we could hear him gargling when we passed. He spoilt one of our games too, for after his time we could never get any more little shrimps out of the taps.

Oldness however was not confined to the Flint Men or the Ancient Irish or even the Normans. Even our immediate predecessors in the Rectory ranked as old; we looked with reverence at their children's names scrawled in tar on the toolshed and at a wooden memorial tablet covered with lichen that they had put up to a cat called Tiger. They had also left us an enormous roller with shafts for a donkey but, as we had no donkey, the roller remained for some years lying on one spot in the lawn. Then on an evil day Annie and Miss Craig and Mrs. M'Quitty got in the shafts and shifted it and later someone took it away. Where it had been there was an oblong strip of sickly yellow on the grass which after some time disappeared, merged in the uniform green. I was sad when this strip disappeared; it was the end—positively the end—of the memory of somebody's donkey.

But no one could do that to the Great Clan McMisque. There were three queens of the clan—the Good Queen McMisque and the Bad Queen McMisque and another. And there were two police forces—the Callers and the Ringers, a thousand of one and a hundred of the other. There was also a family called Corney, all boys, about eight of them. And there were countless Biddy Biddies, the chief of whom was Bumbee. To start with there had only been a few Biddy Biddies but one day I took a newspaper, tore it in little pieces and threw them in the air and they all became Biddy Biddies. More romantic than any of these, except the queens, were Ina Kee and Teddy Bock. Ina Kee lived behind the toolshed and her glamour increased with acquaintance; the first time we went to see her was to consult her about diseases of horses and it was only after some time that we noticed she was younger than the Good Queen McMisque and gentle and very beautiful. Teddy Bock was my oracle, my familiar and my general consolation. He survived all the others and years after they had faded I still used to talk with him secretly whenever I sat in the lavatory.[1]

The strata of our amusements and beliefs through childhood were not arranged neatly, horizontally, but emerged from the ground on the slant. So we managed to retain the older ones side by side, however inconsistently, with the newer ones. This was perhaps partly due to the difference in age – more than four years – between myself and Elizabeth. She drew me up with her into flights of information but I pulled her down into depths of primitive faith. So, while both of us already were talking like scientists about the Flint Men, we both retained a totemistic attitude to Elizabeth's old teddy-bear who by now was weak in the knees and had lost the bloom of his youth. Miss Craig, who may have thought our affection for him pagan, said he was full of germs and one day stole him, hid him on top of a wardrobe. I later found him there, rescued him and hid him in the chimney in the spare room and so he survived as an outlaw.

The games I played with Elizabeth did not include my brother. Archie called him The Boss because he never did jobs in the garden, and Elizabeth and I, with something of Archie's respect for him, took it for granted that he could not take part in our games. He would sit around cross-legged like a little Buddha gazing benignly into nothing. Like my father he belonged in a world not ours. The less I saw of my father – for I saw him less – the stranger I found him. He was suffering now badly from indigestion and, when he was not visiting in the parish, would be sitting alone in the study. I hardly ever entered the study, but once in a way I would sit there awe-struck and look at him reading, moistening his thumb before he turned the pages of the book or sharpening a pencil which was pointed at each end and which beautified all his books with red and blue marks in the margin.

[1] Louis invented this game about the time when we lost our mother. We both played it and we played it pretty well all the time. I half believed in it and I think that Louis perhaps really did. It may be significant that the Clan McMisque was organised as a matriarchy with the Good Queen at its head – an all-powerful figure, somewhat formidable but always on the side of justice. (E.N.)

VII

I was nearly seven when the War came. Miss Craig and Annie were repapering the nursery, doing the job badly, leaving bubbles and pustules and wrinkles. At the top of the new paper there was a little coloured border and as I watched this border advancing round the room under the ceiling I thought it's a long way to Tipperary. It made me sentimental to see the old paper vanish but I was eager for the papering to be completed, for the border to get right around and meet itself. And that would be Tipperary.

People began to give us tins of sweets in red, white and blue with faces of generals in the middle–Kitchener, Jellicoe, Foch. Miss Craig was a devotee of Kitchener but I preferred the name Jellicoe, which seemed elegant and comic at once. It had taken me a little time to make out about the War; all foreigners were foreigners to me and at first I could not distinguish between the English and the Germans. I had heard political arguments before this but they were all about Orangemen and Home Rulers.

In November Elizabeth and my brother and I caught measles and were put in the same room. I had a bandage over my eyes and, to make the room still darker, a wardrobe was placed in front of the window. This was luxury. A bandage over your eyes remits your sense of duty.

When our temperatures were falling our father came in one morning, very unlike himself, and told us our mother had died. Elizabeth began to cry but, being unable to cry, I dived down under the clothes and lay at the bottom of the bed where I hoped they would think I was crying. I felt very guilty at being so little moved but decided that when I grew up I would build my mother a monument. And everyone would know that I had built it.

That Christmas we got a great many presents; they were marshalled on the nursery hearthrug by the crackling of the early morning fire. Everything was gay with colour, there were coloured chalks and coloured wooden rattles and striped tin trumpets and tangerines in silver paper, and a copy of the *Arabian Nights* with princesses in curly shoes and blue-black hair. My father was all smiles at dinner and I had a feeling he was doing this on purpose. During the turkey my brother startled us by asking 'Do the soldiers stop fighting for Christmas?' My father said No.

I thought my father was doing it on purpose because I now slept in his room and found it even worse than the nightmares. Because he was sleeping very badly, would toss and groan through the night, so that, if I was awake when he came up, I would be kept awake for hours listening to him; but I always pretended to be asleep. My great object now was really to be asleep before he arrived with the lamp and his own gigantic shadow.

I could read now very easily and immersed myself in fairy stories. Elizabeth who was eleven warned me against overdoing it; she confessed that she had read too much. Miss Craig also disapproved of book-reading as she called it and forbade it except at certain times. She came in one day when I was reading and I slipped the book into the desk. 'You're book-reading!' 'No, I'm not.' Greatly to my surprise Miss Craig accepted this, and I at once felt guilty of having put over a lie; it weighed on my conscience for several years. But I always felt guilty anyway, especially in regard to my father. I knew it was wrong of me to be frightened of him, to slip out of the room when he came in.

Religion encroached on us steadily. Miss Craig learned us *The Peep of Day* and *Line upon Line* and on Sunday we went to church and watched my father in his surplice which was not too unfamiliar for we often watched Annie iron it. Little by little the *things said* in church began to seep in on me; at first I had only noticed the smell of gas and the wicked coat of mail or the shaggy old sexton blowing his nose loudly on a bright red handkerchief in the middle of the Creed. Then, when I first learned to read, I was always given the Bible open at the book of Revelation the moment my father began the sermon; I was considered too young for the sermon. But now I was old enough for the sermon and I attended to the rest of the service and the hymns made me feel like crying, in a rather pleasant sugary way, but the parts about sin made me terrified. Religion never left us alone, it was at home as much as in church, it fluttered in the pages of a tear-off calendar in the bathroom and it filled the kitchen with the smell of silver-polish when Annie, who might at the same time be making jokes about John Jameson, was cleaning the Communion plate.

In the spring I committed a murder. Down in the hedge by the bottom walk in the garden, where my mother used to walk with my sister, there was a bird's nest. I could hear the little birds cheeping but the nest was too high for me to see into, so when no one was around I reached up for it and it capsized. I cannot remember seeing the nestlings fall out, but when I came past there again, there they were hanging in the hedge, little naked corpses, terrible, silent. I did not let on for years but I avoided the bottom walk.

VIII

It was a terrible day when Annie went away to be married, she had been our bulwark for so long against puritan repression. She was succeeded by Mrs. Knox, a very short little elderly woman with a sharp witch's nose. Everything that Mrs. Knox did was an act of condescension; she was really a lady, she told us, and not only a lady but a wonderful horsewoman. Her cooking was unpalatable after Annie's and her favourite dish was a sodden corpse-white apple-pudding which Miss Craig said looked like a pig's stomach.

On Miss Craig's evenings out we would sit with Mrs. Knox in the kitchen and listen to her moral tales. There was one about a little boy who filled a slice of bread with pins and covered the points of the pins with butter and jam and gave it to his sister and she died. And there was one about a flighty mother who wanted to go to a dance and leave her baby alone, so she made a great bogy and fixed it to the end of the bed to keep the baby quiet if it woke, and when she came back the baby was stone dead. Mrs. Knox used to have screaming-matches with Miss Craig and after a time my father dismissed her. The last we heard of her she was in gaol for working a confidence trick, posing as Lady So-and-so.

By this time the handles were falling off the doors and the house was in general disrepair. My brother was sent to Scotland to an institution and Miss Craig went away—Elizabeth and I wept at her going—and was succeeded by, of all things, an Englishwoman. This Englishwoman, Miss Hewitt, was very easy game after Miss Craig and Elizabeth and I put on the Wild Irish act for her. Miss Hewitt, who was appalled by the way we raised our hands to protect our faces if ever she spoke the least crossly, soft-pedalled her disciplinary instinct and tried to make the house more genteel. She bought a toast-rack and told the new cook to serve the butter in butter-balls and not in a slab. I, who was then about eight and very conservative, considered this a piece of newfangled English foolishness and wrote a polemic against butter-balls on a piece of old wrapping-paper (we never had any proper writing-paper).

Miss Hewitt considered herself an apostle of light but we thought of her as a heaven-sent ignoramus. She was pliable enough to walk anywhere we told her (Miss Craig had always kept us to the roads so that we should not get our feet wet, catch pneumonia) and, as she had no sense of direction, we could keep her three hours rambling through the fields within a mile of home, saying 'It's only a little way now.' And oh how we got our feet wet. While we walked we gave Miss Hewitt general knowledge lessons. As she was English she did not know that the freshwater well in the castle on the rock in the sea was a bottomless well and used to cure lepers. There were not any lepers now but anyway its healing power was gone because someone had cleaned it and removed some bits of old iron. But where did he find the old iron if it had no bottom? We had not thought of that but we dismissed it as a quibble. The old iron maybe was halfway down to the bottom that was not there.

We took Miss Hewitt to see King William's Landing Place down on the pier and, though she was a Protestant, she knew almost nothing about King William, we had to explain to her about blood on the drums. We often heard those drums as we were walking through the country; a couple of men might spend a whole day practising. One would walk in front with a great drum the size of a cartwheel strapped on his back and the sweat running down his face and the other would walk behind with the sweat running down his face and flail the drum on each side with a couple of canes. You might meet them on a desolate road in the hills marching very slowly, only the two of them, but their faces set like Crusaders and the whole country rocking with the noise. And sometimes, we explained to Miss Hewitt, if you did the job properly you cut your wrists on the rim of the drum and the drum got bloody and proved you were a good Orange Protestant.

Miss Hewitt was the first person who pampered me and she took half an hour over my bath. Miss Craig had told me I should have to wear drawers in the bath because Miss Hewitt was English, but this was not so. She used to fill the bath with fleets of paper boats and talk sentimentally about the last little boy she looked after; he had beautiful manners–Miss Hewitt said wistfully–and his name was Trevor.

My father had now engaged a Miss Cranly to come in the morning and give me lessons. Miss Cranly had read some new book about common-sense education and made me write essays on The Button and The Pin, enumerating the qualities one should look for in each. One day my father found some of these essays and his humanist feelings were outraged; a sheer waste of time, he said. He asked Elizabeth and me if we had ever read Shakespeare and we said only Lamb's *Tales*. We were then in such disgrace that we both sat down, read *Julius Caesar* straight off. Not long afterwards I was reproved for reading Shakespeare on Sunday.

About the time of my ninth birthday, in the autumn of 1916, I began writing newspapers. I got sheets of coarse paper, green, brown and white, stitched them together with a needle and cotton and divided the sheets into columns. The columns were devoted to War News (Red Indian wars), verse, archaeological discoveries (illustrated), sensational accounts of improbable happenings and a domestic section of practical suggestions and reproofs directed at Miss Hewitt, Elizabeth, the cook, the dog, the cat and the hens; each of these last items began 'So-and-so is requested to' or more often 'is requested not to . . .'

The dog was a puppy, a smooth-haired fox terrier, who was always killing hens. Miss Hewitt had no control over him and when he dashed off into a farm I would run unhappily after him, dreading the farmers. One day I reached a strange farmyard to find an angry red-faced woman holding him up by the neck as if she would choke him. 'Where are ye from?' she said. 'The North Road.' 'Ye're lying.' Her voice was harsh as sandpaper. 'The North Road,' I said. 'Tal the truth,' she said, 'ye're lying.' This episode increased my fear of people, of what Miss Hewitt called the Lower Classes. The Lower Classes were dour and hostile, they would never believe what you said. Not that the Gentry were much better; even then I was conscious that to be the son of a clergyman was to be something the Gentry only half accepted and that in a patronising way.

So I spent a great deal of the time alone, writing in my newspapers and my diary (for Miss Hewitt was more tolerant than Miss

Craig who had destroyed my first diary because it was bad for my handwriting), and I wrote a number of poems which my father called doggerel. I wrote an Ode to a Parrot beginning 'O Parrot thou hast grey feathers' and an Ode to a Stuffed Monkey beginning 'O Monkey though now thou art stuffed' and also an Ode to Miss Craig. These activities engrossed me and I ceased to be haunted at night. Except for an obsession with the Sin against the Holy Ghost. I had discovered what this sin was and I could not help committing it. It consisted in saying 'Damn God' and once you said that you were lost. I never said these words aloud but I could say them in my mind as distinct from just thinking them. So I would lie awake in bed thinking these words and getting nearer and nearer the verge where I would say them in my mind and be lost. I would use my willpower not to say them but the strain was too great, I could not go to sleep till I had said them, so I said them in my mind and was lost.

But on Good Fridays I made a great effort to be Christian, would read the Crucifixion through in all the four Gospels on end and then walk up and down the garden, keeping my face austere, trying not to be pleased by the daffodils.

While I was nine my father began to teach Elizabeth and me Latin. This was a great adventure but my father's impatience upset me, he thought I was very illogical; 'Sure no language,' he would say, 'could be composed on those principles.' However, I began to introduce Latin words into my newspapers and one day, when I went to a tea-party with tigerskin rugs on the floor, I kept declining the noun '*dux*' in my head and that made everything taste better. '*Ducibus ducibus*' I said, and this private pattern in my mind fitted in somehow with the stripes on the tigers and knowledge was power and a wind blew down the vistas.

And all this time there was War. A little way down the road was the entrance to the soldiers' camp and all day long we could hear the sentry challenging. From our upper windows we could see them sticking bayonets into dummies and sometimes at night they had what looked like a firework display. The soldiers came to Sunday morning service and sat in the gallery; they seemed to be all boots. When you saw them close up they had a strong suffocating smell and faces like underdone meat. Once or twice a week Elizabeth and Miss

Hewitt used to form part of a group of women who made bandages from moss. There was no war work I could do but I used to study very carefully the illustrated papers which were full of sandbags, trenches, barbed wire, howitzers. The whole business already had begun to lie heavy on my stomach.

One weekend a tall blond young man, a hitherto unheard-of cousin of ours in the Royal Field Artillery, came to stay, had trouble at Sunday morning service with his khaki cap in the pew; Elizabeth and I were proud that he had a khaki cap to have trouble with. I sat alone with him in my father's study and he hurt my feelings by pinching my arm, telling me I had no muscle. Then he asked if I could read and said he would test me, handed me a book of Military Instructions. It was all jargon but I read it aloud laboriously and forgave him because of his smile. Not long afterwards we received a newspaper cutting that said he had been killed in action. I liked the phrase In Action; it seemed to confer an aura of daring on the family.

IX

My father and Elizabeth had both gone over to England and I was walking with Miss Hewitt along Love's Loney (which in English is Lovers' Lane) when she told me my father had married again;[1] he had married Miss Greer whom I knew already, she lived in a very big house by the sea—what Archie called a Gentleman's Place—and had attracted my attention many years before by the long white gloves she wore in church. I was very angry and would not speak to Miss Hewitt all the way home. My father had no right to go turning things upside down. When my stepmother came home I would show her what I thought; her life would just not be worth living.

When my stepmother arrived, however, she brought so much comfort and benevolence with her that I dropped my resolution to obstruct. But for my own reading only I wrote an article attacking Late Dinner which she had introduced instead of High Tea. Miss Hewitt went out as my stepmother came in and with her there came a cook and a housemaid who had been employed by her mother, and a great deal of unfamiliarly solid furniture and a stack of books on Foreign Missions. I picked my way through the maze of new furniture and devoured the adventures of the missionaries— in India, Burma, China, Uganda, Paraguay and Ungava. I decided to be a missionary too, preferably in a jungle with lots of wild animals; in the end I should be martyred and clergymen would use me in sermons for a noble example.

My stepmother's family was the wealthiest family we knew, had made their money in linen and had till fairly recently been Quakers. During most of her life my stepmother had spent half each year in the big houses on the shores of Belfast Lough and the other half in one of the great isolated mansions in Regent's Park, London.

---

[1] The children had been told of his intended marriage by their father himself some months previously. (E.N.)

Never mixing in social frivolities, never going to the theatre or dances, never learning to ride or to sail or properly to play any games, never (or hardly ever) reading contemporary literature, and never recognizing Darwin, but doing Good Works and following a daily mid-Victorian routine–cold bath in the morning, Family Prayers, heavy elaborate meals on heavy mahogany tables, for recreation writing-games and puns. Most members of her family had married some kind of cousin and it was considered very daring of her to go so far afield as my father–especially as he was a Home Ruler. But though past forty and without any such experience, she made a very good job of managing the household and was, I think, delighted to be able to particularise her Good Works so visibly.

Elizabeth, who was now fourteen, was sent off to school in England (my stepmother thought it high time she should lose her Northern accent) and I spent the summer alone enjoying the new rich foods and beginning again to show off. I missed Elizabeth very much, as she flattered me by taking my serious proposals seriously and taking my jokes as funny, but I found a certain compensation in the unaccustomed attention given me by my stepmother and her relations; at the same time I felt a little ashamed of myself for playing up to them, for acting the rôle of a dear amusing child, selling my savage birthright for a swansdown cushion. I would salve my conscience by being deliberately naughty, falling on purpose into a pond of mud or turning on the hose to fill the backyard with water. The time I turned on the hose I was caught by the housemaid, a rawboned woman, six foot tall and embittered. She said it was *her* yard (the yard where I had always played) and I had no right to come into it; she would skelp my father himself if he was to come fooling round her yard. This tirade of hers pained me like blasphemy; I had never heard anyone speak like that of my father, and it made it worse that I felt she could skelp him–or anyone else for that matter –if she wanted to; she was my conception of an ogress. Later I found that it was she who thought she was the victim of a tyranny– had spent her life, she told me, carrying coals; carrying coals from six in the morning; break the back on you, carrying coals.

In September I was to go to school in England, in the same town[1] where Elizabeth was but not the same school. I looked forward to it

<hr />

[1] Sherborne.

passionately, being tired of the company of adults (for even Teddy Bock had begun to fail me), but just when I was due to depart, shortly after my tenth birthday in September, I became mysteriously ill. We were about a month late when my father and stepmother took me over to England. Meanwhile I had made my plans. No more self-abnegation, no more lying low in deference to grown-ups who were always having their feelings hurt or else hurting yours. And among the other boys I was going to be prominent; remembering school stories I had read I thought I would exploit the fact that I was Irish; the Irish boys or girls in the stories did what they liked and were always popular.

Waking up in the night train from Stranraer to Euston I said to myself 'I am in England' but could not believe it. There was nothing to prove we were in England; it was night same as anywhere else. I looked into the windows of the carriage but all I could see there were my father and my stepmother and myself sitting in our places just as we might be in Ireland.

But London was more convincing. It was a cab which smelt and a roar of houses and grime, grime, and the yelps of boys selling chocolate and never in the world had there been so much so quickly, the brass bell clanged and we were out once more in the country, the fields were bigger than in Ireland, the hay was all in stacks and never in cocks, there were mellow brick houses instead of the dirty cement, but it was all a waste of time until we got there. I wanted to be rid of my family and start making good.

X

I had never lived in a house lit by gas. The headmaster[1] stood in this miraculous light and his voice filled the room like a bell and his smile filled the room. He was ebullient with health, smelling of tweed, and high up under the ceiling from between the perfect teeth in his classic squirearchic face courteous phrases flowed out, rolled to the walls. Assurance that all was well. Oh yes, the headmaster said, we'll look after him. With great strides rocking the house he led my parents and me to my dormitory.

Its name was Number One and that was glamour. There were two little boys, new boys, in bed already and two older boys would come later. My father asked the little boys their names and where they came from and they answered politely with smiles, but I wished my father would leave us. It was I, not him, who belonged with these smiling little boys. The matron, Miss Meagram, a dried-up old thing in a high collar, told us we must not talk and at last we were left alone. The two little boys began to talk at once.

This astonished me. I had been disobedient in my time but not in this way, not as a matter of course. When disobeying Miss Craig I had felt enormous guilt. That the two little boys should disobey so promptly, easily, even automatically, was disconcerting, contrary to nature. It was my first and greatest shock in an English school. To obey one's elders ceased to be an axiom.

What astonished me nearly as much was the two little boys' aggressiveness. The blond one, who had been so cherubic to my father, changed on the instant into a leering imp, his voice charged with malevolence, his nose twitching like a rabbit's. The dark one backed him up; both were delighted to have someone junior to themselves. 'Where's your little cocky?' they said.

[1] Littleton Powys, brother of Theodore, John Cooper and Llewellyn Powys; 'Owen' in *Autumn Sequel*, canto xxii.

Morning was a harsh bell and bare boards under the feet, an unimagined hustle and breakfast a hubbub. The boys grumbled at the wartime food as they did every breakfast to follow. I sat with the youngest boys at a table presided over by Mr. Cameron who came from the North of Ireland and reminded me much of Miss Craig. He had a jutting underlip which he tugged at between phrases, and while his manner and voice were rough he had a pleasant smile but which suggested something up his sleeve.

I was pleased to get to the classroom, for that was the sphere of ambition. The floorboards were worn away and hairy to set your teeth on edge, nails sticking out of them like nails in a worn shoe. The rows of desks were shiny black with rubbing and scored with initials. The air was full of chalk. The boys coming in from playing in the yard sat on hot pipes around the wall, their clothes steaming, their faces lapsing into coma. Then the bell would break in on us— breakers of brass—we would scurry to the benches and Mr. Powys, the headmaster, would stride into the room, expansively benevolent, a shade pompous, rubbing his hands as if every day were an advent.

Lessons and bells and lessons and bells and meals. It was *de rigueur* to complain of the food. There was a kind of shiny brawn full of hairs and apparent eyes called Pig's Slosh, and there was a coarse yellow maize full of straws which I liked but the other boys said was a disgrace and what did their parents pay money for. At tea each boy was rationed to seven slices of bread and we all made a point of eating our full ration. The thing to do was to pick out slices with holes for the holes would be clogged with margarine.

My first piece of Prep (preparation) was Rep (repetition). I learned by heart 'The Burial of Sir John Moore'. One by one the boys got up from their benches, stood before Mr. Powys, buried Sir John Moore. I felt very proud I could bury him as well as the others.

The little blond boy in my dormitory continued to bully. One night I lay awake and planned my revenge, fixing my mind on his long, long chin, his habit of twitching his nose. Next morning in the play period between breakfast and class, I hunted him out, found him in the changing-room which smelt of Lifebuoy soap and wet flannels, attacked him without preliminaries. I had never done any fighting, but this little boy was weak, pulpy and cowardly, soon I was sitting on top of him. I would not leave him however until I had made him cry. It was rather a problem but I achieved it by pulling his hair, then went off very pleased. But one of the older boys said, 'Is that what they teach you in Ireland?' and the word went around that I was spiteful.

I began, however, to enjoy myself. Everyone knew so much, it spread up and out like a balloon, knowledge was power, there was hardly time to take it in. The things that the boys knew would have been Double Dutch to Carrickfergus. Butterflies, wild flowers, birds, motor-cars, aeroplanes, the County Cricket batting averages. I had arrived in the season of conkers. To make a conker you take a chestnut, pierce it, put it on a string, then you challenge someone else's conker, swinging at it with yours; the combatants have alternate strokes. Conker technique is elaborate; first you have to choose your chestnut carefully, then–or so someone said–you must mature it, then you have to decide what length of string to swing with and whether to hit your enemy's conker on top or to the side. Opinions differed as to the best size for a conker. I, in my first enthusiasm, collected very large ones but these often burst in their first engagement. A few boys had conkers from the last season, usually without shells, wizened and hard as brick, which had disposed of up to a hundred enemies. I looked forward to the day when I should have a veteran conker which other boys would fight shy of.

My object was to become popular. To my surprise I had found that I was no athlete, that the boys laughed at the way I turned my feet out. Very well; if they found me funny I would be funny on purpose, so funny that my company would be precious. Always doing something unexpected. My family helped me by sending me from Ireland a new pair of boots much too big for me. They were very uncomfortable, kept filling with pebbles and grit, but a great asset. I turned my feet out all the more, and oh how the boys laughed. The headmaster took me aside, told me it was bad to be a buffoon, but I paid no attention. The laughter of the boys was intoxicating.

I also decided to be generous. Twice a week we were allowed to buy sweets, and now and again I would try giving all my sweets away. I did this hardly at all from altruism but mainly in order to be

66

popular and a little to mortify the flesh. In order to prove I could abstain I would sometimes hoard my sweets for days.

Life was now largely dominated by the names of local institutions. 'Break' for instance. Break meant the quarter of an hour in the middle of the morning when we could go into the yard and play games, but the word 'Break' itself was something irrefrangible, magical. To have the word 'Break' on your tongue gave you an advantage over the ignorant masses, over the People at Home. When I went home for the holidays I sprung these new names on my family with the pride of a religious convert. I relished being institutionalised.

Very soon, I preferred school to home, felt I had everything in hand. Popularity was achievable by recipe; at school one was a person, at home one was just a child. At home I felt at the mercy of strangers, winced before gutter urchins, crossed the road to avoid the mill-girls, but at school we felt superior to the town boys whom we called Cadgers—another magical word to buttress our own reality.

At the beginning of term, if I got there early, the pegs in the passage would still be naked, then, as they flowered with hats, my excitement would rise and bubble and soon all would be parrot-house. I welcomed even the smells—boots and gas and antiseptics—and found even the changing-room much more romantic than the bathroom at home. There were six basins in a long counter of slate and the slate slabs were scalloped at the edges where the boys used to sharpen their penknives. It must have taken years to wear away the slate like that; I felt proud and assured to have such vener-able contacts.

My first summer term was so exciting I felt like the princess in the fairy story—you open your mouth and out come golden guineas. In the stand in the passage, empty in winter, there was now an efflorescence of butterfly nets—the first thing I noticed the first day of term. Nets of emerald green or peacock blue, voluptuous as ladies' dresses, suggesting sunswept prairies; even to handle one indoors was to feel yourself lord of summer.

And then came bathing. One day all the boys appeared at Break with bathing-drawers on their heads. Striped in different colours according to their powers of swimming. When we came back from

67

bathing we fastened these drawers on the wall of the yard, stretching them out on two nails. From our classroom window we could see this wall and, as these garments dried, the colours became carnival-gay; sometimes when fully dried the wind would belly inside them, the wall would dance, beyond Latin grammar and sums we knew there were wind and water and a chute down which those boys who had passed a test would come sailing out of the sky like Jacob's angels.

XI

Sherborne is built of a rich yellow sandstone and surrounded by yellow quarries, the water comes yellow from the taps and the clay in the fields is yellow. The Abbey is yellow but stained with red from a fire, the Dorset voices are lazy and the Abbey chimes are comforting as embers. Mr. Powys was a lyrical nature-lover and expected us all to collect things. Because the other boys seemed so far ahead with butterflies and birds' eggs, I chose to collect fossils; the yellow quarries and the yellow fields were full of them, you could even hack them out from the walls of the houses. When I came home with my hands bright yellow from fossil hunting, I would feel an achievement in my stomach. And fossils were so old. I kept them among my books and the books became stained and so prehuman themselves. I made plasticine models of diplodoci.

On May Day Mr. Powys read aloud Herrick's appeal to Corinna. Get up, get up for shame. He read it with such gusto, booming like a belfry, you felt you must rush out at once, jump over hedges. And summer in Dorset was a series of lyrics, the names of Hobbs and Hitch were scarlet stars. Nearly all of us were fetichist towards cricket, identifying ourselves with well-known cricketers. I was first the Rev. F. H. Gillingham because he was a clergyman; but Essex did so badly, I changed into Woolley, because he was left-handed and I liked the name.

Things and actions were more important than people. I assessed the other boys by the things they did. Being hardly conscious of them as characters I treated them as sounding-boards, mechanical partners in play or figures who were there to be rivalled. There were a few boys however who could not be so relegated to the wings of the stage, who impinged on my island of ego with their brute unamenable otherness. This was usually due to their physical appearance, not that such boys were necessarily either handsome or strong. There was a lanky boy from Cornwall, with a long thin face, a long pointed nose and a double-barrelled name. He had fitted up his locker inside to represent a High Church altar, with a purple cloth and tiny gilt crosses. For me he represented Cornwall, Cornwall was a land of witches, and his double-barrelled name itself was a word from a pagan liturgy. I did not of course express this make-believe in words. When talking to him or about him I treated him just as a schoolboy, but his real significance had nothing to do with school; the life of the school I could assimilate, but here was something I could not assimilate, hence its fascination. Then there were two brothers, bullet-headed, close-cropped little boys, backward at their lessons. They had the resilience of a solid rubber ball, caning did not affect them and I could not imagine them away. Many of the boys only existed if I chose to let them exist but these little bullet-heads would go on existing anyway. They were flatly, undeniably there, and I resented it only rarely. Usually it was nice to know they were so much *there*, but sometimes it was like looking for a door in the dark and finding only a wall.

After a little time at Sherborne I became intolerant. The faces of some of the boys, especially among the new boys, maddened me. To an unobservant adult little boys of that age look all much alike; to me it was the adults who looked alike whereas the boys ranged from Adonises to gargoyles. I could not suffer ugliness gladly. Each term on returning to school I inspected the new boys and there were always some whose faces disgusted me. Embryonic ugliness, necks like naked fledglings, pallid wattles of skin beneath the chin, ears like snowploughs, eyes like brandy-balls, dental plates in their mouths and–worst of all–an expression that lacked shame, these half-baked creatures were not even aware that they were hideous. Sooner or later I would pick a quarrel with these boys, punch them on the nose which made them cry the quickest.

I noticed the War more when I went home. The trains were full of troops singing 'It's a long, long trail a-winding', and it certainly was. Often I sat in the corridor wedged between kitbags and rifles, half-choked with the smell of sweat, brass-polish, beer. A long long trail to Crewe, Carlisle, Stranraer. And words I did not know but knew were bad, the four-letter words I had seen on lavatory walls. It would never end of course. But if it should ever end the world would all light up; more light than I could imagine, the sluice-gates opened full.

A sallow clergyman came to tea with my father and talked about the War, self-important, bitter. 'You wait,' he said, 'till the French get into Berlin!' His face shone as he thought of the bayonets. We had two kittens then, one called Mons and one called Flu.

In my fourth term at Sherborne the incredible happened. Armistice in Europe, gala in Sherborne. Little boys whooping and junketing—*non Angli sed angeli*; hang the Kaiser and no more rations. A friend of mine nicknamed Flounder had a little painted man made with a fretsaw. We decided to sacrifice him, rechristened him the Kaiser, burned him in a hole in the wall. Yet even at the time I felt that this was cheap.

The next spring I returned to England through Dublin, my father having put me in charge of a dear old man in the train. The dear old man had rosy cheeks and a watch-chain tight on his paunch. We sat opposite a tipsy American soldier, large and raw and angry, who insisted on talking politics. 'England,' he said to the dear old man, a Unionist, 'England's no better than Germany. Kings and dukes the lot of them,' and he told us about German atrocities. Germans, he said, they nail you to boards and they leave you to rot and the English royal family is German. No more wars for him, fighting for God-damned dukes. And as for the dear old man, what did he think of Carson? The dear old man drew himself in, his watch-chain sagged on his belly, he said he admired Carson. The American soldier turned to me; 'You're only a kid,' he said, 'but you look like an American kid. What do you think of Carson?' Feeling shockingly disloyal to the dear old man but remembering my father and Home Rule, I said I thought Carson was a pity. The American soldier was delighted, asked the old man if he was not ashamed, a whitehaired old man like himself and a little boy like me had more sense. I felt very uncomfortable. In the station at Dublin I was met by my stepmother's sister and given sandwiches and tea in the buffet. Up at the bar I could see the American soldier, drinking strong drink and talking loudly and coarsely. A world that I did not know and did not like, and yet, as regarded Carson, he agreed with my father and, apart from that, it was true, they

71

nailed you to boards and the biggest collection of butterflies or birds' eggs—or even of fossils—will never cover up the havoc and the hatred. I pretended to enjoy my sandwich. 'Oh yes,' I said to my stepmother's sister, 'I am glad to be going back to school.'

XII

Peace. The novelty of it soon wore off, we stopped having maize and Pig's Slosh and, bread being no longer rationed, few of us ate more than three or four slices for tea. I was conscious about 1919 of a new power in myself, the power–and the wish–to criticise. Many of the other little boys were aggressively critical too and we could not tolerate those who remained snugly and stubbornly in prejudice. Thus I had a bitter argument with a boy who said there were no white foxes. I said Yes there were, it was a question of climate. Bally nonsense, he said. I said I would show him a book to prove it. Wouldn't believe it, he said; his pater had never seen a white fox; he believed his pater. My anger nearly burst me into tears.

In the holidays Elizabeth and I used to bait my stepmother about Evolution. She was immune even to my father who mentioned Evolution in the pulpit. No, my stepmother said, passing it off as a joke but piqued nevertheless, she for one was not descended from a monkey. 'But now your appendix,' Elizabeth would say, 'you only have one because you once had a tail; the appendix is no use now.' 'You mustn't say things like that,' my stepmother rejoined, at last getting red in the face at our precocious importunate blasphemy, 'of course it must be some use; otherwise God wouldn't have put it there.'

It worried me too to watch my father cutting cake. If it was a round cake he would approach it with, it seemed, a certain embarrassment, holding the knife inexpertly in a too white hand, and cut it never from the centre but from some point which would give a shorter slice. This struck me as unscientific; oh yes, I knew my father did this out of modesty but couldn't he see that it made the cake lopsided and that later on someone would have to have slices longer than half the diameter?

At school I no longer assumed that the masters were all my

73

superiors. Some of them were ninnies. Mr. Cameron left us for a time and in his place we had a master from Galway—seedy, embittered, with a powerful brogue, a bad cough and always the same suit. He could not manage the chalk on the blackboard; the pieces of chalk from day to day, from month to month, harassed him with unending guerrilla warfare, breaking in his hand, deploying to all corners of the room. 'Damn the chark!' he would shout, hurling the remaining stub away from him. 'The square on the hypotenuse is equal— Damn the chark!' And then, conscious of our grins, he would look ashamed, on the verge of tears, and surrender to a spasm of coughing.

Powys, however, remained rather the demi-god, though we often resented what seemed his too pompous righteousness; if he caught us ragging he would treat us like God the Father with Cain and we found that out of proportion. But he was so full of health and Natural History, so handsome, a walking tower, and his voice so beautiful and bronze, we forgave him his disciplinarianism, his occasional sentimentalities. I had always enjoyed hearing my father read the Lesson, weighting the biblical names—Abana and Pharpar —with all the ore of the East, but Powys was the first who thrilled me by reading poetry. On Saint Cecilia's Day he would assemble the whole school and read us Dryden's Ode; the classroom would fill with marble columns and the cracked ceiling and the incandescent burners would vanish in hanging velvets, brocades. When Powys taught us to scan Latin hexameters he would stride up and down the room slowly, yards to each stride, intoning 'Spon-dee! Spon-dee!' Spon on the left foot and Dee on the right.

I tried to combine science with fantasy, told a serial story in dormitory which lasted for five terms, a Jules-Verne-like romance of life on a square planet; one of my friends made a map of it in water-colours. And going home through London I was taken to the British Museum, fell in love with the Egyptian cat-headed goddess, Sekhet. Because I had always been devoted to cats and because Sekhet was so self-assured in granite, in her tight fluted dress, her serene but athletic elegance, her momentous undeniability.

During one summer holidays my father took us to the salt-mines. We went on an outside car, clopping of hoofs and scuttling of pebbles, the country a prism for the sun was shining on the patchwork, but Elizabeth and I were impatient till we got there; we had always wanted to go down under the earth to the caves of crystal and man-made thunder, to the black labyrinth of galleries under the carefree fields, under the tumbledown walls, the whins and the ragweed. We descended a pitch-black shaft in a great bucket, at the bottom was a cross of fire and there sure enough was the subterranean cathedral and men like gnomes in the clerestories, working with picks.

Some time later I dreamed the gnomes had caught me, imprisoned me under the ground until I should find a certain jewel. A hopeless task; I wandered under the vaults groping through heaps of shattered quartzite rocks. Then met another prisoner, a girl; we decided to give up the hunt, to brave the gnomes and make our escape to daylight. No sooner decided than we found ourselves in a lift, an enormous lift fitted up as a teashop; a middle-aged man was eating bacon and eggs; no one took any notice of us. So there we were going up, sometimes the lift would stop, people come in and get out, but no one took any notice. It was frightening but almost hilarious. Then as we rose to the light I do not know what became of the girl but I woke up.

When I was about twelve my brother came home for a fortnight. Having forgotten what idiocy meant I built him in advance a hut in the shrubbery which could only be entered through a trapdoor in the roof. He and I were to sit in there together, eating leaves of nasturtium and sorrel, making believe to be explorers. But when he arrived he was changed, had forgotten how to go even up or down stairs. When he left in a fortnight to return to his Institution I felt a great relief but a guilt that more than balanced it. And the bloom, I felt, had gone off the Dorset hills. And the boys at Sherborne seemed suddenly terribly young; I had learned their language but they could not learn mine, could never breathe my darkness.

I invented a prayer to keep off the evil, would say it to myself any hour of the day in the house or the street, putting my hands over my ears to keep out the noise of the world. My stepmother asked me if I had pains in my ears, perhaps I really ought to see a specialist.

XIII

But Sherborne was gay enough once I went back to it. There was a new master from Oxford, a Mr. Charles, who arrived to teach us English, History and Geography. He told us we need not bother with History and Geography; all that really mattered was Keats. He was tall and slim, with small features and a mouth that could sneer, he wore a grey check suit with a grey check shirt and a grey check tie and grey check socks, and he left little islands of scent behind him in classroom and garden. He filled his room with a bust of Dante and Keats's death-mask, and wrote Greek verses on the wall which we thought were his own composition. Cricket, he said, was a classical game, an art, but rugby football was barbarous.

For some time we thought that being taught by Mr. Charles was a picnic, he flattered us by denouncing Philistia and aligning us with him against it. It was our first taste of aesthetic snobbery and was sweet enough in the mouth; poor Mr. Cameron was out of it. Then one day Mr. Charles said to a boy in class: 'Have you ever heard of Mazzini?' and the boy said, 'No and I don't want to.' Mr. Charles, who had been born in Italy, flared into a rage that dwarfed Mr. Cameron's. 'Damn you,' he said, 'little middle-class brats.' It was all a mistake, he saw now, trying to assist us to culture, pearls before swine. He left the room in a tantrum, banging the door, and we were too appalled to enjoy the rest of the hour's idleness.

He had a worse tantrum later. He had offered a prize for an English essay—to be done in our own time and the entries voluntary—on some subject like the Poetic Function of the Imagination. The eldest among us were thirteen and none of us understood the title but Mr. Charles seemed very keen on it, was always giving us hints, and a few of us—many weeks after the competition had been announced—were about to begin an assault on the Imagination when Mr. Charles suddenly in class asked us which of us were entering. No one was brave enough to hold up his hand. Mr. Charles went white and tense; this, he said, was the end. He had done all he could to no purpose. Very well, in future he would meet us on our level. Savagely he tore a quire of foolscap into quarters, threw them at our heads. 'Spell,' said Mr. Charles, spitting the words like a machine-gun, 'spell. It is all you are good for. Spell erysipelas, symmetry, asyndeton.'

Mr. Charles by these outbursts put himself in the same category as the others, was no longer an exception to the rule that masters do not belong. We had been fools to try to accept him; masters are always outsiders. But it did not matter so very much; we went on with our collecting of stamps, butterflies, fossils, our catalogues of brands of car and motor-cycle, our mimicries and private jokes, our paper aeroplanes and trove from Sunday walks—an old sheep's skull, the corpse of a stoat, a bunch of cowslips. Things and statistics and names are more important to boys of twelve than friendship with any master.

Inspired by Mr. Charles I had read Malory's *Morte d'Arthur*, sitting in a windowseat and reading with such concentration that my hair stuck to the paint of the woodwork. The book was very long but by no means too long for me; I revelled in the reiteration of incident; to go from joust to joust and count how many knights Sir Tristram or Sir Pelleas unseated was as exciting as reading the County Cricket batting averages. My friends and I found a table in an old summerhouse and became the knights ourselves, drawing lots for the leading names. On Sundays we rode about the country on branches of trees, each with an ashplant for a sword, and tried to use the Malory diction. It was my last open make-believe before my adolescence, after which time, like everyone else, I lived half the time in fantasy, but craftily, deceiving both others and myself. This adult make-believe is something we have foolishly ignored. Teddy Bock is always with us, and in the epoch of Hitler—Siegfried Redivivus—it is not only a mistake but a disaster to ignore those underground motives which cause both art and war. Economic factors? Yes, but they aren't the whole story. Man is essentially weak and he wants power; essentially lonely, he creates familiar daemons, Impossible Shes, and bonds—of race or creed—where no bonds are. He cannot live by bread or Marx alone; he must always be after the Grail.

Together with the *Morte d'Arthur* I studied astronomy which combined the excitement of collecting with the glamour of Church. I would read about the nebulas and the stars that had gone black, and that was like organ music; and I would learn by heart the distances of the stars and the diameters of the planets, and that was like Sir Pelleas or Hobbs. Then when the night came I would go out collecting, and this was made attractively difficult at school by our early hours and in Ireland by the cloudy sky—you might just pick up a star here or there in a rift. In January 1921 I found myself wonderfully alone in an empty carriage in a rocking train in the night between Waterloo and Sherborne. Stars on each side of me; I ran from side to side of the carriage checking the constellations as the train changed its direction. Bagfuls and bucketfuls of stars; I could open my mouth to the night and drink them.

In my last two terms at Sherborne I took things easy, for I had got an entrance scholarship to Marlborough College and felt that this interim was only marking time. When I told Mr. Powys there were seven hundred and fifty boys at Marlborough he said he hoped I would keep my head above water. I was a little alarmed at this remark, decided that at Marlborough I would behave quite differently; no more buffoonery. At Sherborne I had become established as an eccentric and that gets awfully boring.

On the Twelfth of July Powys came into my dormitory and said: 'What is all this they do in your country today? Isn't it all mumbo-jumbo?' Remembering my father and Home Rule and the bony elbows of Miss Craig and the black file of mill-girls and the wickedness of Carson and the dull dank days between sodden haycocks and foghorns, I said Yes it was. And I felt uplifted. To be speaking man to man to Powys and giving the lie to the Red Hand of Ulster was power, was freedom, meant I was nearly grown up. King William is dead and his white horse with him, and Miss Craig will never put her knuckles in my ears again. But Powys went out of the dormitory and Mr. Cameron came in, his underlip jutting and his eyes enraged. 'What were you saying to Mr. Powys?' Oh this division of allegiance! That the Twelfth of July was mumbo-jumbo was true, and my father thought so too, but the moment Mr. Cameron appeared I felt rather guilty and cheap. Because I had been showing off to Powys and because Mr. Cameron being after all Irish I felt I had betrayed him.

Before I left, Mr. Powys gave me a sex-talk, putting it very delicately, working up from butterflies to birds. I could not make head or tail of it and when he said, 'You know what part of the body I mean?' I said, 'No, I don't.' So Powys began again with a joke about a baby wetting its bed, and that put me off the whole business because I was very prudish. I felt a chill in my bones and a weight on my stomach, and when I got back to dormitory I was silent and thought about it. But decided it was best not to think about it.

Once a week we used to go and shoot in a miniature rifle range. The entrance was at the far end and the path which ran along outside the range had a border of snapdragons. They were very gay in that last summer, opening their mouths and snapping, the name reminded me of the raisins burning in the brandy and the harsh reports of the shots inside the wall counterpointed them oddly, both colour and noise were vital. If only one could live the life of the senses and have no problems, no need to keep one's head above water! But even the senses had their problems—there was always that baby in the bed.

That September, before I went to Marlborough, my family took me to Anglesey and we attended a church service in Welsh. Religion in Welsh seemed more primeval and in the pew behind was a woman suckling her baby. Her breast was round and white and, though I did not like the noise of the baby sucking, I was not disgusted. It was talking about these things that was disgusting but the things themselves seemed all right. They sang the Gloria in Welsh and I thought what fun—always moving on, Sherborne to Marlborough, sandstone to flint, Glory be and Glory be and the world is there for the having.

XIV

The public schools of England have been written down *ad nauseam*. To flog these dying horses is no longer very daring and there have been more than enough autobiographies of rich boys faring ill, of sensitive plants wilting on the playing fields. The public schools profess to build character and we all know now what that meant—a very limited, narrow, but not unattractive brand of character, all right on a short-term view but all wrong on a long. In the intervals of character-building they gave one not a bad education. As for the playing fields I for one never objected to them; to be rolled in the mud satisfied one of my instincts.

Physical discomfort and futile ritual—those were the first things I noticed. I entered a junior house where boys of about fourteen lived for a year or so to be hardened before they moved on. Boys of that age being especially sadistic, life in the junior houses was more uncomfortable than the supposedly more frightening life we moved on to. The house itself looked like a prison, a great square building of ugly brick, with a huge well down the centre surrounded by railed-in landings; you could look up from the basement, see the prisoners listlessly parading on every floor, their shrill voices echoing metallic, the air sombre and stale, steaming in the morning from the bathrooms and dense in the afternoons with frying fat. There were often one or two little boys trudging down and up the stairs from the ground floor to the basement, turning automatically at the bottom step or the top, just down and up, down and up; these boys were doing 'Basements'—a punishment inflicted on them by boys one term or more their seniors.

We had our meals in a great bleak hall with more than five hundred other boys. The walls were distempered a sombre red and ornamented with a great number of dingy plaster busts. For the first few meals I got very little to eat because I did not understand the custom of Rushing; as soon as you entered the hall you were expected to stick a fork in your patty, a spoon in your porridge plate and so on, otherwise anyone else could 'rush' them as well as his own. There was also Condescending, the word 'condescend' being perhaps a corruption of 'Can't you send'. No one in the junior house could condescend till he was in his third term, then he could pass the word down the table 'Condescend the sugar—or the milk—third-termer', and the milk or sugar had to be sent up to him unless a fourth-termer or a fifth-termer liked to intervene and condescend it for himself on the way. Thus a new boy was always like Tantalus, about to help himself from a bowl or jug which just as he was reaching for it would be harshly condescended away.

For my first two or three days at Marlborough I did not go to the lavatory because I did not know where it was and was too embarrassed to ask. One was expected to know these things on arrival; no one helped one.

The caste system limited my circle of acquaintances. I was very glad to make friends with whom I could but the junior house, compared with Sherborne, was dull. There was not the same multiplicity of interests, the same variety of play; everyone was careerist, obsessed with getting on in form or in games, with getting into a senior house, with keeping his place in the weekly or fortnightly class-lists and so avoiding caning. Their conversation, when it was not shop, was infected with the social snobbery they brought from home. During term we wore uniform black but at the end of term we were allowed to wear ordinary suits to go home in. At the end of term accordingly everyone was jealously competitive and those boys were despised whose clothes were not well cut. As for the boys who went home in their school clothes—of whom I was one, for I was ashamed to ask my family for a decent suit—they were almost pariahs.

Ill-qualified for social climbing and not an athlete, I spent a lot of time in the Reading Room, specialising, as I had done for years, in the fantastic—in ghost stories, legends, medieval romances. I was particularly fond of a large edition of Dante with illustrations by Gustave Doré. I had a strong objection to smutty talk, but I liked Doré's naked women with great round breasts marked with concentric circles who floated on the whirlwind or were tumbled into morasses.

81

During my third term, while still fourteen, I passed an examination called the School Certificate, after passing which one specialised. I had not been expected to pass, so felt very jubilant, had a joyful holiday in Perthshire with my family during which I helped to save Elizabeth from drowning. My stepmother hurt my feelings by saying 'We must thank God you can swim so well' but my egotism survived this injustice. I had passed the School Certificate, I had rescued Elizabeth, I would soon go into a senior house and in my fifth term there I could wear coloured socks.

In Perthshire we were shown over a ruined castle by a white-haired, rosy-cheeked curator, biblical in speech and heartily God-fearing. My father said he was a very fine type—you would find that all over Scotland—and took the occasion to deplore the defects of the Irish peasantry. The pious old man reeled off his dates with gusto till he came to a crumbled stone relief showing the rear view of a woman with her dress drawn up revealing her buttocks. His face lit up, he asked us if we knew what this was. None of us knew; my father looked a little displeased. Ah, said the old man, it was a good old custom; pity it had gone out; in the good old days if a woman misbehaved herself they would hold her down like this and anyone that came by was welcome to give her a pandy. I was secretly delighted; what fun it would be to have a grown-up woman held down for you to smack her on the bare behind.

Another day in Perthshire we met a company of film actors including a girl with yellow yellow hair and tight-fitting riding-breeches. She was very fragile and no taller than I was, and a little-boy lust took hold of me though I had not yet reached puberty. Wherever we walked afterwards, in the glens or by the lake, I imagined little fantasies—how I would come here and find this girl alone and how I would wrestle with her. Her walking about in breeches was a challenge; I would chase her through the pine trees and catch her, then I would show her. Show her what? I really didn't know but there was a big word Pandy in the sky and it would be much more exciting somehow than wrestling with boys, though that was enjoyable enough.

Returning to school I went into a Classical form and was made to buy a full-size Liddell and Scott Greek lexicon. From that date I was taught no more modern languages, modern history, science or mathematics. Certainly I was advancing. The next term I went into a senior house, the big boys were very big indeed but they took no notice of me, the chief unpleasantness was fagging. When you were on coal-fagging you went down with a bucket into a cellar that was deliberately unlit and not provided with shovels; you groped in a mass of coal-dust trying to find lumps, for if you failed to bring enough lumps the big boys cursed you; then you stumbled with your buckets up stairs and stairs and the big boys cursed you. When you were on milk-fagging you had to fetch milk for eight or more of the bigger boys across a hundred yards of courtyard and again upstairs; this milk had to be carried in eight or more tin mugs, you were not allowed to transfer it to a jug and redistribute it in the mugs the other end; and you had to carry all the eight or more mugs in one journey so that you were always spilling the milk and getting cursed. But the cursing was really more important than the milk. This was long before Mussolini made his chieftains jump over tanks.

When a boy first entered a senior house such as mine he spent most of his day in a building called Upper School. It had been built about 1850 and, though enormously large, hardly seemed like a building at all. It was just a great tract of empty air, cold as the air outside but smelling of stables, enclosed by four thin walls and a distant roof. One half of the floor was covered with desks and benches, the other half was empty; there were only two doors and two fires. These were coal fires and radiated heat for not more than two or three yards. One fire was called Big Fire and reserved for less than twenty boys who were the oligarchy; the other fire, Little Fire, was open to the rest of us who numbered about a hundred. To be elected to Big Fire was a great honour but could only be hoped for by athletes or by boys so stupid that they had remained in Upper School longer than the normal span; if you had any brains you were soon moved on elsewhere.

I have never been anywhere like Samoa, but I fancy that the rites of Upper School should interest professional connoisseurs. Our last meal in the great dining-hall was at 6.30 p.m. and an hour's preparation of work began in Upper School at 7.15 Those of us who belonged to Little Fire were expected to be sitting at our desks by 7.0 at the latest. The next quarter of an hour was a babel while we watched the members of Big Fire at their antics. Big Fire, although the oligarchy, had no responsibility except to be exhibitionist. Above them there were four Captains, aged about sixteen and invariably athletic. During the rest of the day these Captains belonged to Big Fire but from 7.0 to 7.15 they were Big Fire's enemies. The Captains were not due to appear until 7.15 when they would come in with canes in their hands and preparation would begin. Anyone out of his seat when the Captains entered was caned. This applied to Big Fire too, but whereas Big Fire would not have brooked our leaving our seats during their sacred quarter of an hour they were expected by themselves and by us to be on the floor till the last half-second. So they would spend the time barricading the doors against the Captains or making them ingenious booby-traps or else running whooping out of the building by one door, around through a yard and in at the other. Round and round till the Captains caught them. Sometimes all of Big Fire would be caught out of their places at once, and after preparation we would have the treat of a mass caning, standing in a large semi-circle while the Captains took a run and laid into their bosom friends.

The Captains entered at 7.15 but that did not mean we could all start working. The Captains marched up and down the alley-ways slapping the desks with their canes and inspecting the lids to see if they were flush; if the lid of any desk were even a quarter of an inch raised its owner was booked to be caned. Meanwhile the junior boys had to go round the hall 'scavenging', gathering up in their hands the fruit-peel, match-ends, fluff, muck and paper which had been lavishly thrown on the floor during the day, and carrying these nasty little handfuls to an enormous wastepaper-basket. The Captains would keep an eye on the scavengers and flick at their ankles with their canes if they scavenged too slackly.

The wastepaper-basket had another purpose. Once in a while – not more often than once a term – Big Fire decided that someone was undesirable and could therefore provide a Roman holiday. They would seize him, tear off most of his clothes and cover him with house-paint, then put him in the basket and push him round and round the hall. Meanwhile Little Fire, dutifully sitting at their desks, would howl with delight – a perfect exhibition of mass sadism. The masters considered this a fine old tradition, and any boy who had been basketed was under a cloud for the future. Because the boys have an innate sense of justice, anyone they basket must be really undesirable. Government of the mob, by the mob, and for the mob.

It was hard to do much work in Upper School. The cold kept everybody shuffling, and every so often a boy would put up his hand and ask the master in charge (who had entered later than the Captains): 'Please, sir, may I cross Court?' Crossing Court was a euphemism for going to the lavatory. The school lavatories–or the rears, as they were called–consisted of a large shed with brick walls and a corrugated-iron roof, open at each end to the wind and rain. The centre of this shed was occupied by two long rows of cells, set back to back and without doors, and each containing a fixed seat with a round hole in it; underneath was a channel which was flushed from end to end automatically every quarter of an hour; the time to excrete was of course immediately after this flushing. As it was one of the few places where a boy could speak to a boy two or more years younger than himself without being observed by the masters, you would often see older boys prowling up and down there in the morning after breakfast, looking for their favourites on the stools.

Building of Character. At the age of fifteen or sixteen we were expected to be confirmed. The Confirmation candidates assembled in the chapel each week to have a special talk from the headmaster. One day he gave us a full hour's talk on the Commandment, Thou shalt not commit adultery. What does that mean? It means much more than it says. Whenever you meet a girl or a woman you must think of her as if she were your sister; otherwise it is adultery. Self-abuse is adultery too; it destroys your body and your mind and you end in the madhouse.

From the British public schools come the British ruling classes. Or came till very lately. It was from the public schools that our Governments caught the trick of infallibility. The public-school boy, after a few years of discomfort, has all the answers at his finger-tips; he does not have to bother with the questions. It is only the odd public-school boy who thinks that there are any questions left. This is why the public schools will die like the dinosaurs–from overspecialisation and a mortal invulnerability.

XV

No, character building from my point of view was a flop. Not like
the Wiltshire Downs or making Welsh rarebit or even Greek grammar. Once you can make a Welsh rarebit—which we did on half-
holidays on gas-flares—there it is and you eat it. But all this moral
fibre . . .

The town and the school of Marlborough are set down in a
hollow and on all sides the downs rise in curves, bevel and grey and
serene as perching doves; on the skyline there are one or two clumps
of trees like hippopotamuses. On days too wet for games we were
sent running over these downs with a time limit out and back; if
you were late either way you were caned but, once you got used to
this strenuous effort, these runs were exhilarating. I liked it even
when it hailed—hard clean hail whipping the throat and the ears and
not a bit of shelter within a mile; I would run my fingers through my
hair and be pleased to find the water in it warm. Then when you got
back into the communal bathroom even lukewarm water would bite
you until gradually getting reacclimatized you sunk into your tub,
wonderfully relaxed in an underworld of steam and dim pink bodies
humming Gilbert and Sullivan.

Even within the school grounds there were objects of glamour.
There was an allegedly druidic mound which had been brought up
to date by an eighteenth-century countess who had carved a spiral
pathway round it and added a couple of grottoes: it was now covered
with trees and in the trees was a rookery. Beyond this mound was
the bathing place, a converted castle moat overhung by laburnums.
My senior house was a Queen Anne mansion and the chief dormitory
was a long high room with lime-green panelling, egg-and-dart
moulding round the cornice and a series of majestic windows which
looked out on an elegant velvet lawn bounded by scalloped yew
trees.

These things atoned for the many rawnesses. I had never before

86

lived in a chalk country, and after the clay of County Antrim and the sleepy yellow sandstone of Sherborne the chalk of Marlborough and the sheep-cropped turf and the flint seemed spare and hard and invigorating. Chalk goes on for ever. The white horses cut in the hillsides in the time of God knows whom defied the encroachment of the grass. To stand alone on the downs made you feel powerful. As if it was you who with a razor had shaved the rubbish from the world.

Atmosphere and technique were two categories of pleasure. Lessons were mainly technique; I was not yet immersed in humanism. Grammar is nearly always badly taught, but even so, once we got the hang of it, Greek grammar was a pretty toy to play with. You find there are things you can do in Greek you never could do in English. The two negatives for instance– *ou* and *mē* –and even more the exquisite subtlety of the double negative *mē ou*. And the wealth of particles. And that wonderful Greek word *an* which you can even tack on to a participle, so that where in English you would say 'Those who would have done this', in Greek you can get rid of the wretched relative, say 'Those *an* having done this', but 'having done' itself would be one word and not two. The same with hockey; we learnt the economy of the wrist-flick, began to aspire in all things to a grace that was apparently effortless.

And the third category was friendship. There was an inky little boy called Graham Shepard[1] who did not quite fit into the Marlborough pattern. He had been brought up to believe in 'breeding' and the importance of being a gentleman, so he paid due deference to the 'bloods' and to people who were out of the top drawer, but in appearance and manner he was a stray from some other place or era, a surprising blend of precocious worldly-wiseness and faunal innocence. His feeling for fantasy geared in with mine, we would dress up in bracken in Savernake Forest, jump out on the road to scare old gentlemen. He lived by right of himself, untidy and often unwashed, and he gabbled so that people found him hard to follow. Something like a cockney leprechaun, he had an enthusiasm not encouraged at Marlborough and when he said 'Let's go a bicycle ride' he meant it would be fun and it was. One day in May, when

[1] Drowned on active service, 1943 (cf. 'The Casualty', *Springboard*, p. 41); he appears as 'Gavin' in *Autumn Sequel*, canto ii.

we were both sixteen, Graham said 'Let's go a ride' and all the white horses were wishes.[1]

As we skimmed down southwards over the chalk country the hedges were still fresh and lathered with mays, the laburnums were tumbling gold and the sun raking the downland. Upon wheels we were free, were We, and as we passed under the beeches the light fell through in confetti. A green and amber combustion of trees, an unfolding, unshuttering of sunlight, and the droning of an aeroplane somewhere in the dome of the sky, an indolent sleepy noise that had no foreboding. Just a silly old plane wool-gathering, taking a wee dander—to use an Ulster phrase—taking a wee dander over England.

The oracles all were with us. We rode along the towpath of a canal, decided to bathe. The water was a tepid purée, but bathing in the country was forbidden and nakedness on a towpath seemed a beautiful bravado, so we undressed quickly and stepped in. The canal was not more than four foot deep and one foot of that was slime which came up between the toes obscenely caressing. We stood in the middle splashing each other and hallooing when a deep mocking voice came and hit us like a flail.

On the bank was a very ragged tramp with several days' growth of beard. He had an open shirt with a mat of black hair on his chest and a leering, tipsy face and he was accusing us huskily, incoherently. We felt on the instant like unfledged birds, both guilty and outraged. Easy for us, he was saying, it was easy enough for us; how would we like to do a hard day's work? Graham said that we had to work too. The tramp laughed and spat. Never done a day's work in your lives, he said. His swarthy male contempt felt like a bludgeon on our puny white bodies. 'Books,' Graham said. 'Books!' the tramp said and shambled away swearing. Graham and I made an effort to laugh it off, climbed out of the canal, wiped the slime off our legs in the long grasses and danced ourselves dry among the buttercups. But we could not quite laugh the tramp away. As if in the middle of a harpsichord recital a steamroller came through the wall and ran over the harpsichord, the gavotte dropped dead in its tracks. 'Poor old bloke!' said Graham but he had spoiled our afternoon and we knew he was the enemy.

[1] Cf. 'The Cyclist' (*Holes in the Sky*, p. 38).

XVI

A parade of masters:–

Masters to a new boy are always impressive, gradually they shrink, begin to repeat themselves, their mannerisms stand out further and further like Pinocchio's nose, you realise that their intellect is static, you cease to care what they think of you, you write them off as mere 'beaks', inhuman, bored and embittered.

A young master comes up fresh from Oxford or Cambridge, full of ideas and charm; after a few years the ideas shrivel away, the charm becomes a convention. In order to do their job well they have to become more or less mechanical. The nicest masters are the eccentrics, but these are eccentric before their time in a way which belongs to the old, have little tricks and crotchets dipped in a petrifying stream, spinsters and proud of it too.

There were fifty masters at Marlborough, half of whom were insignificant, pleasant enough but incurably trivial, fawning on their seniors, saving up money for a sports car, backbiting each other in the Common Room. Of those who were academically brilliant the majority had stuck at a point. And the great athletes were getting stiff in the bones and short in the wind, still changed into flannels, exposed their thinning hair to the weather, but their souls lingered in ancient *Wisden's Almanacs*, in framed and crested photos of forgotten teams.

There was a fighting parson, a mathematician and housemaster, who flogged his house into winning all their matches and terrified his classes by his staccato method of teaching, throwing books at their heads, saying 'Do this sum quickly; it is Corban–a gift.'

There was another parson, a chemist, very long and weedy, with an unhappy Adam's apple, who spent his holidays bicycling in France, taking photos of cathedrals which he made into lantern slides so that afterwards, as a balance to science, he could talk about culture to a half-empty lecture hall.

There was a little old man, a housemaster, F.R.G.S., who could not be bothered to cane and punished his boys by making them grind his coffee.

There were masters notorious for playing with their parts or for puns. There were many who had been in the War whose tempers had been ruined by shell-shock or military boredom.

There was a humane dapper little Oxonian, with a print of a Patinir on his wall, who was said to drink a glass of absinthe each Sunday and to weep in his Thucydides class whenever he came to the collapse of the Athenian expedition to Syracuse.

There was a sad alcoholic whose pupils brought dogs into his classroom on the assumption that he would think them unreal but who took them out to dinner and gave them Burgundy.

There was a brilliant classicist who had been an Oxford Fellow but preferred schoolmastering and, while he was at it, preferred teaching the lower forms. Obese and unwieldy and shabby, with a great strawberry face, he was a recluse and could be seen every afternoon lumbering alone over the downs, his head swinging like a drunkard's. He had no use for humanism in the classroom, concentrated with gusto on grammar and syntax; he said that 'Honour Mods.' at Oxford, the examination which lays such stress on textual commentary and minute scholarship, was the Greatest Examination in the World. He was a stickler for tidiness in his classroom, made his boys write their answers on pieces of paper the size of postcards. Proud of his isolation, he did not mind what he said about his colleagues; 'I hear Mr. X has been making a fool of himself again' he said to us when Mr. X had been trying to repress a romantic intrigue. On half-holidays he would go by train to Bristol and back for the mere pleasure of train-riding, all the way stuffing himself with chocolates. There were three things he hated, he said – God, girls and cricket. His favourite author was Anatole France.

My last three years were spent under the two leading classical masters who thus had almost a monopoly of my education. The master of the Classical Lower Sixth was very brisk and efficient, appearing each day on the stroke of the clock, taking a long, firm and yet self-conscious stride to his desk, jutting out his jaw and looking us up and down like an inspecting colonel. He always wore the same clothes – dark grey flannel trousers, a buff-coloured Harris tweed sports jacket, a stiff white collar and a dull green tie which every so often he would push up into position with a quick movement that implied 'What must be must be.' A moralist and a logician, very precise in diction, he was never tired of asking: 'What exactly do you mean by that?' But he had his sentimental quarters of an hour when he read us *The Shropshire Lad*. In spite of his bonhomie and briskness and his optimistic belief in Progress, he struck me as a melancholy figure, more lost than he would ever have admitted; looking over his shoulder were the shades of a thousand retarded progressives, of the one-time promising stars of the Oxford and Cambridge Unions, of earnest modernist Christians who reconciled Christ with T. H. Huxley, of those pre-War devotees of Reason who had whittled away their doubts with a razor and were left with nothing but a razor.

G. M. Sargeaunt, the master of the Classical Upper Sixth, was very different. Apart from his pupils few boys in the school had spoken to him. He was aloof and austerely Olympian, had a private religion of his own founded on ancient Stoicism. He had once been a housemaster but had resigned because he refused to give religious instruction to the boys in his house who were about to be confirmed. Tall and slim, with grey hair sweeping back from his forehead and suffering innocent blue eyes, he dressed with a lazy sophistication and spoke with a beautiful contemptuous drawl—as if he had one foot in Heaven and were just dragging the other foot after him. But could hardly be bothered to finish the sentence, left the other foot where it was because Heaven after all was perhaps a little crude.

Though he made the least effort to inspire us he was the one master we really found inspiring. He expected so little from us that he never got angry, he expected so little that he put us on our mettle. Occasionally he would forget how stupid we were and speak with emotion. As when he defended Cicero whom he thought historians had maligned. In opposition to Mommsen who represents Cicero as a double-dealing, weak-kneed, opportunist reactionary, Sargeaunt thought of him as the one sympathetic figure in a period of thugs and crooks, a doomed liberal who had the courage of his culture. And Sargeaunt was homesick for fifth-century Greece. He liked the Greek attitude to Fate, their refusal to bank on Utopias, their courage in going on living without the stimulus of heaven or heady idealism. 'The Greeks,' he would say, 'didn't expect such a *lot* out of life.' Then with long nervous fingers he would put away his lexicon and slope back to his Dutch wife and his little modern villa, full of first editions and reproductions of Tintoretto, where he would read Thomas Hardy or Dante or write–but only once in a way–neo-Hellenist articles for unpopular journals.

XVII

When I was just seventeen I was allotted a study, a tiny room ten foot by five which I shared with a boy called Reckitts who was going to go into the Church; it contained four chairs and two tables. Reckitts and I, who had been new boys together in our house, had been very friendly. He too was the son of a clergyman but unlike most sons of clergymen at Marlborough, who became would-be fast, Reckitts remained true to his family's puritanical traditions; he even refused to drink ginger beer from stone bottles in case it might have fermented, and he went white and tight-lipped when he heard a dirty story. I had hardly begun to share a study with him—something we had looked forward to for a year—before an antipathy blossomed between us. Being with Reckitts was too like being with my family and what was forgivable in them seemed intolerably priggish in Reckitts.

As was my custom, I focused my resentment on his personal appearance. He was small and dark with a high bulging forehead, a pale mauve face and large purple hands and on a cold day he would sit reading at his table in woollen mittens. His mittens and his morality and, even more, his occasional sentimentality exasperated me into malice and, while letting him do all the cooking and tidying which he did with the zeal of a Boy Scout, I invented little games to annoy him, suddenly pointing at the top of a little cupboard in the corner and saying: 'Look at that thing up there. Look at the way it's grinning.' Then Reckitts would look up at the empty corner and at me and either lose his temper or shrink back into himself (I could see the suspicion growing in him that perhaps I was really crazy). After a few weeks it was a stalemate; we would both sit and work in sullen silence. Reckitts had covered the tables with strips of green baize which enhanced the atmosphere of a vestry-room; he regarded me as a backslider because two years before I had told him I was going to be a missionary.

It was unfortunate for Reckitts that 1924–5, the year when we shared a study, was the year of my most rapid intellectual development; I began it a shy little boy and ended it trailing my coat. I should have liked to share a study with Graham but that was impossible because Graham was in another house. However when our study became spiritually suffocating I would visit Graham's study which was only suffocating physically. Graham never opened the window and, in order to be warm, kept his gas-flare burning all day. He often left a kettle on the flare, the water would evaporate, the room would fill with steam, and the nearly empty kettle would dance and clank while Graham would gabble away, drop ink and butter on his books and take no notice of his surroundings. His mind was hardly on Marlborough at all. He had begun to brush his hair and spent much of his time thinking about dances in Surrey or bathing parties in Cornwall. Where he came from in Surrey the families lived in half-timbered modern houses, had army connections, played a good hand of bridge, sent their daughters to finishing schools in Paris, read Kipling and insisted on 'breeding' and went to hunt balls. Graham, who considered this life of theirs inadequate, still wanted to cut a figure among them. But what he wanted to do most was to write. He and I were both itching to write. If you can describe a person you somehow get a magic power over him. Like the witches who made wax dolls and stuck them with pins.

Marlborough, unlike many public schools, had a strong highbrow tradition; there was always a group among the older boys that was openly against the government, that mocked the sacred code and opposed to it an aesthetic dilettantism. Down the passage from Graham's study was a door with an inscription above it –

Here thou, Great Anna, whom three realms obey,
Dost sometimes counsel take and sometimes tea

–and inside sat John Betjeman writing nonsense on his typewriter or polishing his leather books with boot-polish. John Betjeman at that time looked like a will-o'-the-wisp with Latin blood in it. His face was the colour of peasoup and his eyes were soupy too and his mouth was always twisting sideways in a mocking smile and he had a slight twist in his speech which added a tang to his mimicries, syncopating the original just as a slightly rippling sheet of water jazzes the things

94

reflected in it. He was a brilliant mimic but also a mine of useless information and a triumphant misfit. I felt ill at ease with him, not understanding his passion for minor poetry and misbegotten ornament, not knowing how many grains of salt to take with each of his pronouncements.

In my own house the dominant intellectual was Anthony Blunt, who had a precocious knowledge of art and an habitual contempt for conservative authorities. He was very tall and very thin and drooping, with deadly sharp elbows and the ribs of a famished saint; he had cold blue eyes, a cutaway mouth and a wave of soft brown hair falling over his forehead. His features were far from classical but he had at times a pre-Raphaelite beauty; when he was annoyed he pouted and stuck out his lip, his good looks vanished and sulkiness was all. He had specialised in mathematics, but outraged the masters of the Modern Side by putting most of his energies into a society of his own to which he read papers on Cubism. He truculently admitted that he preferred Things to People. He considered it very low to talk politics.

In the autumn of 1924 I joined Anthony's society and read them a paper on Norse Mythology. This estranged me still more from Reckitts, and I began to frequent Anthony's study and borrow his books on painting. One day when Reckitts was out I borrowed three small coloured prints and put them up in our study—a Duccio Madonna, a Greco Holy Family and some picture by Altdorfer.[1] When Reckitts came back and saw them he was so angry he almost burst into tears. The Madonna especially struck him as blasphemous, disgusting; he said that her face was green. Shortly afterwards he picked a quarrel with me over the Giant's Causeway which I said was well worth seeing. No it wasn't, Reckitts said. 'But you've never been there,' I said. No he hadn't but an uncle of his had been there and it was not worth seeing at all. The rift was final. Reckitts, I decided, was incurable, and I was relieved when in our third term together he portentously announced that he was going to leave a year early because Marlborough got one into a groove. All right, I thought, let him get out of his groove and get himself into the Church. Reckitts was hurt that I expressed no sorrow to be losing him. He was more hurt still when his grandmother died and I

[1] By Patinir according to L.M.'s later account (p. 228).

95

showed no sorrow over that. I concluded to myself that as one gets older one cannot be friends with just anyone. You would think people's minds would get wider, more elastic, but they don't. Quite the contrary. There was that little boy at Sherborne who denied the white foxes, you could put that down to childishness but when you began to grow up you found that your own contemporaries, some of whom had been open to ideas before, were all denying white foxes. And you could not thrust white foxes upon them because their whole world hinged on the denial of white-foxiness. So you had to choose between the white foxes and them. So you chose the white foxes.

I arranged to share a study for my last year with Anthony, and went away for the holidays determined not to yield to my family an inch of the ground which I had won from Reckitts. My family were touring Scotland and I behaved very sourly, regarding Scotland as a Philistine country and regretting I was not on the Continent. Occasionally I would see a field of corn which I thought was like a Van Gogh but in general I was irritated by my stepmother's praise of the scenery. Scenery! Samplers! My stepmother was viciously Victorian. I was emulating Anthony's antagonism to the generation of our parents. My stepmother and father were hurt by my lack of enthusiasm, not realising that this was a deliberate façade hiding a brand-new enthusiasm, the bacchanalian chorus of adolescence. I was reading a book on Greek philosophy in order to prepare for a scholarship examination at Oxford and was swept away by Heraclitus, by the thesis that everything is flux and fire is the primary principle. There was a little girl whom I admired from a distance. I wrote her name on a flat pebble and threw it, like a prayer or like bread upon the waters, into the Caledonian Canal.

XVIII

Anthony and I made hay of our last year. Before Christmas we had both got scholarships, Anthony to Cambridge and I to Oxford, so that after that we had nothing to do but amuse ourselves and infuriate everyone else. Anthony had whitewashed the study and had a double row of art books running along one wall. On top of this bookshelf we had some photographs of pictures by Picasso and a small coloured print of Cézanne's inevitable Montagne Ste Victoire. There was one distorted still-life by Picasso–a jug and a bowl of fruit–which seemed to me especially real, the distortion bringing out the jugness of the jug and the bowlness of the bowl. That was my chief reason for liking it, but I did not say so as Anthony believed in Pure Form and entirely discounted the representational elements in painting. He continued to read papers on Cubism. I read a whimsical paper attacking both Common Sense and Science.

In our study we anticipated the life of the University, spending hours and hours in Socratic argument, in gossip, malice and risqué wit. We used the fashionable phrases of the highbrow twenties– 'too *devastatingly* baroque'–and practised the fashionable child-cult. I painted deliberately naïve water-colour pictures of goldfish in imitation of Matisse, and we bowled a hoop around the school and played catch on the playing fields with a huge painted nursery rubber ball. We found it only too easy to outrage the Boy in the Street.

My father had played with the idea of sending me to Glasgow University, as being both more moral and more industrious than Oxford, but I had got my Oxford scholarship almost before he realised I was entering for it. I wrote home, however, to deprecate this performance and to explain that I saw through Oxford completely. On my way back to school after Christmas I missed my train connection at Cheltenham and sat up all night in the Ladies'

Waiting Room in the station, huddled over a tiny coal fire and reading *Prometheus Unbound*. This was one of my sacred books – along with the *Golden Ass* of Apuleius and Dasent's translation of *Burnt Njal* and of course *Morte d'Arthur* – and I felt uplifted, reformist, anarchist, escapist simultaneously, as I listened to the goods trains grunting on their sordid errands and swilled the rhythms of Shelley, the sweet champagne of his wishful thinking and schoolboy anger, his Utopias of amethyst and starlight, and I thought how wonderful to miss one's connections; soon I shall miss them all the time.

Anthony and I went in for eclectic reading; it was either stark and realistic or precious and remote and two-dimensional. We read Tolstoy and Dostoievski and Beckford's *Vathek*, Thomas Hardy and Crébillon *fils*, Blake and Lucretius and books about Blake and Lucretius, lives of Cézanne and Van Gogh, the three Sitwells, Lord Dunsany's fairy stories, Edward Lear and T. S. Eliot and Aldous Huxley. Anthony had a flair for bigotry: every day he blackballed another musician; he despised Tennyson, Shakespeare, the Italian High Renaissance and Praxiteles, was all in favour of the Primitives, of Uccello, of the Byzantine mosaics, of Brueghel and Negro sculpture. Our view of history was conveniently false. The Middle Ages, the Elizabethans, the Eighteenth Century were all oversimplified and falsified. I thought of the Middle Ages as *merry*, almost *à la* G. K. Chesterton, and of Elizabethan England as through-and-through glamorous, ignorant of its appalling chicanery and crudity and ignoring the cheeseparing old harridan who sat on the throne, starving her navy, double-crossing her favourites and giving the lie to the myth of Gloriana.

Graham Shepard was suspicious of Anthony's aestheticism and rarely attended the meetings of our society. He did not prefer Things to People and thought that Pure Form was nonsense. He was becoming more and more interested in the spectacle of contemporary English society, was trying his hand at writing social satire. He and I also collaborated in verbal fantasy, not that we had ever heard of Joyce or surrealism or automatic writing; we just liked to play about with words. 'Mr. Little Short of Extraordinary was little short of extraordinary. He went to bed with his wife and dislocated his jaw. And that was the night the Isms came to Auntie.

General Useless MacNess was always in a mess. The Boy stood in the Burning Bush. "What are ye doin' the day?" quoth the cat. I'm minding my pees and peeing my queues. Oh the Harp that Once and never got over it!' That sort of thing. I was especially fond of parodying hymns—every little blasphemy a blow for the Better Life.

Graham left a term early to go and take a course in France and I was left with Anthony and my third great friend, John Hilton. John Hilton was physically tough but hesitating in speech, with a matted chest and a red parroty nose. He was good at mathematics and endowed with some horse sense but was willing to be seduced into fantasy and took up the child-cult with alacrity, painting a gay still-life of a Dutch cheese and writing a very catchy nonsense poem about oranges and wine and carmine crinolines. The child-cult was money for jam but the trouble was that at the age of eighteen we had caught up with the outside intellectuals, had nothing to move on to. Life had to be turned into Art and Art was a patchwork quilt. Since a boy of eighteen can make a patchwork quilt as well as, or better than, a man of forty, we were about to transfer to Oxford and Cambridge without any incitement to emulate our elders.

That summer term, our last term, was an idyll. I used to run over the downs with Anthony, Anthony wearing a blue silk handkerchief floating from the strap of his wrist watch, and we would come back with our arms full of stolen azaleas and sitting in our study whose white walls were golden with reflected light would eat an iced walnut cake or bananas and cream. And we would spend whole afternoons lying naked on the grassy banks of the bathing place, eating strawberries and cherries and reciting the *Pervigilium Veneris* or 'An hendy hap ichabbe y-hent'. One day Anthony took an easel and canvas down to the bathing place to do a composition of a corrugated-iron shed. The Bathing Master, who did not know about Pure Form, rushed up scandalised, told us it was strictly forbidden to take photos or paint pictures of the bathing place. When Anthony explained that he was only interested in the shed, the master grudgingly gave him permission to continue; provided, he said, you don't put in any *figures*.

Anthony did not like games but I used to have wonderful afternoons playing tennis on the headmaster's court surrounded by an old-world yew hedge. My conception of tennis was to volley and smash all the time; I disliked playing off the ground. It was very satisfactory when the balls went into the yew hedge, smacking in so plumply, the hedge at once closed over them, you felt you had battered through a wall. In the intervals between the sets I would argue with my friends as to whether a laburnum in flower really looked like scrambled eggs.

[Sometimes I was conscious that Anthony and I were spending too much time in being *enfants terribles*; it is so easy merely to do the opposite. Our habit of precious cerebration too ran counter very often to the integrity of our senses. When you keep trying to think up a simile for laburnums—scrambled eggs or anything else—the burst of yellow evaporates and all you are left with is words. And one's mystical self was sidetracked. Sometimes I would lie on my back on the downs and fancy I heard the earth spinning, but most times the impression was forced; I got down on my back in order to have the impression for my mental scrapbook rather than because the ground called me down to it. What was true, however, was our animal spirits; they made us dance even if the steps were affected, anti-social, exhibitionist.][1]

Sweating and shouting and swimming and trailing one's coat. We felt ourselves the cream of the world and life was one big party like Matisse's picture *Le Bonheur de Vivre*—distorted pink nudes under undulating trees, dancing in a circle innocently naughty, and a nude girl playing the double pipes. There was no nude girl at Marlborough, that was the pity of it. As nearly all the elder boys had their mild homosexual romances—an occasion for *billets* and giggling and elaborately engineered rendezvous—I picked on a dark-haired boy of sixteen who had large grey feminine eyes and asked him illicitly to tea. I then wrote a poem about Circe on a marble balcony and Anthony told me I must beware of the influence of Tennyson.

We drew an important distinction between intelligent people and clever people, had a great contempt for those who were merely clever. The only real values were aesthetic. Moral values were a delusion, and politics and religion a waste of time. I had now given up saying my prayers. Anthony too had a father a clergyman and we

[1] Passages in square brackets are taken from the rough draft; see Editor's Preface, p. 12.

both resented the fact that our parents assumed us to be Christian, though neither of us would have dared to stand up in their presence and die for our lack of faith.

One night, lying in the great green dormitory, I found myself walking with my father over the downs. We were ascending a slope that was cut off blind by the sky and I was walking some way ahead. As I came near the skyline there was the noise of a funfair and a tall scarlet soldier standing stiff in a bearskin, woodenly abstracted. I reached his level, topping the curve of the world, the brass music blared up full and down below me was Calvary. Not on a hill – that was the first correction – but far down below me in an amphitheatre cut in the chalk. Tiers and tiers of people in gala dress – bunting, rattles and paper streamers – and in the arena were the three bodies on the crosses. A sight to make you retch and I knew if my father saw it all would be over. He was drawing up behind me when I woke.[1]

At the end of term Anthony and I gave a tea-party in our study. When we had stuffed ourselves full we took the tea-set piece by piece, lovingly fondling the china, and threw it out of the window to smash on a blank wall opposite that was divided from our block by a narrow alley. Piece after piece fell in tiny fragments into space but we kept the best till the last; the sugar bowl, still full of lumps, burst on the wall like a round of machine-gun fire and the large teapot sailed to its doom trailing tea from the spout. 'Ruins of Carthage,' we said and washed our hands of Marlborough.

It was in this summer of 1926 that the English General Strike occurred and was broken. The most publicised blacklegs were the undergraduates of Oxford and Cambridge who regarded the strike as an occasion for a spree; a comic phenomenon due to the Lower Classes; a comet that came from nowhere and dissolved in rubble and presaged nothing to come.

[1] Cf. *Autumn Sequel*, canto xxii.

XIX

At first it was a delight to find myself with two rooms of my own and a little man to wait on me, bringing me my tea in a battered pewter teapot and with a deference as traditional as pewter encouraging me to think myself grown up. My family were allowing me—a year and I had my first cheque-book. Each undergraduate paid £10 a term for tuition; the rest went on college and tradesmen's bills.

I continued my classical education which had already come to condition my whole outlook. This traditional English form of education is rooted in that same class system which conduces to an ethics of self-interest; it thus came about that when I was nineteen I joined to a dislike of science a disbelief in altruism. Skimming the cream off the milk; skimming the cream off the cream; you begin to forget there are cows. Our classical course took four years and was divided into two parts, each terminating in an examination—'Honour Mods.' and 'Greats' respectively. All examinations are a racket and these two famous examinations were no less of a racket for being famous. Honour Mods. involves a great deal of futile memorisation and Greats encourages jargon and false profundity. But four years of study, however desultory, in the Oxford School of *Literae Humaniores* (humane letters) is likely at least to check one's dehumanisation, and seems preferable, at least from a human or humane standpoint, to any brand yet patented of more useful, sensible, all-round or modern education—both to the kind that teaches you to make a living but forbids you to live and to the kind that equips you for everything and nothing.

I had not, however, gone to Oxford to study; that was what grammar-school boys did. We products of the English public schools went to Oxford either for sport and beer-drinking, in which case we filled in time deriding the intellectuals, or for the aesthetic life and cocktails, in which case we filled in time deriding the athletes; our feuds were between ourselves, for the grammar-school boys did not enter the picture (they were to enter it after the Slump when Oxford discovered politics).

Oxford in 1926 was just at the end of its period of postwar deliberate decadence–the careful matching of would-be putrescent colours. At the first party I went to there was no drink but champagne, a young man played by himself with a spotted stuffed dog on a string and the air was full of the pansy phrase 'my dear'. I discovered that in Oxford homosexuality and 'intelligence', heterosexuality and brawn, were almost inexorably paired. This left me out in the cold and I took to drink.

Coming of a temperance family, drunkenness had always been for me a symbol of freedom. It was a kicking overboard of the lumber of puritan ethics; it was a quick road to fantasy; it achieved a communion among those whom sobriety divided. I had heard a temperance lecturer explain that alcohol impairs the mind through weakening the synapses of the brain, and I was willing to believe this; we have more mind than is comfortable anyway, the same again and to hell with the synapses. And the distortions of drunkenness made objects more real, more 'significant', even on a morning-after emphasising, as Picasso did, the jugness of the jug and the bowlness of the bowl. John Hilton told me that he felt the same way when he had a bad cold; he recovered that vividness of visual objects which we all had had as children and had lost. We continued to envy or think we envied children.

My father had never mentioned synapses but I knew that *his* chief objection to drink was that the drunkard loses his self-respect. But that again from my point of view was all to the drunkard's credit, self-respect being one of the roots of evil. Miss Craig had self-respect, Sir Edward Carson had self-respect. Self-respect was the Evil Genius of half the world's trouble-makers–of the sectarians and the militants, the nationalists and imperialists, the captains of industry and the moral reformers. To get tight therefore, to stagger round the quadrangles being sick or making water, even if it was not always enjoyable, was all in a good cause; one was laming and debilitating one's private Satan, one's Tempter, one's self-respect. For the same reason I was not altogether displeased when I was attacked by a gang of athletes and 'debagged', i.e. had my trousers torn off. The athletes attacked me because they disliked the ties I wore and because they assumed I was homosexual. I was indignant but at the same time recognised that this was another good step down the ladder. One's self-respect must go.

After the first exultation of having two rooms of my own and listening to the crickets in the college kitchen and watching the Jacobean buildings turn plum-coloured at tea-time, I became depressed by Oxford. The climate was muggy and there were none of the geniuses around that there ought to be. I used to get up very late and cut my lectures, because the lecturers were inaudible or dull. I hated my tutorials—the endless interpolation into Greek compositions of phrases carefully collected from writers of the proper period; I thought that was a game for the 'monsters', i.e. the grammar-school boys, those distorted little creatures with black teeth who held their forks by the middle and were set on making a career. I used to sit wedged between these monsters at dinner, listening superciliously as they discussed Noël Coward and Bernard Shaw; in my opinion no one intelligent would mention such writers.

For the banner of Intelligence had to be kept flying even though Anthony was at Cambridge and Oxford seemed hardly to have heard of the Post-Impressionists. I continued to read the Sitwells and to write a rococo kind of poetry. Until I read Joyce and D. H. Lawrence and swung over to the cults of the Back Street and the Dark Blood.

My snobbery left me lonely in a small college which contained comparatively few public-school boys and still fewer 'intellectuals'. The person I liked best was my 'scout'—the servant who brought me my meals and supposedly made my bed. He was a tiny elf, seventy years old, with a greasy bowler hat, a thick moustache and a chuckle; he was always telling me stories which were built up carefully to a climax; when the climax came he would shut himself out of the room, timing the bang of the door to endorse his wit. He used to romanticise about the landscape of Devonshire—'dead red cows on dead green grass'—and had seen the moon under an arch at Tintern Abbey. Like most college servants he was a money snob and liked to see people entertaining, used the word 'gentleman' very often and thought that the old days were better—the days when the Warden was the *Honourable* Brodrick[1] and the future Lord Birkenhead, being tutor in History,[2] got drunk every night and hung up his trousers over the pictures on the wall. Both of them real gentlemen. When my scout heard that my sister was becoming a doctor he said: 'Funny thing that, sir, the way brains runs in families.' 'Like wooden legs,' he added and shut the door on himself with a bang and a chuckle. He was very charming but a parody; Oxford with its Fellows and scouts and tradespeople is as full of walking parodies as any Anglo-Indian club. Nature in England has a way of imitating *Punch*.

The servants varied from college to college. In Magdalen and Christ Church the scouts were like Hollywood manorial butlers; in the more plebeian colleges they were often like caricatures by Rowlandson of inn-keepers or ostlers. Under the scouts in all colleges there was a host of menials, many of them badly paid. A surprising number of these looked half-witted; their features were often wildly haphazard, their bloodshot eyes splodged askew on their faces, their mouths unable to shut, hair growing out of their ears. Some of them were lobster-red from drink, others decayed as if from centuries of malnutrition. Their gait too was abnormal—slouching or walking crab-wise, cow-hocked or bandy or sagging at the knees. Like an inbred race apart—superannuated relics of the Dickensian tavern or poorhouse, apes in green baize aprons. And oozing out of them all a traditional automatic sycophancy—a leering, smug, half-imbecile, half-cunning, self-abasing consciousness of class. Themselves barely articulate, they gauged the undergraduate by accent.

As for the dons, they might just as well have been at Cambridge; I should hardly have missed them. Few of them were interested in teaching. They lived in a parlour up a winding stair and caught little facts like flies in webs of generalisation. For recreation they read detective stories. The cigar smoke of the Senior Common Rooms hid them from each other and from the world. Some of them had never been adult, their second childhood having come too early. Some of them had never been male, walked around in their gowns like blowsy widows or wizened spinsters. They had charm without warmth and knowledge without understanding.

[1] G. C. Brodrick, Warden of Merton 1881–1904.
[2] F. E. Smith, later first Earl of Birkenhead, was tutor in Law (not History) at Merton, 1896–9.

In appearance they were nearly as grotesque as the menials. There were exceptions of course, maybe the exceptions were a majority, but for me at least it was the grotesques who typified Oxford. When I think of Oxford dons I see a *Walspurgisnacht*, a zoo—scraggy-necked baldheads in gown and hood looking like marabou storks, giant turtles reaching for a glass of port with infinitely weary flippers, sad chimpanzees, codfish, washing blown out on a line. Timid with pimples or boisterous with triple chins. Their wit and themselves had been kept too long; the squibs were damp, the cigars were dust, the champagne was flat.

The word 'don' was uttered by most of my friends in a tone of superior pity. 'You're the sort of person would become a don' was a serious insult. Becoming a don meant ossification. There was one old man, for instance, who had been lecturing for decades on the Origins of the Greek Drama. I heard him recount in one of his lectures how that very morning he had been passing the College bathrooms and what do you think he had overheard–the bathroom attendant saying 'Hurry up, gentlemen, please; there are other gentlemen waiting'–a classical hexameter line. The old man had done his human touch, got his laugh, but I was told that he over-heard this every year. Yet some of the dons, we had to admit, were very good indeed of their kind, masters of Socratic dialectic. It was an excellent weapon though they never went out into the world with it. You have to have left Oxford and seen the mess that is everywhere caused by wishful thinking before you can be properly grateful to those dry old inheritors of Reason who seemed to have no wishes at all but at least could think.

When the tourist thinks of Oxford he thinks of the colleges. Living in the colleges ourselves we found it more amusing to explore the poor streets which smell of fried fish or the residential district of North Oxford with its neo-Gothic architecture and its population of cranks. Anyone driving into Oxford from the north could know where he was from the spectacle of fanatical and fantastic old maids upon bicycles, in mushroom hats and shapeless timeless clothes. Ecclesiastical porches, baronial turrets, bad stained glass in the lavatory window; the Englishman's home is his ragbag. John Betjeman used to tour this district with a camera. I visited three homes in North Oxford during my first term. One belonged to an aggressive hypochondriac old lady who, as soon as she met me, said, 'I hear you're a clever young man. Are you interested in Peter Piperisms?' In another house Graham Shepard and I were entertained by a don and – more entertainingly – by his wife who made her whole conversation out of sexual *doubles entendres*; she had a dog and a canary to help her out.

The third house I visited by mistake, having found in my room in college a note of invitation intended for an undergraduate who was a Plymouth Brother. Arriving at the unknown house I found myself in the midst of Plymouth Brethren – young men in dark Sunday suits and stiff collars and dowdy girl undergraduates mainly in spectacles and with clumsy embarrassed hands. The room was full of cake-stands and suspense and suddenly everyone stood up and Mr. Moore, our host, a genial, cunning old man, began praying in an over-familiar way which implied that we and God were all one jolly family. Then we ate. Mr. Moore was puzzled by my presence but he took me into a corner and said I was welcome all the same and would I come again, they did this every Sunday; there was a young man from the Colonies, he said, a very fine athlete, who had told him just before he went down that there had been moments during his university career when he felt like going wrong but, whenever these temptations arose, he used to say to himself 'I'll just go up and have a cup of coffee with old Moore' and the situation was saved.

At this time one of the popular songs was *Red, Red Robin*, which like many jazz songs combined the nostalgia of the thwarted with the philosophy of 'Whistle owre the lave o' 't.' When the red, red robin comes bob, bob, bobbin' along, there'll be no more sobbin', etc. The choice for many undergraduates was between this and Old Moore or some other form of naïve and self-gratulatory religion. There were many Anglo-Catholics. One of these was a tall, gross young man with a sweeping Jewish nose, rich wet lips and a wish to convert people. He kept saying 'My dear, my dear', and when he neared the sacred topic his bosom would expand like a prima donna's; he wanted the limelight and cultivated people with reputations, especially bad ones. He used to say: 'I can't bear Jews; I suppose it's because I have a very slight strain [*sic*] of Jewish blood in me myself.' When he left Oxford he did arduous and efficient slum-work in the East End of London, afterwards entered the Church and spent some time in India in association with Gandhi, evolving in place of his early passion for purple and candles a programme of Christian socialism.

Graham Shepard and I and most of our friends regarded all persons who had any religious faith as museum specimens. We did not deplore their existence any more than we deplored the existence of the absurd buildings by Butterfield in Christ Church and Merton or the existence of the would-be county families around Graham's home in Surrey. Without this caste of grotesques the world would be dull. For in every sphere we had a perverse taste for the grotesque.

For instance we used to organise readings of plays such as *The Jew of Malta* or *The White Devil* in a room lit by candles stuck in beer-bottles and a skull on the table with radishes in its eye-sockets. We bought strange fruits such as persimmons and passion-fruit, and I got myself an ashplant in order to be like Stephen Dedalus and trained it to carry tram-tickets in its mouth. Going to a concert by the Dolmetsch family I tried to induce a trance-state and, while listening to the harpsichord, secured a picture of a chimpanzee hobbling along a street, holding above its head a large basin into which people were throwing coins from the windows.

In the summer of 1927, when Graham and I shared a canoe, instead of going up the Cherwell as was the custom, we used to paddle along the evil-smelling canal through the slums or up the Isis past the gas-drums. One May morning we were on this stretch of the Isis watching a dragonfly among the cow-parsley and shards on the bank when a goods train came over the railway bridge and we made a chant out of the names on the trucks—Hickleton, Hickleton, Hickleton, Lunt, Hickleton, Longbotham. This incantation of names at once became vastly symbolic—symbolic of an idle world of oily sunlit water and willows and willows' reflections and, mingled with the idleness, a sense of things worn out, scrap-iron and refuse, the shadow of the gas-drum, this England. Hickleton Hickleton Hickleton—the long train clanked and rumbled as if it had endless time to reach wherever it was going. The placid dotage of a great industrial country.

XX

Graham and I were always searching for phrases. The right phrase was something with positive, or even absolute, value—even if, as so often, it was conveying denunciation, irony, scepticism, defeatism, nihilism. (If Nil is a word it can't be nil.) Our experiences with words being a long way ahead of our experience, we accepted ideas with much less discrimination than we accepted phrases. Reading William James's *Varieties of Religious Experience* we said 'That's that.' There were no flies on Graham or me; we saw through the whole damn peepshow.

In spite of this hardboiled attitude I remained childishly romantic, was always talking about the Not Impossible She. Few of my friends, excepting the homosexuals, had as yet had sexual experience, but I was exceptionally shy because I did not even know any girls to speak to. One day that summer, 1927, someone said to me: 'If you want to meet your Not Impossible She you must come to a lunch party I'm giving.' So I went to the lunch party and there were four men, including myself, and two women; one of these talked all the time—very whimsically, it seemed to me—and the other, her daughter, Mariette, said nothing. Mariette just sat there like a Japanese doll, slight and dainty, her hair very black and her skin very white and garnet rings on her fingers. But her mouth looked sulky and, when our host asked me afterwards if she would do for the Not Impossible, I said No, she would not.

Having no sex-life I was building myself an eclectic mythology. Peopled with the Disappointed; Orpheus and Persephone and Lancelot and Picasso's earlier harlequins. This world was girdered with odd pieces from the more heterodox Greek philosophers, especially Heraclitus and Pythagoras. For Heraclitus recognised the flux—and one has to do that to be modern—and Pythagoras brought back order with his mathematics and music. I equated Pythagoras with Thor, the Norse time-god, the hammer-bearing lord of the thunder, and at home one holiday this was confirmed from the mouth of my brother who described the thunder to me as a man with a hammer and who on another occasion sat cross-legged looking at the clock, his head on one side, and listening intently said, 'Time is going very fast, very fast.'

Reading for Honour Mods. was on the whole repellent to me—I could not bear niggling over textual commentary—but I sweetened it with side-dishes, was delighted for instance by Nietzsche's *Birth of Tragedy*, though I know it to be perverse and historically upside-down. It made the Greeks seem much more human because it made them as gloomy as the moderns and as orgiastic as D. H. Lawrence. 'Up Dionysus!' became my slogan; it was a good come-back to that authority on the Greek Drama who overheard hexameters in the bathrooms.

I had never been abroad (my family were as unwilling to send me abroad as they were to allow my sister to go to dances), so that, when I went to Paris in the summer of 1927 with John Hilton, I went there in a bubble of naïve expectations. All I wanted to see was poetic-looking poets sitting in cafés. John would have preferred to go a walking tour and get in a sweat (he got in a sweat very easily) but I persuaded him to spend hours every day sitting in the Boulevard Montparnasse waiting for romantic encounters and drinking Benedictine. We were disappointed; the people looked so bourgeois. We were disappointed too by the picture shows; where we had expected the colours of the early Matisse all we seemed able to find was conscientiously muddy landscapes by painters like Segonzac. *Mais où sont les Fauves d'antan?*

One night John and I were locked out of our hotel and I was delighted at being forced to spend the night in the street. John however refused to drink all night and, when the piles of saucers before us were high, he went away to sleep on a bench. Towards dawn I felt cold and rose to go for a walk. The only other person in the café got up and followed me; he was a fat greasy double-chinned old man, dressed in black with a broad black hat. I was always well-disposed to people with that kind of hat and was very pleased when he caught me up and asked where I was going. I said I was locked out. He said he would be delighted to put me up for the rest of the night. I said I was delighted. He said he was a poet. I said: '*Moi aussi.*' We walked a long way, had a cup of coffee, went up to his apartment at the top of a four- or five-storey building.

His apartment disappointed me; a couple of wicker chairs and an empty bookcase, no disarray or glamour. He showed me a bed and retired to another room but when I was in bed came back and made overtures. I was astonished. Since I pretended not to understand, he began to make signs with his fingers, ogling me tipsily. At last I said: 'All right; you go back to your bed and I will join you; your bed appears to be bigger.' The old man shambled off, I dressed as fast as I could, snatched my ashplant and ran downstairs. The sun was up and I was enormously elated at having eluded the old man. John merely said I was a fool.

We were only abroad a fortnight but we tired each other out with Significance. I would look at a bridge over the Seine and say, 'That is significant' and John would say, 'What do you mean by significant?' I could never adequately explain, so the only thing to do was to eat more camembert and drink more Benedictine. However, when I got back to London I felt Continental and triumphant.

My family and a host of my stepmother's relations, one of whom was about to get married, were staying in a private hotel in South Kensington. The only other people in this hotel were permanent residents—rice and prunes for ever. These old ladies who lived in a forest of family trees, including Royalty's, were delighted to find their hotel the take-off for a wedding. 'But *when* will the Prince of Wales . . .?' I went on feeling Continental.

In September I drove with my family to Connemara; my father had not been back there since settling in the North,[1] so that all the time my reactions to the West were half my father's. That is, I was not seeing the West for the first time; I had been born there sixty years before and this was my home-coming. When we drove over a hill-top and there was the Atlantic gnashing its teeth in the distance, my father rose in his seat and shouted 'The sea!' And something rose inside me and shouted 'The sea!' Thalassa! Thalassa! to hell with all the bivouacs in the desert; Persia can keep our dead but the endless parasangs have ended.

Down through Ballysodare in County Sligo where my ancestors were buried under brambles to the Island of Omey where my father

[1] This is in fact inaccurate. (E.N.)

had been born. In Ballysodare we stopped outside a little thatched cottage and my father asked the woman in the doorway if there were any MacNeices now in the neighbourhood. 'Sure I married one myself,' she said and took us inside to see his photograph.

Omey was home-coming too. It is a small roadless island covered with crisp grass and when the tide is out you reach it across the sands. My grandfather had gone there as a sort of self-appointed Protestant missionary, had built a house for himself and a school for the island children.[1] My father was trying to make out where his house had been, had discovered a few stones on a knoll exposed to the Atlantic, when a bare-footed weatherbeaten woman came over to him, gripping the rocks with her toes, and said to him, 'Which of them would you be?' The brogue she spoke in was as rich as a pint of stout and she reeled off a list of Christian names. My father told her which he was. Sure she knew he must be one of them, she said, the way he knew the lie of the ground. When the MacNeices went away, she went on (my father had been then about nine), the potatoes had stopped growing on the island and everyone had gone to America. 'If my mother was alive now you could hear her crying the length of the island.'

It was a country I had always known, mournful and gay with mournful and gay inhabitants, moonstone air and bloody with fuchsias. The mountains had never woken up and the sea had never gone to sleep and the people had never got civilised. My father was remembering the stories the fishermen used to tell him about the houses and the towers were down there under the sea, and he was looking around for rookeries all the rooks had left, and his nostalgia would make him walk fast, swinging his stick, and then break off impatiently. 'Terribly backward,' he would say, 'terribly backward.'

[1] In fact, Louis's grandfather was a schoolmaster on the staff of the Society for Irish Church Missions and served in this capacity for a time on Omey. The school and the master's house on the island were built by and belonged to the Society. (E.N.)

XXI

In the New Year of 1928 I hastily learned by heart some textual emendations by Wilamowitz, Scaliger and Co., got my First Class in Honour Mods. (I was a natural examinee, an intellectual window-dresser.) When the examination was over I went on a drunk for several days, beginning with marsala at breakfast—in homage to Edward Lear. Dazed with alcohol I went for a walk with Graham in the twilight. In the suburbs among the jerry-built villas we saw on a sudden a blind woman being piloted over the road; as Graham said, it gave you a jolt. It was not so much that she was blind but what were we?

I could not face the world of the blind woman nor tackle the problem of evil. I denied that there was any problem; evil was a mere illusion. In the next term, summer once more, I began to read philosophy—an exquisite engine of destruction—but still spent most of my time experimenting with poetry or in playboy escapades. I had come up to Oxford with a belief in the Practical Joke as a principle of ethics and in the Enfant Terrible as an unacknowledged legislator. I now had a new friend, Adrian,[1] who was indolent and pliable and willing to abet my career of minor anarchism. Every so often we got ourselves creditably fined, for giving a party in the dons' private summerhouse or for stealing a stone angel from the sacristy. If I did enough of these things I might be sent down, and that would be still better than missing a train connection or being locked out of a hotel.

The only serious activity was poetry. The most prominent poets among the undergraduates were Wystan Auden, Clere Parsons and Stephen Spender. Spender was the nearest to the popular romantic conception of a poet—a towering angel not quite sure if he was fallen, thinking of himself as the poet always, moving in his own limelight. He was already taking upon himself the travail of the

[1] Adrian Green-Armytage. Cf. p. 252.

world, undergoing a chronic couvade. Redeeming the world by introspection. Physically clumsy, he combined with the glamour of the born martyr the charm of some great shaggy animal and—a saving grace in my eyes—you always could make him giggle. Clere Parsons was a bleached frail little man, who brought special bread with him to lunch because he had diabetes, and who had an invalid's fanaticism in politics (he was the first of those poets to turn political) and an invalid's too trustful or unjust likes and dislikes of individuals. Like all of us he was obsessed with technique and had just discovered E. E. Cummings. The Cummings method, he told me, was something he himself had been fumbling for; it was so essentially *contemporary*. Parsons, whom the doctors had doomed to a death in the near future, was eager above all to be contemporary.

Auden, then as always, was busy getting on with the job. Sitting in a room all day with the blinds down, reading very fast and very widely—psychology, ethnology, *Arabia Deserta*. He did not seem to *look* at anything, admitted he hated flowers and was very free with quasi-scientific jargon, but you came away from his presence always encouraged; here at least was someone to whom ideas were friendly—they came and ate out of his hand—who would always have an interest in the world and always have something to say.

Neither Auden nor Spender had as yet shown the slightest interest in politics and, with a few exceptions such as Clere Parsons, the cult of Soviet Russia was something almost unknown. John Hilton had a book about the U.S.S.R., and he and I used to laugh over it in the same way that Graham and I had once laughed over Kipling. The conception of mechanised collective man seemed to us as crude as the White Man's Burden. I judged Soviet Russia chiefly by its attitude to the arts, and that attitude seemed to me false.

The branch of philosophy most pertinent to my needs was aesthetics but I soon decided that all aestheticians were blind. I was particularly disappointed by Croce whom I had heard so praised and whose name itself was so seductive. As I understood Croce, he was maintaining that the artistic activity lies almost completely in the vision, the work of art itself being merely an epiphenomenon, a sop to the public. This I considered a blasphemy; the artist does not see the thing completely till he has made it. Otherwise why make it? My contempt for Croce was confirmed by my observation of a little Hindu graduate who was writing a thesis on Hegel but who thought that Croce's statements were final. When this Hindu first appeared in the college, he continued vegetarian and said his prayers in the bathroom with the tap running. Later he took to eating meat and getting drunk, became paunchy and unhealthy and incoherent. That, I thought with satisfaction, that is what comes of Croce.

Apart from my instincts I was now almost without principles. For example, if I felt sorry for people, I might be ready to do them a good turn, but I would have vigorously denied that there was anything morally good in this good turn. So-called altruism was merely a projection of egotism. Spinoza and Nietzsche had been right to repudiate pity. On this basis it was hard to choose–unless one's appetites came into it–between one course of action and another; it meant weighing one's ultimate self-interest and that was a bore. When in doubt I used to play over and over to myself a gramophone record–the Rondo of Mozart's E flat Horn Concerto– and then do what came into my head.

That summer I was taken to call on Mariette and her mother whom I had not seen since our first meeting a year ago. They lived in a grandiose eighteenth-century house with enormous windows, scented like a potpourri and full of untouchable *objets d'art*. Mariette and her mother moved through this house as if they were in a Russian ballet, coloured handkerchiefs over their heads or flowers in their hair. The mother was always talking; and Mariette, when she was not dancing in a room upstairs with one of her beaux–'*Tant que la vie durera Mariette dansera*'–would be lying on a sofa covered with Moorish draperies as if she would never sit upright, much less stand, again. She said standing made her feel faint.

I talked mainly with her mother–I had never met anyone so cosmopolitan or with such a Santa Claus' bag of reminiscences–but Mariette fascinated me by her bijou unreality. She had spent her infancy in Constantinople and much of her girlhood travelling in Italy and France and had gone to a progressive self-governing school in North Oxford from which she was nearly expelled for her 'un-forthputting' influence, but in spite of all this had remained wonderfully uneducated, could not do the simplest mathematical sum and did not know whether Queen Elizabeth was earlier or later than Queen Anne. She weighed less than seven stone and looked as fragile as porcelain, dressed in the primary colours–pillar-box reds and canary yellows–and was always scented with chypre. She told me she had relations in India who were jewel merchants and whose daughters did nothing all day long but measure each other's eye-lashes, run pearls through their fingers. I could well believe it.

This was the first Jewish family I had known and I got in the habit of leaving two-thirds of myself outside when I entered their doors. This combination of Oriental indolence and elfin vivacity, of sophistication and primitive superstition, of sentimentality and worldly scepticism, I could only treat as a spectacle; I did not even try to take it seriously. I was as much amused by their serious discussions of horoscopes and the Evil Eye as I was by their deliber-ate jokes which had either the tang of the ghetto or a nuance of *La Vie Parisienne*.

I asked Mariette and her mother to lunch, with two other men and another girl to complete the party. This was a gaffe. Mariette told me later that she and her mother had gone to countless lunch parties in Oxford, sometimes with a dozen men present, but never, never had any of their hosts even dreamed of inviting another woman. When she had entered my room and seen a girl there she had been *utterly horrified*.

Going home that summer I found it duller than usual. Mariette might measure her life by dance-cards, keeping them in a lavendered box tied with ribbon at the bottom of a drawer, but was it any better to measure by the Collects for the Day? I was detailed to accompany my father on a pleasure trip up the coast of Norway; a huge boat packed with middle-aged Americans and with English spinsters who were blowing their savings. I talked to hardly anyone on board, read John Stuart Mill's *Logic* and medieval Latin poetry. When everyone was in bed I would stand on the upper deck under the midnight sun and recite one of these poems, the 'Nun's Lament'. It seemed to me very appropriate.

When we reached Spitzbergen we all went ashore just to say we had been there. The only vegetation was lichen, the only inhabitants some bearded Danish miners who worked the inferior coal. The trippers looked at the miners and the miners looked at the trippers.

When zoo meets zoo. That evening we had a gala dinner, liverish old men and mammose but crack-voiced women wearing paper caps, blowing whistles. A gramophone was playing 'Dance, dance, dance, little lady'. I felt alone and wretched, got up very early next morning to see the last of Spitzbergen. Diamond cut diamond; hard in the brilliant light the spikes of painful peaks. Striped pyramids of khaki, black and white; the only softness was where a glacier flowed into the sea. It reminded me of Hans Andersen's fairy story of the Ice Queen with her geometrical puzzles. The view was a consummation of abstract art; it was not any more what I wanted.

XXII

Immediately after the beginning of that autumn term, 1928, I had to return to Ireland for my sister Elizabeth's wedding. I felt guilty because I had no strong feelings on the subject. The wedding reception was given in the Parochial Schools, the blackboards and multiplication tables being removed for the occasion or concealed by flowers and ferns. C-A-T spells Cat. That evening one of the bridesmaids and I took one of Elizabeth's wedding presents, a huge and hideous china jar–the sort of thing you put a palm in–and rolled it downstairs to smash at the feet of my stepmother. Full stop. Exclamation mark. Anyone who got married–so I felt–had left the world on a tangent.

Back in Oxford I was more than usually lonely. Graham Shepard and John Hilton were both too busy working and Adrian and I were finding it harder to keep up the rigolade. We hired a car to drive to Cambridge and had a very bad smash but even that was an ephemeral excitement. [One morning I bought some modelling clay and with frantic haste made a more than lifesize head of myself, using a mirror. My scout said no one but Mr. MacNeice would have thought of using a mirror. I stuck on the eyebrows and ears instead of squeezing them out of the mass, and when the clay dried they fell off. I had modelled the head on my Liddell and Scott lexicon and I let the lexicon remain as a pedestal. When anyone asked me 'Who did that?' I said 'Bechstein.' As long as people thought it was Bechstein's work–whoever he was–they admired it.]

Style remained more important than subject. The magic words– Relativity and the Unconscious–were always on our lips and we were pathetically eager to be realist (which meant the mimesis of flux), but we always fell back upon Form. This paradox came out in our admiration for contemporary novelists–Joyce, D. H. Lawrence, Virginia Woolf–who give you the flux but serve it on golden platters. We considered them good because they were the acolytes of

Flux, but it was the gold and the ritual that fetched us. For they each had something positive to offer: Lawrence had his crusading enthusiasm, his wonderful pictorial sense; Joyce had the solid ground against which he kicked; Woolf had at least a precision of picture and cadence. The flux is the reality, so has to be recognised, but you can make this recognition with style. What you do does not matter, but how you do it; Picasso can make a picture out of anything. We took great trouble with our dress and deportment.

As I had no religion and no exciting personal relationships, my approach to ideas was very emotional. Even when it came to metaphysics. Metaphysics for me was not something cold and abstract; it was an account of reality, but an artistic account, not a scientific one. I did not believe that one system of philosophy was truer than another and thought that philosophers themselves were fools in so far as they fancied they were getting to the bottom of anything; on the contrary their work was always superstructure, largely a matter of phrases, and these phrases were employed not as the physicist employs them but as the poet employs them; the philosopher's job—to use our favourite word—was stylisation, building a symphony which should sanction his emotional reactions to the universe. When you boil them down they are all alike. I found it amusing to collate a sceptic like Hume with one of the downright idealists. Hume denies the latter's Universals but he brings them back with an 'as if'. That was just eighteenth-century good manners —there's no such thing as blue blood but the world must go on *as if* there was.

I tried to orchestrate my philosophical reading not only with other literature but with the random details of life. Our elders and instructors were conscious of this adulteration. It puzzled them that young men who obviously had a keen sense of logic should occupy themselves so much with the byways of the Unconscious, with idiosyncrasies of manners and dress, blind alleys and baubles, rhyme without reason. Other generations of undergraduates had been silly spontaneously or by accident, whereas we were silly of a set purpose, mortifying the mind as the early Christians had mortified the flesh.

While we expressed a contempt for Oxford our world remained Oxonian. Only occasionally something came in from outside. Thus one day Graham and Adrian and I were sitting by the fire in my room when a foreign voice said 'Excuse me' and there in the doorway was a seedy little man in a green slouch hat who looked like a crook detective. He had yellow eyeballs and long black nails and wanted an introduction to Walter de la Mare. An adoptive German baron, he was writing up English life for papers in Germany and his thick-skinned determination to get copy had already carried him into all kinds of British inner shrines. For months we were unable to get rid of him and had to listen to his sickly sentimental or unsavoury man-of-the-world reminiscences–how he had seduced his best friend's wife or how he had met Lenin in Switzerland and been particularly struck by his *humanity*. One day he picked up a Swinburne and began reading aloud 'The Hounds of Spring' in his German accent and with a fruity Germanic intensity. Some time, he said, we must go out with him and 'have a dash up channel, as they say in the navy'; he emanated a sordid sexuality. But as well as sex and alleged cosmopolitan culture he had a finger in politics, told us he was a follower of Hitler and, if Hitler got in, was booked for a Government post. At that time, 1928, we knew almost nothing of Hitler. Political ideas were those which concerned us least.

Tired of University life–I knew all the moves in advance–I took to calling more and more often at Mariette's. Mariette and I went a couple of walks together which I found very flattering, and I was agreeably surprised to discover that she had a passion for nature, identifying owls and telling me about the farm they used to have in Kent and the baby goats she cuddled under the cherry trees. But that was in the last war and she had never got over the air-raids–when she first went to school had had visions of headless men. I was astonished to find Mariette so sensitive; I had thought of her at first as a brittle little houri.

One day, aided by rum and the Mozart Horn Concerto, I found myself engaged to Mariette. I could not quite take in what it involved, having always thought of marriage as something not to be thought about and hardly knowing Mariette. I was just twenty-one and she was a few months younger.

During the Christmas holidays (I had not of course mentioned my engagement to my family) I wrote to Mariette and told her about my brother whom I had been too frightened to speak about before. Her reaction surpassed my gloomiest expectations; I had not known what enormous stress certain Jewish families lay upon eugenics. But it was not hereditary, I wrote. Mariette wrote that she accepted my word for it but her family would have to have official confirmation, a doctor's certificate or something. I answered that I would see to that in due course, being unable at the moment to get any such thing from my father. In thus shelving what I thought was a mere formality I did not realise the rift I was preparing with her family. I was much more worried by what my family would think about it all. Mariette was not the sort of girl they ever came across in their parish, and besides she was a Jewess. She for her part had only just forgiven my being the son of a clergyman, told me that when she was little she always held her nose when she passed a clergyman or priest, assuming that, because their collars were the wrong way round, of course they must never wash.

When I returned to Oxford I saw Mariette every day for two or three weeks and found it exhausting; she was like a little volcano that is never off the boil. I went to a lunch party in my college, mixed my drinks deliberately, got wildly drunk and began to run through Oxford, making through a drizzle of rain for the open country. And never again would come back. A policeman arrested me and put me in gaol. The College authorities debated whether they would send me down, but one of them, who hoped that I should get a First in Greats (and Firsts were rare in the College), told me to write a letter of apology to the Warden. I wrote a long letter arguing that it is good for young men to get drunk because they need a spiritual catharsis. Adrian told me that if I sent this letter it was the end of me, so I reluctantly tore it up (I considered it brilliant) and wrote the Warden something more conventional. He decided not to send me down but told me he was writing to my father.

As my father had a horror of drink, I decided that now was the occasion to precipitate everything. I sent him a telegram to outstrip the Warden's letter, in which I announced that I had been put in gaol for drunkenness and was engaged to marry a Jewess: At the same time I wrote him a long letter explaining that after all I was a poet and did a lot of good in the world by amusing my friends. John Hilton also, unknown to me, wrote him a letter asserting that Mariette was a wonderful girl and that marriages between Jews and Gentiles *could* be a success, for he was the product of one himself.

My father and stepmother came over to Oxford and everyone interviewed everyone. The families agreed that we were both very young and that our engagement was a whim which would most likely pass. I had more than four terms to go at Oxford and no prospect of making a living. In the meantime Mariette and I might as well see each other and it would be desirable to clear up this question of eugenics.

During the next vacation Mariette and I wrote to each other every day, and when any of my letters failed to arrive she would send me a telegram. Both the families deplored the inconvenience of our mutual fixation. I had now, encouraged by opposition, committed myself to the prospect of marriage. Mariette, when she was not being hysterical, prevented me feeling lonely. At the same time I missed the company of my friends, for the time left over from Mariette was not even enough to read my books in.

We spent that summer term having picnics and going in a canoe on the river, though Mariette could not swim and was terrified of water. The eugenics question had not been cleared up and I was also generally censured for my idleness. But Mariette wore gingham dresses and looked like a nursery rhyme shepherdess, and the Upper Isis, placid between banks of yellow flags and great empty meadows, was empty of everything except the present moment. There were lapwings and mayflies and one evening at twilight a squadron of swallows swooped down over the water, their reflections were been and gone, a moment of annunciation. I felt very near to Mariette and it was a relief not to have to discuss if the descent of swallows was 'significant'. For Mariette could not have discussed it.

XXIII

In spite of the two families' hopes of hushing up our engagement Mariette had to be accommodated. She and I spent August 1929 with my family in the island of Achill and September in her uncle's villa in St. Tropez.

Ireland was something new to Mariette and obliged her by appearing very Irish. A local peasant girl, who had been engaged to do the work, turned out delightfully incompetent and committed all the Irishisms beloved by English humorists. When told to clean a pair of shoes she asked 'Do you mean both of them?' and when sent up to a bedroom with a hot-water bottle she would hang it on the knob of a chair. There were three itinerant butchers who visited the house in rotation and sold us whole sides of sheep. And when I walked along the road with my arm around Mariette, an old woman called out, 'That's a grand way for a girl to be—linked to a boy.'

The world on the whole was gay. One day Mariette and I drove across the island to buy lobsters. The fishermen had only a dozen which they had contracted to send to the mainland, but Mariette's Mediterranean persuasiveness was too much for them and one of them gave us two lobsters, saying to his colleague who was in charge of the box for the mainland, 'Throw in a couple of herring; they're all fish.' The lobsters sat on the back seat and clacked their claws like castanets as we drove home. On the whole gay, though Mariette was afraid of the wind and of open spaces; how can I marry, I thought to myself sometimes, someone who does not like the wind?

Autumn comes early in Achill. We were walking along a road through a bog that had once been a forest—stumps of grey bog-oak like bones—when Mariette's face went under its own shadow and she said, 'Do you hear that?' It was only a robin singing; 'Yes,' I said, 'I hear it.' 'But it is his winter song.' His winter song so early.

Mariette beneath her childlike vivacity had a deep primeval – perhaps also childlike – melancholy.

On our way to France we stopped a night at her grandmother's house in London and Graham came round to see us, tripped over the end of the heavy Victorian window-curtains and down they all came; it was most reassuring to see that Graham could still make a fool of himself. To put the curtains back he fetched a step-ladder and preached us a Salvation Army sermon from the top of it. He was almost the only one of my friends whom Mariette liked; the rest she found too purely intellectual. As we left for France I felt I was leaving behind with Graham my whole Gentile background. My rôle in life was to be the Good Jewish Husband.

Provence with its garlic cooking and rowdy cicadas and stars drowned away most of my doubts and I joined Mariette in building castles – but very domestic castles – in the air. 'And now,' her uncle said to her, 'perhaps you will grow up?' The trouble was, though I only rarely admitted it to myself, that Mariette's growing up seemed to imply my staying put at a point. And I could no longer write poetry; Mariette required a soundproof room and you cannot write poetry in a soundproof room.

When I returned to Oxford for my last year, I went into lodgings, sharing a room with Adrian. It was very difficult to work. We had two scrannel-voiced landladies, half-sisters, who had just bought a vacuum cleaner and could not leave it alone. Mariette would arrive every day at two o'clock and sit with me five hours. I gave up altogether going to her house and the five hours would be spent in a recital of what went on there, of Mariette's anxieties and nightmares. After dinner in the evening I would try to get on with my philosophy. Adrian would fetch a jug of beer from the pub next door and I could only keep awake by reading aloud to him.

I enjoyed metaphysics very much and hoped for a world-view. Whereas Mariette only hoped for a house of her own. But it will be possible, I thought, to achieve a compromise; I can live with Mariette in her house and still have a private wire to the cosmic outposts.

In philosophy I was drawn two ways. I wanted the world to be One, to be permanent, the incarnation of an absolute Idea (though the word 'Idea' is inadequate since this Idea must be as much superintellectual as God, if there were a God, would be super-human). At the same time any typical monistic system appeared hopelessly static, discounting Becoming as mere illusion and hamstringing human action. My tutor,[1] one of Oxford's few remaining neo-Hegelians, maintained, in face of the pigeon-hole philosophy flourishing at Cambridge, that neither logic nor ethics could be separated from metaphysics. I found his attitude sympathetic since my instinct was to drag in ultimate reality everywhere. The attempt of semanticists to narrow philosophy to the clarification of language was in my opinion as mere a parlour game as the traditional formal logic of bottled syllogisms. Reading F. H. Bradley's *Logic* I was delighted to find him saying that any judgment about anything whatsoever is a judgment about the Universe; I tried to suppress the feeling that in that case it becomes impossible to assess a judgment without subpoenaing the Universe (and how difficult it is to get that witness into court).

The stress laid upon Ancient Philosophy in our course repeated the pattern of our social position as public-school boys; we spent a great deal of time pitting Aristotle against Plato but had no adequate foil to the school of idealism which both represent. Nobody mentioned Democritus. On this select arena of ancient idealism my sympathies were divided. The Platonic hierarchy mounting up to and subsumed under the Form of the Good inevitably appeals to anyone whose childhood has been fed on Christianity and his adolescence upon Shelley. The Form of the Good, the One, may be food or it may be dope but it stops the hunger of the waifs of Here and Now. Many people therefore are ready to plump for the One until the wind blows under the door of that supposedly soundproof system – 'But where,' says the wind coldly, 'where are the other eleven?' Aristotle, if only by contrast with Plato, appeared as the champion of the Other Eleven.

Aristotle the biologist was anxious to avoid the gulf between Being and Becoming established by Plato the mathematician. His concept of *energeia* – significant and so, in a sense, eternal movement exemplified in the time-world – was an antidote to the static and self-contained heaven of Plato's transcendent Forms. But when you look into him you find he does not go far enough: reality, rescued

[1] Geoffrey Mure.

125

from the One, is traced back to the *infima species* but not to the individual unit, while his distinction between *energeia* (significant and absolute movement) and *kinesis* (movement which is merely relative) restores the Platonic gulf that he has just been trying to fill in. Or so I thought. Aristotle allows that what is *energeia* from one angle may be *kinesis* from another; but in that case, I thought, *kinesis* also should be a permanent principle, whereas Aristotle supposes a highest grade in which mind thinks only itself and this he exempts from *kinesis*. Complete fusion of subject and object; a full stop; death. Being opposed to this full stop, it will be seen that I was ripe for Marx whose basic thesis, translated into Aristotelian, is that *energeia* can only be achieved by the canalisation and continued control of *kinesis*. But, Marx being then hardly known in Oxford, I had resort to the flashy dynamic idealism of Gentile's *Mind as Pure Act*.

That the Oxford philosophers were riding for a fall was pointed out in the Autobiography of R. G. Collingwood, who denounces their activities as merely frivolous cerebration, the desperate attempt of figures in a picture to refute their frame by ignoring it. We who were undergraduates in the twenties were equally frivolous but more consciously desperate; we felt the frame cramping us. There is nothing to be done, however, with a frame like that but to break it, and we were too young for that and England too old. Hickleton Hickleton Hickleton–the long train settled with a jolt or two in a siding and the engine was uncoupled for the night.

XXIV

Although marriage with Mariette promised a life where the clocks had been put back or even replaced by sundials, I still clung to the importance of being modern and, as my last public gesture in Oxford, read a paper entitled *We are the Old*. I had got the phrase from Gentile and my thesis was this: traditionalism is the death of tradition; to keep a tradition alive means constant change and that means change of forms. Tradition preserved by revolution – but only by revolutions in technique. Technical experiment was still the Ladder of Perfection.

My aesthetic hedonism sanctioned Mariette and her lack of any sense of proportion. Reading Plato for examination purposes I was reacting against the view that reason dominates instinct, soul body, and subject-matter form, and found support for my attack on these three Platonic tenets in the psychoanalysts, D. H. Lawrence and the Post-Impressionist painters respectively. Plato had thought he was condemning the bodily pleasures when he compared them to the pouring of water through a sieve. I was willing to accept this comparison but argued that life is like that; life is like water and water must always be on the move, it is the only way it can realise its value; see for yourself, put a rose on your watering-can and water your garden, see the pattern and prismatic colours of the water in the air. For pattern is value and a *static* pattern dies on you.

Dr. Johnson had said that the poet is not concerned with the minute particulars, with 'the streaks on the tulip'. This, I thought, was just where he was wrong and just where I met Mariette on a common ground. Mariette was crazy for the streaks on the tulip. At the same time I felt she made much ado not about nothing but about the obvious or the trivial. Her conversation was like a barber's scissors when he is giving his last touches to the back of your head, clicking away very fast, very deftly, but apparently not making contact.

Graham and John Hilton and Auden had all left Oxford and, even when I could steal half an hour from Mariette or an hour or even two from work, I had few opportunities for intellectual conversation. But I had met Father D'Arcy, the great Jesuit and authority on St. Thomas Aquinas, and he alone among Oxford dons seemed to me to have the glamour that medieval students looked for in their masters. Intellect incarnate in a beautiful head, wavy grey hair and delicate features; a hawk's eyes. I suspected his religion, of course, but it at least, I thought, has given him a *savoir-faire* which you do not find in these wishy-washy humanists; it was a treat to watch him carving a dish of game.

And Stephen Spender was still around—around and around—and his great beaming messianic face was an antidote to our conventional Oxford nonchalance. He showed me the manuscript of a novel in which he had featured Auden as a kind of Lord of Death. This figure was not in the least like Auden but was an exquisite example of Stephen's lust to mythologise the world in which he walked. He was not yet influenced by communism, so was still building what castles he could out of personal relationships. I criticised the novel as not being very like Oxford. Oh that does not matter, Stephen said, I am thinking of transposing the whole scene to a lunatic asylum.

Shortly before my examination I went up for an interview to Birmingham and was appointed, for the next academic year, to a Lecturership in Classics at Birmingham University. That meant that, as soon as the Oxford term was over, Mariette and I could get married. I carefully did not mention this appointment in my letters home to my family. 'But my dear,' my friends said, 'you will not be able to live in Birmingham!' Birmingham was darkest Africa. [But I had hardly breathing-space now to assess my future, I was so busy working and, when not working, opposing those who opposed our marriage. Had it not been for this opposition we might well not have got married, but we both felt that our self-respect would be ruined if we let other people even think they were dictating our lives.]

On the first day of Greats, my final examination, Mariette was sent to see a prominent neurologist who allegedly told her I was mentally unsound; I had a psychosis and would sooner or later commit suicide. But why, she asked, would I commit suicide? Because I had a psychosis. But how did he know I had a psychosis? Because people who commit suicide always have psychoses. Unable to answer this logic Mariette asked if it wouldn't be a good idea for him to see me. Quite unnecessary, he answered; he knew all about me that he wanted to. Besides, he had read one of my poems. The interview was a stalemate; the neurologist got his fee but Mariette was depressed. I went on writing examination papers.

Mariette and I were married on the last morning of term in a registry office at Carfax in the centre of Oxford. It was Midsummer Day; *vive la bagatelle!* Our marriage coincided with a formal visit to Oxford by the Princess Royal, and as we arrived late at the registry and stepped out of a taxi with a bouquet of roses, people began to cheer us from the house-tops. This particularly tickled Graham Shepard who had come to Oxford for the occasion. I said goodbye to Graham sentimentally—to Graham and the world of Graeco-Roman fauns—and went away with Mariette into the Cotswolds where the stone of the houses contrives to be grey but warm and the lanes were foaming with elder and little rivers like the Windrush wind their way through quite straightforward valleys merely for the love of winding. There is no hurry in the Cotswolds; all the little rivers will puddle through in the end. Mariette and I were very tired. Now, we thought, we can have a long rest.

XXV

Tant que la vie durera Mariette dansera. Tant que la vie—or at least in 1930, the year of the liquidation of the Kulaks. And even in Birmingham, that sprawling ink-blot of nineteenth-century industry. Chimneys to right of us, chimneys to left of us, someone had blundered. But *we* were not the keepers of the badgered employees or the badgering unemployed, of the slaves of the assembly-belts, the fodder of the mills. Ours not to reason why and we might as well keep out of it.

South of Birmingham is Shakespeare's England, Flower's Ale dominating Stratford; north lies the Unknown Country, the black country, the Potteries, vistas of pit-heads and slag-heaps till you reach the Eldorado of Cotton but the conquistadores are dead and the looms have been shrivelled by the Rising Sun of Japan. For all them saints what from their labours rest—St. Arkwright, St. Hargreaves and St. James Watt—let the hooters cry in the deserts of old iron and the numb dumb queues of workless workers cross themselves once beneath the hungry smoke-stack.

The Slump was on the way, but Mariette and I, who had never had any money of our own, found ourselves very comfortable living in a converted stables on the south, the genteel, side of Birmingham. As we had no household belongings, our chief activity for a couple of months was buying. Since Mariette regarded this as an almost sacred ritual, I accompanied her whenever possible to the stores where she showed a childlike delight in bargains that was quite divorced from mathematics. Mariette bought like a jackdaw, was almost uncritical of anything that glittered.

The University building was a mass, a mess, of grimy neo-Gothic, the rooms designed to be dark and the stairs and the benches in the lecture rooms designed for discomfort; the whole could have passed for a typical block of insurance offices. In the square outside stood a drab stone statue of a frock-coated worthy, very like hundreds of other statues in London and the provinces; the Victorians had many philanthropists and they all had to be mortified in stone. This one was Josiah Mason who in 1880 had founded Mason College which later became Birmingham University. He had of course been a self-made man, had risen from a blacksmith etc. etc. to a pin-manu-facturer after a flirtation with imitation gold jewellery (Birmingham in the nineteenth century had led the world in imitation trinkets – 'Brummagem buttons' and as-it-were mother-of-pearl).

I entered Josiah Mason's foundation without realising that it was as different from Oxford as Josiah was from Walter de Merton. I had to take a course of Plato and intended to teach Plato dynamically; before getting up on the morning of my first class I had been rushing through Tolstoy's *What is Art?*, for Plato would come more alive to the students if they could link him with Tolstoy. An hour of the students' faces punctured my good intentions. I felt like Mr. Charles when he had said: 'All you are good for is spelling.'

They were all so unresponsive, so undernourished, I just could not be bothered. My snobbery was by this stage willing to accept a clean-cut working-man but it could not accept these hybrids. Many of them came from working-class homes but they were all set on finding a berth in the lower middle or the middle middle classes. This meant that of those taking courses in the Arts an alarming proportion were preparing to be school-teachers. And it meant also that Plato must not come alive for them, for that might queer them with the education authorities, the local boards, the headmasters.

With no more desire to be a good teacher and doubtful now whether I could be a good writer, I fell back on the home. For Mariette at least, in her own way, was advancing. Before her marriage she had never done any housework or cooking, had never done anything strenuous except playing tennis and dancing, could not even poach an egg; but already she was cooking from Czech and Italian recipes, greatly to my admiration and her own. In her spare time she was painting the house–walls, ceilings and furniture –picking out every available panel, lintel and knob in different colours. It was like living in a gypsy caravan. She got very annoyed if anyone used the phrase 'colour-scheme'. A colour-scheme for Mariette was an affectation of aesthetes, a sheer fiction. She had met too many aesthetes in Oxford. To have colour-schemes was a sign of infertility. No, no, you paint your chest of drawers as the bird sings, and you paint your wardrobe also as the bird sings, and if it is a different bird so much the better.

Graham had procured for us a tiny ginger tom-kitten. His ears were so big that he seemed to be swinging between them, his purr was so big that it shook him like a standing car when the engine is left running too fast, his paws were the colour of butter and melted on your hand like butter, he chirped like a bird to draw your attention. Mariette winnowed the finest ashes for his ash-box. He became a Sine Qua Non, a household god. He became a symbol of security, a sexual go-between, an absolute. Mariette and I made love to each other by referring to him.

When the wind blew from the south the air would thicken with chocolate; we were only a mile from the Cadbury Works. The Cadbury family, being Quakers, were unusually humane employers, had built around their works the first garden city in England, but its whimsical little residences, originally intended for the employees, were by now largely occupied by small business men or clerks. The Cadbury workers were given voluntary culture in the evenings—an opportunity it was diplomatic to use. In spite of the good conditions at Cadbury's many young men and girls were frightened off by this voluntary culture; it was also said that the girls there got very fat and that the atmosphere could give you T.B. And some workers prefer to know where they stand, to have an employer who does not meet you halfway. I thought myself that, if I had had to be employed in mass-production, I would rather not mass-produce chocolate. The girls in their white aprons each with her own little monotony, flicking a pink bauble accurately on to a bonbon, for ever and ever and ever—a million baubles on a million bonbons, and another girl puts them in a million frilly paper cradles and then they are marshalled in boxes with perpetual June on the cover and are shot around the world to people's best girls and mothers and the frilly paper is trampled underfoot in cinemas and railway trains and stadiums and every day is somebody's birthday.

XXVI

For five years Mariette and I lived together in Birmingham and all that time we were living on an island. We ignored our Birmingham context as much as possible—Mariette said someone had left the salt out of the Midland accent—and spent most of our free time driving into Shropshire in a Baby Austin car given us by my father. We never went abroad, because Mariette said she was sick of travelling, and I saw very few of my old friends. Auden and Spender were both in Germany building up their new *Weltanschauung*, John Hilton was in Germany learning to be an architect in the functional manner of Gropius, Adrian was in Vienna learning German in order to get a job at the British Museum, Graham was working full-time for the *Illustrated London News*, writing captions under the illustrations, nearly got the sack for describing a shrewmouse as a rodent. Anthony Blunt had stayed on at Cambridge where he was tutoring in French and doing research in the history of art; he had abandoned the crusade for Pure Form and was now palpably academic.

Later, Graham, John and Adrian got married. Mariette and I were not altogether pleased; people, excepting ourselves, seemed to get duller after marriage. And they got so preoccupied with money. We were better off than the others, thanks to Mariette's investments and an annual allowance from her grandfather.

Many people considered us a romantic and comfortable couple, but we had our rows. The first was at breakfast in an inn where I failed to finish my boiled egg. Mariette, peering into the eggshell, exploded into righteous raciality; no Jew, she said, would start a boiled egg and not finish it. Just as no Jew would ever by accident step in muck in the road. Whenever Mariette was annoyed she remembered that I was a Gentile. She had certain unsurmountable prejudices—for instance, against strikes, religion and drink. I was tainted with the two latter but did not bring up the question of strikes; her view of society was so patriarchal—or matriarchal—that we had no common ground for argument.

She was especially suspicious of the Labour Movement because our landlord and landlady, who lived across the yard, were militant socialists and we had to pay them £100 a year rent. Two or three times a summer they would lend their garden for Labour Party garden parties and our doorstep would be littered with orange peel. All the people who attended these functions seemed to belong to the organising committee; it was like the old Spanish army—all officers and no men. There were coconut-shies and loud-speakers and treasure hunts and everyone was red in the face with righteousness and self-importance. At least so it seemed to Mariette and me, and we knew several workers who suspected the local Labour Party in the same way that they suspected the parish church.

Our landlady was American, had a charming smile, violent red hair and vitality, had spent her life furthering causes; an evangelist in her teens, a deputy on Henry Ford's peace ship, a protagonist of Birth Control in England. In her time off from political committees, peace campaigns and protest meetings, she would chop down trees with a long-handled axe or give evening parties to those who were elect and correct, to those who were Left and jolly.

Many Leftist writers came to stay in her house—Maurice Dobb, A. L. Rowse, John Strachey, Naomi Mitchison. The word Proletariat hung in festoons from the ceiling. And yet I felt that they all were living in the study. The armchair reformist sits between two dangers—wishful thinking and self-indulgent gloom. The phrase 'I told you so' is near to his heart (the *New Statesman and Nation*, our leading Leftist weekly, lived upon prophecies of disaster—and was never disappointed) but when he fancies an allegro movement he has—or had, rather—only to turn to Moscow. Naomi Mitchison after a fortnight or so in Russia gave a lecture at Birmingham University about the joy in the faces of the masses. It all seemed to me too pat. Our landlady's friends had a gospel-tent enthusiasm and quivers of prickly statistics, but the gospel of Marx as sifted through Transport House seemed to me hardly more inspiring or more broad-minded than the gospels of Dr. Arnold or Cecil Rhodes.

1931 was a black year for Labour. The country was rocking from the collapse of Wall Street, there were two million unemployed, the old gang of Labour leaders – the deplorable trinity of MacDonald, Jimmy Thomas and Snowden – suddenly called themselves 'National', sold their birthright. Our landlady put more than usual energy into electioneering, but everyone knew that Labour was down the sink; old MacDonald had posed for the camera pulling the plug out. Mariette and I, sitting in a cinema, watched the results of the election thrown up on the screen – loss after loss for Labour. All the Birmingham boroughs returned 'National' candidates. Mariette was amused and almost pleased; she had not forgiven the orange-peel on her doorstep. I was not pleased but I wondered to myself if it mattered. They were all racketeers anyway – look at the Trade Union leaders. Look at Jimmy Thomas and Derby. As Thomas Paine had written: 'Can ye give to prostitution its former innocence?' Up in the industrial district on the north side of Birmingham the air was a muddy pond and the voices of those who expected nothing a chorus of frogs for ever resenting and accepting the *status quo* of stagnation.

XXVII

I would look down my list of students: 'Mr. Green, will you translate now?' After a pause a voice would come from somewhere on the benches but nobody was opening his mouth. So I never learned who Mr. Green was.

But the Professor of Greek, E. R. Dodds, made me feel rather ashamed. Most members of the Birmingham staff had the outlook of business men and the seriousness with which they took their work was for me further evidence of its futility. But Dodds was no business man. He had been expelled from Campbell College in Belfast for 'gross, studied and sustained insolence', had in the Great War had the courage of his Irish nationalism but served with a hospital unit in Serbia, had—for all his academic brilliance—nearly been sent down from Oxford for his Irish Republican sympathies. He had specialised in Neo-Platonism, a subject hardly known at Oxford because it was outside the syllabus. He had written poems in the Irish romantic tradition. He was a member of the Society for Psychical Research but ruthlessly insisted upon scientific evidence. He combined a razor-keen rationalism with an unusual humaneness. His chief pleasure was gardening and his head would have been wonderful to sculpt. And with all this he took his university work—and even the university committees—seriously.

[The Doddses were a godsend to Mariette and me, because while I talked to Dodds Mariette talked to his wife about animals. Mrs. Dodds had a parrot called William and a Sealyham terrier called Gregory and she treated them—which is of course common in England—as members of the family. But her love of animals did not strike one as either sentimental or silly or escapist; it was married to her wit, and the tone of her voice did not change when speaking of Gregory or to him. It was just a fact that she preferred Gregory to the Joneses. It was not that she had any inferiority complex in face of human beings, for she was extraordinarily clever and very capable of asserting herself. Many women take to dogs because they are fools and cannot have communion with people. Mrs. Dodds on the other hand preferred dogs because she recognised that *other* people were fools; and she did not suffer fools gladly though she had a liking for eccentrics. Mariette and I amused her because we were so unlike the rest of the faculty and the faculty wives.]

Dodds resented the contempt for the provincial universities expressed, or tacitly implied, by Oxford and Cambridge. I endorsed this resentment on paper but when in contact with the students I merely felt '*Qu'allais-je faire dans cette galère?*' For instance I was tutoring an older student, an ex-clerk who had got a State scholarship, and we were reading the *Symposium* of Plato. But there was something, he said, that he did not understand; these philosophers—how was it possible they should have sat together drinking?

If I wanted to get on in the profession, Dodds told me, I must do some research. Edit a Greek play perhaps. He recognised that much of the 'research' done at universities was done merely from careerist motives and much of it was a waste of time. But provided you had a critical faculty, provided you had imagination and provided you did some work you might contribute something to Scholarship. Scholarship for Dodds was a living and humane activity, an antidote to sentimentality, to our more muddled or trumpery brands of civilisation. Wilamowitz's edition of the *Heracles* was in Dodds's eyes a high work of human genius, an education, an inspiration, a resounding defeat for barbarism. I was moved by Dodds's enthusiasm but I felt that the halo of Wilamowitz was not for me. I did not want to be a scholar; I wanted to 'write'.

The trouble is that you cannot write in a hot-house. Mariette would plug a leg of lamb full of rosemary and cloves and that was the event of the day. To write poems expressing doubt or melancholy, an anarchist conception of freedom or nostalgia for the open spaces (and these were the things that I wanted to express), seemed disloyal to Mariette. Instead I was disloyal to myself, wrote a novel which purported to be an idyll of domestic felicity. Faking, I thought, doesn't matter so much in prose and one must at least keep one's hand in.

We turned on the gramophone the moment we got up—Sophie Tucker or Elisabeth Schumann or Segovia with his guitar. Most of our records were worn out, if not cracked. Once in a way Mariette would get a new record, play it all afternoon. And all the next morning and the next afternoon. And on the seventh day she rested, played something else.

Four or five times a week we went to the cinema, going solely for entertainment and never for value, holding hands like a shopgirl with her boy-friend. The organist would come up through the floor, a purple spotlight on his brilliantined head, and play us the 'Londonderry Air' and bow and go back to the tomb. Then the stars would return close-up and the huge Cupid's bows of their mouths would swallow up everybody's troubles—there were no more offices or factories or shops, no more bosses or foremen, no more unemployment and no more employment, no more danger of disease or babies, nothing but bliss in a celluloid world where the roses are always red and the Danube is always blue.

One day a blue-check pigeon descended at our doorstep worn out. Our landlady's gardener encouraged us to keep him and Mariette discovered that she had an ancestor who was a pigeon-fancier in Bagdad. Very soon the air was whirring and rumbling with pigeons; when we came out of the door they landed on our shoulders and flowed over our feet. We kept an enormous sack of Indian corn; dipping our hands into this sack became one of our daily sensations, an assurance of physical good; your fingers came out mealy under the nails.

We also took up dogs. Having a liking for the less usual breeds we bought in turn an Old English sheepdog called Cherry, a pug called Prunella and a borzoi called Betsy—a haystack, a little Dutch cheese and a film-star to take out on strings. Each week we bought two weekly dog-papers and read the reports of the shows, talked dog-jargon with Dodds's wife. Mariette and I began to visit shows and even to show at them—in Birmingham, Manchester, Cheltenham, Oxford and Maidenhead, at Ranelagh, Cruft's and the Crystal Palace.

An English dog show is very very English; you meet all the people you never would have thought of inventing. Dog-fanciers can be divided into two classes—those who look very like their dogs and those who look exactly unlike them. While there are old ladies showing Pekinese who look like Pekinese themselves, there are also gigolos with bulldogs or bruisers with Yorkshire terriers. The show is a wonderland of non-utilitarian growths. Through the smell and the noise and the clouds of chalk you can distinguish dogs that have been passed through the mangle and dogs with permanent waves, Bond Street ladies in veils and Amazons all boots. The human beings talk to each other roughly and curtly but twitter and coo to their dogs. There are sportsmen and sportswomen who work their dogs in the field, and there are hermits from caves of melancholia who might have been artists or had lovers. You feel his nose to be sure that he is not ill, you chop up his meat so neatly, you put in his codliver oil and a spoonful of lime for his bones, you brush him and comb him and pluck him and every so often you worm him—you are proud if he passes worms and proud if he doesn't.

It's not fair, that's what it's not, judge don't know a dog from a carthorse, I tell you straight been showing for forty years and never in my life I mean what I say, see the dog he put up well would you believe it, no it's not fair, that's what it is, it's not.

XXVIII

Educated people in England, if they consort with members of the working classes, tend to think of them as 'characters'. You may throw darts with the yokels in the village pub but all the time the yokels are on the stage and you are in the stalls. Instead of a bouquet for their performance you give them a pint of bitter.

Mariette preferred the working class to her own because they did not talk about colour-schemes whereas they did talk about pigeon-racing and the price of food-stuffs. Also she had a dream of being the Lady of the Manor with dozens of domestics and under-gardeners and tenants all of whom would adore her and whom she would treat with the greatest kindness and educate in birth control and hygiene. In default of a manor she assembled a little circle consisting of our maid and all her relations and her younger sister's young man and our landlady's gardener and his son and the plumber, Mr. Wilkins. They were all more or less characters and gave Mariette an inexhaustible subject of conversation.

The gardener, Robinson, belonged, like my scout at Oxford, to the old order of things. Like most gardeners he was conservative, approved of the social hierarchy, wanted the boss to be the boss and suspected the radicalism of his present employers. He looked as if he had walked out of a comic strip, had a long hanging moustache and eyes that through cracked glasses fastened on their object like corkscrews. He preferred carpentering and other odd jobs to gardening and was delighted when we asked him to knock down the wall of our house in order to move in a divan. All such problems were easy for him—'That's easy, you get your two by four if you understand what I mean, you get your two by four . . .' He spoke in the old Birmingham dialect and would tell us long stories filled out with circumstantial details and expletives—'Good God Almighty, Hell!' He had spent the Great War in the trenches and told us how he had come across a Frenchman fishing in the Somme—'he were landing them one after the other, do you see, one after the other like that'; and his bait was cheese. But Robinson didn't want any more war: 'They won't get *me* for another of their wars, not unless they fight her with pigs' bladders.'

His son, Young Robinson, was a handsome, sensitive boy with beautiful natural manners and half one finger missing that he had lost in the rolling mills. Working an eight-hour day in a hell of noise, he found it a change to come and clean our pigeon-house or paint for us, would swing off his bicycle smiling like a seraph, say 'How's yourself?' in answer to Mariette's greeting. He talked to us on the assumption that we always knew what he meant. 'Fellow at our place yesterday got in trouble for throwing.' 'Throwing?' 'You know. *Throwing.*' He was surprised when he had to explain to us that the hands in the rolling mills were accustomed to relieve their feelings by throwing at one another; it had been forbidden because they thought it was dangerous, someone might get hurt and that. 'Throwing what, Young Robinson?' 'Oh, spanners and that.' All he wanted was to live on a farm; then he'd be in his oil-tot. Young Robinson was always whistling. Until he got married and went to live with his mother-in-law. He became pale and haggard and his wife started a baby. It was born paralysed and after a little died. Young Robinson still came to work for us but he hardly smiled as he got off his bicycle and he did not sing or whistle any more.

Janet, our maid, was pretty but pale and delicate; once a month she used to nearly faint (which was why she could not aspire to a job in a shop) and I would drive her to her back-street home. 'Here's Our Janet' her mother would say and arrange her on the couch in the kitchen and give her a cup of strong tea. The kitchen of course served as the living-room; no one entered the parlour next door except to polish the furniture. Janet's family consisted of Our Dad (pronounced almost Our Dud), Our Mother, a serious elder sister, a gay younger sister and a married brother who lived elsewhere. The kitchen in the evenings was always overheated and full of arguments about the Football Pool. Our Dad, who had been a commercial traveller and enjoyed it, had long been out of work and went nearly every day to the public library to study the ads for a job but, as Janet said, of course he would never get one, they said he was too old, it wasn't really fair. But he remained *au fait* with the railway time-tables and could tell you how to get anywhere. Our

Mother had had a couple of strokes but did all the cooking and most of the housework. Janet helped her a little, but the two sisters, proud of their jobs in shops, considered they had done their bit by contributing part of their wages. Janet's brother had a job in the Austin Motor Works, which he hated, and according to Janet was unhappily married; his wife was a bit touched, spent all the house-keeping money on canned foods which she hoarded and never opened. His escape was fishing; he belonged to a club which on Sundays would have angling competitions along the Severn; the members of the club would line the Severn for miles.

Janet's younger sister's young man, George, was an electrician, would often come to our house to fit up gadgets on the cheap. He was unlike the rest of them in that he was not class-conscious. When I went to the pub with Janet's brother I felt a barrier between us. He was affable, very polite, but he minded his p's and q's. One day he told me that he voted Labour but if he were me he would vote Tory. This kind of realism precluded intimacy. But George was no realist; very short, very young, he was perky as a schoolboy and did not vote anything. With his heavily greased hair and ill-cut mouth he looked like a soccer pro. He had little schooling, his grammar was shocking and his vowel sounds never less than a triphthong (Janet's family thought him a rough diamond); but he was full of himself in the same way that Mariette was and had the same abundance of anecdotes. His first job in life had been wiring the slaughterhouses—put him off meat for months. Them slaughter-houses, they was full of Italianos, great big fellows with moustachios, who had played a trick on George, locked him in in the dark in a Bluebeard's chamber with blood to his ankles. But George had now gone up in the world and was the right-hand man of his boss who owned an enormous car and an aviary and had a porcelain elephant in his garden that made a fountain with his trunk. One day when George came to see us, he was grinning like a gargoyle; the boss's Alsatian had eaten the boss's toucan.

About the beginning of 1933 Mariette decided to modernise the house with a view to having a baby and George introduced us to the plumber, Mr. Wilkins, who had plumbed for Queen Alexandra. Mr. Wilkins was a heavy powerful old man, slow and momentous in speech. 'Young George,' he would say, 'there's a pity now; he ain't got no education.' For he himself was a great reader; toughest job he ever took on, he told me, was a book called *The Decline and Fall of the Roman Empire*; didn't mean much to him but he got through it. He had a sister who attended a spiritualist church–'I don't hold with them things myself'–and who used to get in trances and start painting pictures or playing the piano. 'Now there's a funny thing, my sister she ain't no musician, don't know one note from another hardly, but when she gets that way, down she sits and plays like someone at a concert; a real pleasure to listen to–you know what I mean. But I don't think it's right. Gives me the creeps sometimes. And you know what she says? There she is at that there piano playing away real high-class concert music–out of her head if you follow me–and you ask her what's got into her, she says it's the Spirit of Wagner.'

Characters all. That spring Mariette and I visited Cambridge and were entertained by Anthony, playing charades with an assortment of Cambridge dons and undergraduates and Bloomsbury intellectuals. A charade was good if it was risqué or blasphemous, and I felt I was back at Marlborough. The same private gossip and tittering, the same disregard for everybody not ourselves. Perhaps it was better to live among the characters. But is it a fact that nobody ever gets anywhere?

[Sometimes in the nights I woke and wondered where we were going, but most of the time I was doped and happy, most of the time except when I thought about time that most of the time is waste but whose is not? When I started again to write poems they were all about time. We had an old record of 'The Blue Room', one of the most out-and-out jazz sentimentalisations of domestic felicity –far away upstairs but the blue began to suffocate. I wrote a novel which was basically dishonest and ended in a blue room as if that solved everything.[1] I followed it up with a very different novel called *The F. Vet*, a purgation of my grudges against my family, after which I felt more kindly to them.[2] And after that I began to recover stamina; the dope-dream grew a little thinner. Mariette too was recovering from her earlier life; in 1930 all she had wanted was rest but now she was almost rested.]

[1] Published as *Roundabout Way* by Louis Malone (Putnam, 1932).
[2] So far as I know this novel was never published and no manuscript of it exists. Title: perhaps *The Family Vet*?

XXIX

While Mariette was modernising the house and preparing to have a baby I found that I again had the time—and the inclination—to think. A temporary colleague of mine, who had won all the prizes at Cambridge and who shared my room in the university, had gone off his head. This disillusioned me about madness which I had still tended to think of romantically. He was one of the dullest men I had ever met. Shortly before his collapse he had taken to automatic writing; I found on my table a sheet of foolscap with this sentence written very neatly in the middle—'My academic successes are enough to blazon my name for all time through every school and university in the world.' I had to drive him to the mental hospital in my baby car; all the way he kept talking about suicide, occasionally quoting A. E. Housman, saying he was sure they would certify him. And so they did; it was schizophrenia, a hopeless case.

He had been notably egocentric. Madness after all, I thought, is the *reductio ad absurdum* of personality. The gospel of the twenties, Self-Expression, taught us that the more you indulge your personality the more you become free; you can trace this back to Shelley but it is wrong. Push your personality as far as it will go and you end in a padded cell. There is an antinomy between Freedom and Egotism. I began to take more interest in the Soviet Union of which I knew next to nothing. Having a child presented the same problem as teaching in Birmingham University. You teach these students merely to enable them to get degrees and teach other students who will get degrees and so on and so on—an infinite regress. So you grow up in order to marry and have children and they grow up . . . For Mariette having a child and bringing it up appeared to be now her be-all and end-all. She had always been obsessed with keeping alive, avoiding danger and armed with disinfectants, and now she was going to project this on to her children. What you did did not matter as long as it enabled you to be; work was merely a means of making a living. Maybe, I thought, we should turn this upside down–what you are does not matter but what you do. Or, seeing that what you are is conditioned by what you do, it would be more correct to say '*That* you are does not matter', mere existence does not matter. I got very irritated when Mariette suggested we should save against the time we were sixty. For thirty-odd years we were to save money and gargle our throats– for what?

[I used to walk round the suburbs with my borzoi slowly digesting the world I had lived in almost without knowing it. I was aware of a dichotomy. Living with Mariette was not only pleasant but good, Mariette was a 'real person', she at least meant what she said, her enthusiasms, however whimsical or frivolous, were genuine. But outside Mariette was the Rest of the World, intellectually stimulating and in ways more real than Mariette but horrifying.] Living in Birmingham had reconciled me to ordinary people; I found re-assurance in silent gardeners, inefficient hospital nurses, in a golfer cupping a match in his hands in the wind, in business men talking shop in the train. I found no such reassurance in the intelligentsia. I remembered how under the Roman Empire intellectuals spent their time practising rhetoric although they would never use it for any practical purpose; they swam gracefully around in rhetoric like fish in an aquarium tank. And our intellectuals also seemed to be living in tanks.

I looked around at my friends. Graham was still writing captions for the *Illustrated London News* but he was not *writing*. John Hilton after taking architectural courses in Germany and London could not decide whether he would not prefer to be a university lecturer in philosophy. Adrian owing to the Slump had failed to get his job in the British Museum and had consented to enter a stockbroker's office in Bath. Anthony, still at Cambridge, could now tell you where any picture was in Europe, where it had come from and who had bought it and when.

But there was an important exception–the group of poets who had appeared in *New Signatures*, published in 1931. They were all politically Left, but it was not the jogtrot, compromising Left of my landlady's garden parties. The English Labour Party is notori-ously lacking in glamour; these young poets had turned to the tomb of Lenin, the great flirtation had begun with the Third International. The strongest appeal of the Communist Party was that it demanded sacrifice; you had to sink your ego. At the moment there seemed to be a confusion between the state and the community, and I myself was repelled by the idolisation of the state; but that was all right, it is written: 'The state shall wither away.' Young men were swallowing Marx with the same naïve enthusiasm that made Shelley swallow Rousseau.

I had a certain hankering to sink my ego, but was repelled by the priggishness of the Comrades and suspected that their positive programme was vitiated by wishful thinking and over-simplification. I joined them however in their hatred of the *status quo*, I wanted to smash the aquarium. During Christmas of 1933 Mariette performed her usual rites–the rustle of coloured paper–and I sat down deliberately and wrote a long poem called *Eclogue for Christmas*. I wrote it with a kind of cold-blooded passion and when it was done it surprised me. Was I really as concerned as all that with the Decline of the West? Did I really feel so desperate? Apparently I did. Part of me must have been feeling like that for years.

In May 1934 Mariette went into a nursing home called The Dingle (since 1930 we had not spent a night apart) and I suddenly found I had a son and at once becoming terrified that something might happen to him tried to remain detached and an observer. Another woman having a baby there had flown over for the purpose from Iran; how odd, I thought, to fly all that way to a place called The Dingle.

While Mariette was in the nursing home I went a long walk with George the electrician along the towpath of one of England's many superannuated canals. I left my ashplant, my Oxford talisman, behind in a pub. Well, never mind, I will go back and fetch it. For years I had been leaving it behind, had gone back and fetched it. But this time I kept putting it off and after a few weeks George told me the pub was being demolished and I gave up all thought of recovering it. I found to my surprise that I no longer missed it.

XXX

For the next year Mariette hardly went out of the house; she would not trust anyone with her child whom she was looking after according to Truby King. Truby King's methods are unnatural but supposedly scientific. Just as the mechanistic view of the world was once scientific.

I regretted that Mariette immured herself but I was happier than I had been for some time. Instead of a prolonged elopement I suddenly found I had a family and more time to play with or to work with rather than less. I went out one day in September and bought our last dog, a bull-mastiff puppy, and a few days later I paid a flying visit to Dublin to join Dodds who was editing the life and letters of his friend Stephen MacKenna and had gone to Dublin to collect reminiscences. I felt I was born again, to be able to go to Dublin on my own. Dodds and I walked up the Wicklow Mountains and, as I looked down on Dublin Bay, I felt that the world was open. Dodds felt something too, for he suddenly plunged from a crest and ran half a mile downhill hurdling the tussocks. I was wearing cityfied suède shoes and finding them afterwards soaked and scratched by heather had a sense of having cut loose; a great wild star of space was smashed in the hot-house window.

Dodds and I went to tea with W. B. Yeats in Rathfarnham. Yeats in spite of his paunch was elegant in a smooth light suit and a just sufficiently crooked bow tie. His manner was hierophantic, even when he said: 'This afternoon I have been playing croquet with my daughter.' We were hoping he would talk poetry and gossip, but knowing that Dodds was a professor of Greek he confined the conversation to spiritualism and the phases of the moon, retailing much that he had already printed. Burnet, Yeats said, was all wrong; the Ionian physicists had of course not been physicists at all. The Ionian physicists were spiritualists.

He talked a great deal about the spirits to whom his wife, being a medium, had introduced him. 'Have you ever seen them?' Dodds asked (Dodds could never keep back such questions). Yeats was a little piqued. No, he said grudgingly, he had never actually seen them . . . but–with a flash of triumph–he had often *smelt* them. [As he saw us out at the gate he was urging Dodds to remember that Julius Caesar was killed at a full moon.]

I came back from Dublin exhilarated and spent a placid winter reading and writing and training the bull-mastiff puppy. We had a new friend Ernst,[1] a lecturer in German, who now lived in a flat at the top of our landlady's house. I used to go up there continually and get Ernst to listen to me; he listened just as John Hilton or Graham used to; it was very flattering. I was now getting poems in print and that was flattering too. I had recovered a kind of undergraduate gaiety. In the spring Ernst and his sister and Dodds and I made an expedition to Twickenham to watch Ireland play England at rugby football. What a lot of amusing things one might have been doing before.

The papers said that Ireland had no chance, so we had the excitement of being the under-dog. And the stands were like a museum, packed with specimens of the land-owning Anglo-Irish, a species almost obsolete in Ireland; these were juxtaposed here with the scions of the new Ireland, self-assertive young hobos, each with a green beret and a loud guffaw. As we sat very high in one corner, the ground was a great box padded with human faces and lined with baize. The figures on the baize, in emerald or white jerseys, were like the little balls in a child's puzzle under glass that you have to joggle into holes. We joggled all we could but Ireland lost.

The bull-mastiff puppy got enteritis, followed by fits and tics and paralysis. I nursed her for thirteen weeks and by that time she was hobbling as if made of wood, could still respond to orders but her eyes were blank as an idiot's. I had never seen an idiot dog and I had her put away. I still had Betsy, my borzoi, and I used to take her long walks with a lecturer in English, Waterhouse, who had been in Birmingham all this time but whom I had only just begun to know closely. We took Betsy up into a derelict industrial region near Dudley and sent her racing down slopes among the pitheads where

[1] E. L. Stahl, now Professor of German at Oxford; Aloys' in *Autumn Sequel*, canto xiii.

the wind sang shrill through long black grasses and where the presence of this aristocratic beast in ostrich feathers seemed an impertinence. Waterhouse had always seemed reserved but he capered about on the lost black hills just as Dodds had capered on the Dublin mountains. Perhaps there was something in Mariette's belief that inside all the best people there is a well of nonsense.

For August of that year, 1935, we took a large old farmhouse in the Cotswolds, the floors and stairs on a slant and the garden full of stone mushrooms. We brought with us our new cook, large and red and formidable like the cook in the *Spook Sonata*, and a decrepit old woman called Miss Higgs who Mariette thought needed a rest because she lived with a nagging sister; she was supposed to help with the housework but one morning there was screeching in the kitchen. Miss Higgs had left her false teeth in the sink and the Spook Sonata cook was telling her to keep out of the kitchen for the future. Mariette, who was playing her rôle of the Lady of the Manor, was disappointed at this outcome of her good intentions. Both the cook and Miss Higgs had voices that carried.

However, the sun shone every day and we had a succession of guests. First there was Ernst. He and I used to take the car and drive very fast over the hills to play golf, a game we could enjoy because we were bad at it. We found a little nine-hole course at Broadway poised above the Vale of Evesham so that when you drove from the tee you felt you were knocking the top off England. Ernst who was rather formal in Birmingham became childlike in the country, improvised a Negro spiritual with a refrain 'Rattlesnake, rattlesnake' and sang it for a whole hour's drive. When Ernst left, Waterhouse came and entered into banter with Betsy who had to be lifted over stiles and who was hailed by the little village boys with cries of 'Here comes the sissy dog.' Waterhouse opined that Betsy's absent-mindedness was due to divided personality; every so often she would notice herself doing something, say 'Oh there's that Betsy again.' When Waterhouse left Tsalic came; we had been asked to invite him because he was poor; I had met him once and Mariette never.

Tsalic was a Russian Jew from America doing graduate work in Oxford. He had been an American football star and weighed two hundred pounds, had the good looks of a Jewish heavyweight boxer and the charm of a shaggy sheepdog who expects to be laughed at. Although his voice too was shaggy and he spoke very slowly he and Mariette understood each other at once. And he and I had long talks about football.

We took him back to Birmingham to stay with us because he had nowhere to go. [Then things happened quickly and crazily. The Oxford term was starting and Tsalic was due back on Friday but he wanted to play in a football match in Birmingham on Saturday, so I drove him down to Oxford on Friday to fix things up with his tutor. Driving back again I was very tired from lack of sleep, and a mile from home in a Birmingham suburb a heavy car hit us broadside on at a crossroads, knocking our little car 90 feet; it mounted the pavement, waltzed round two lampposts and came to rest again in the road. Tsalic and I had fallen out on the way. I woke up as if from a long long sleep and found myself sitting on the road, and there was the car. Car? I must drive it home. I got into the driving seat and the car would not start; then I noticed that all the little gadgets on the dashboard were hanging out by the roots as if in some picture by Dali. I gradually realised there must have been an accident. Tsalic who had bad concussion was taken to a hospital. I walked home covered with mud and blood and told Mariette who had long been keeping dinner hot for us that Tsalic was in hospital in a very bad way. Mariette and I went off to the hospital together. Tsalic was in a hushed corner behind a screen and the nurse asked us where were his nearest relatives. His nearest relatives being in America we were told to be prepared during the night; if there were a crisis they would call us on the phone.

There was no crisis, but the next morning I felt as if my neck were broken. I wanted never to drive a car again and I wanted never to have any more problems. Full of self-pity I washed my hands of problems. Anyone could do what he liked but damn my neck and my head.][1]

The next two months were mad. Tsalic returned to our house to convalesce and I sprained my ankle, could only walk with two sticks. Before my ankle had recovered Tsalic left for London and our sitting-room caught on fire. This fire, I felt, was cathartic. I carefully changed my trousers, got our landlady's long-handled axe

[1] Much abbreviated in the final draft.

and smashed the cement base of the hearth, for the beams underneath it were burning. The only other person about was one of our landlady's lodgers and he worked a hose on the spot from the disused stable below while Mariette threw buckets of water into the fireplace above. Soon there was a large hole in the floor and the bucketfuls of water and fragments of cement were falling on the head of our landlady's lodger. Mariette's face was tragic but I was in the height of never-again don't-care spirits. By the time the fire was extinguished our sitting-room looked like a scene from a war-play. The next morning Mariette left for London, there to join Tsalic and not to come back again. She told me later it was because she was 'lonely in her mind'.

XXXI

There were other things that Mariette explained later: everyone, she said, had always treated her as either a freak or a doll; even I had admitted I thought of her as some kind of changeling, a creature crept out of a wood and making believe to be human; whereas Tsalic treated her as someone like himself. This was understandable, but the day Mariette left I felt very desolate. It was after a week or so I began to feel free. I started divorce proceedings almost at once and entered on nearly a year of intrigue, spiritual squalor and anxiety. All very out of proportion; I could not understand why a purely private affair should be considered worthy of all this underground diplomacy, this ultra-diplomatic stupidity. Among other things I received a poem—a bad poem—from the son of a rabbi apologising on behalf of the House of Israel for Mariette's behaviour.

I became immediately concerned with domestic problems, the household income being halved and the expenses doubled. The Spook Sonata cook tried to cheer me up with a series of roast ducks and enormous joints (the butcher had not been paid for months). Going up to Scotland to interview a nurse for my son who was now eighteen months old, I suddenly realised I was under no more obligations to be respectable; Mariette had followed Miss Craig and Reckitts off the map. Since being arrested in Oxford I had not got seriously drunk, because Mariette disliked it. Now I could do what I liked.

Knowing no one in Edinburgh I called on a young man who had written to me on green paper to tell me he was a poet. I found him the eldest of ten children living hugger-mugger in an under-furnished house full of cats; those of the children who were not in bed with flu were discussing in their mother's presence a new cat they intended to give her as a Christmas surprise. Later in the evening the father of the family got tipsy, asked me was I descended from an Irish king. I said yes—from Conchobar MacNessa.[1] Right,

[1] More correctly, Conor MacNessa. (E.N.)

152

he said, we must have some champagne. (Someone had made him a present of some bottles that had gone flat.) We sat up late drinking the flat champagne, and the father of the family became more and more morbid. 'I'm a dead man,' he kept saying, 'I'm dead today and you'll be dead tomorrow.'

The next day I attended a drunken party the guests at which spent half the evening looking for each other all over Edinburgh. There was a keen frost, and Prince's Street is the ideal street for the drunkard as it has only one side to it; the other side is original night and floating in it somewhere a castle. I was seen off on my midnight train to Birmingham by a Scottish Nationalist young man who was holding in his hand a glass of brandy. We drank perdition to the British Empire and smashed the glass on the platform. I did not wake up till the train drew into Birmingham. I had a throbbing head and a filthy mouth but felt somehow purified.

Not liking the idea of Christmas in our house without Mariette to rustle the paper, I spent it with Graham Shepard and his wife in a little country inn looking over the Severn near Tewkesbury. To reach this inn you drove along a side road and then along more of a side, less of a road, and then along the muddiest merest lane which came to a dead end on the river. The day we arrived the mist was so thick that the river had no further bank. A Lethe where everything ends and nothing begins. I stayed on a day after the Shepards left. The landlady thought I looked moody, said 'You ought to get married.'

I did not sleep very well these days. In bed in a big yellow room with a ten-foot skylight (we had had this room built to our own design) I felt the skylight encroaching, tried to dodge it; sometimes it was a falling tent and sometimes it was the gap that cannot be closed. The room too was sometimes too silent and sometimes full of voices; I would open the door quickly and no one would be there. In this room I had two precise visions, both by electric light, both solidly planted in the air about five foot up from the floor. The first was a human eye a yard or so long; the rest of the face was invisible but on both the upper and the under eyelid there were worms instead of eyelashes, transparent worms curling and wriggling. The second vision was of a sky-blue little beast like a jackal but with horns; he sat there pat on the air, his front feet firmly together.

So I did not like being in the house, especially as the new nurse and the cook did not get on together. I began to go out a great deal and discovered Birmingham. Discovered that the students were human; discovered that Birmingham had its own writers and artists who were free of the London trade-mark. The intellectual students were not so obsessed by politics as their contemporaries at Oxford or Cambridge, since, coming from the proletariat themselves, they were conscious of the weaknesses of the Prolet-Cult; some of them in fact were trying to achieve the old Oxford manner just at a time when the Oxford undergraduates were trying to declass themselves. But the best of the Birmingham students were not poseurs, were fully occupied having affaires and lending and borrowing money and being witty and foul-mouthed. [Reggie Smith, the son of a working man in Aston, and the one Birmingham student I met who had no complex about class, thought nothing was so funny as the Oxford and Cambridge proletarianisers. Not that he was one of those whose tastes are conditioned by reaction against their origins. Reggie was perfectly at home with all classes and equally happy— and what is more, equally acceptable—drinking half-pints with factory hands and talking literary criticism with Mrs. Dodds. Being naturally a realist and having a great supply of animal spirits and a natural taste for poetry, he did not confuse realism with escape. The sons of the upper ten, when going Marxist, think they have found escape but they call it realism. Reggie, immune to this fantasy, was hard to draw into a crusade.]

At this time, 1936, literary London was just beginning to recognise something called the Birmingham School of novelists. Literary London, hungry for proletarian literature, assumed that the Birmingham novelists were proletarian. Birmingham denied this; take John Hampson, Walter Allen, Leslie Halward—Hampson was a friend of E. M. Forster and was not employed as a labourer, Allen was a graduate of Birmingham University, Halward was a plasterer's labourer but even he could not be counted as of the sacred proletariat—his father had been a small pork-butcher. It could be conceded however that they wrote about the People with a knowledge available to very few Londoners and that their view of the novel as social history had grown naturally out of their background instead of being, as in London, an apostasy from the view that the novel is primarily art. Though not accepting their theory of the novel I found these Birmingham writers very refreshing; they at least were not hybrids; they were writing – and writing efficiently – on subjects they really knew.

But Birmingham also had–what was much more surprising though less impressive–its clique of surrealists. There were two brothers who were small clerks; one was a surrealist painter and one was a surrealist poet; they saved from their scanty wages to visit the exhibitions in London, and they had a little circle of friends who considered social consciousness anathema and met together to indulge in mutual confessions of insanity. I was present that spring when some of them fell foul of Auden whom they considered a traitor to art. Auden trailed his coat, said that in his opinion Low was the greatest living artist. But I felt sorry for his opponents; they looked on the verge of tears, had no reputation or position or logic with which to defend themselves. And yet, as one says, they had got hold of something–something they were clinging on to through their long office hours and the gritty jarring atmosphere of this soulless commercial city.

Lastly, there was Gordon Herrickx[1] who went his own way and had no sense of publicity. He worked all day as a stonemason and did sculpture at night in a shed behind his little gimcrack house in the suburbs where he lived with a wife and a child. He spent all his spare money on records of classical music. It was only in summer he could do his sculpture; in winter he was too tired from hacking the frozen stone in the stone-cutter's yard. It took him a summer to finish one piece of sculpture. He had made some very good portrait heads but was now chiefly interested in semi-abstract or symphonic pieces founded on some natural *motif*. The year before he had completed a 'cyclamen' and this year he was at work on a 'chestnut-bud'. To achieve these he had made a great many drawings of real cyclamens and chestnut-buds in every stage of their development, had then–without hurrying–allowed these to synthesise or crystallise into one dominant pattern, and had then taken a great slab of Hoptonwood stone (which cost much more than he could afford) and cut the arrested flame in it. Hoptonwood stone polishes beautifully and Herrickx polished and finished every facet; his sculpture

[1] 'Wimbush' in *Autumn Sequel*, canto i.

was meant to be seen from every angle, the cyclamen could even be rolled bottom upwards and still look in order, in key. This sculpture was a very pleasant change from the take-it-or-leave-it and better-not-finish-it modernist school then fashionable in London. The Chestnut Bud, which was about four foot high but placed on a pedestal, dominated the little dim toolshed with the precise dignity, the controlled momentum of a Rameses. Herrickx was delighted to show his work to anyone–'That's pretty good, old man, isn't it?' he would say–but he had no idea how to sell it. He almost seemed to prefer keeping it out there in the shed like a dog that was too big for the house.

I offered to drive the Cyclamen to Cambridge, told him I thought I could sell it to a friend of Anthony Blunt's. He was gleefully grateful. With difficulty we hoisted it into the car and with still more difficulty at the other end I got it up into Anthony's room in his college, a coquettishly chaste room with white panelling and Annunciation lilies. But Anthony's friend had just had a baby and Anthony had now gone Marxist, was no longer so eager to push the sale of a work that was primarily abstract or decorative. So the Cyclamen was not sold. Sidestepping the purpose of my visit I let Cambridge entertain me very much as it had entertained me three years before. But now there were two differences. One: Cambridge was still full of Peter Pans but all the Peter Pans were now talking Marx (Anthony himself was writing Marxist art critiques each week in *The Spectator*, extolling Diego Rivera and deprecating Picasso). Two: Mariette was not with me.

The next morning while Anthony was teaching I found a gin-bottle in his room and drunk myself blind before lunch; it seemed an exquisite outrage to the room and also to Dialectical Materialism. Anthony had invited to lunch a very elegant evergreen don whose gestures were always timed, who never put a finger-nail wrong. I made this don a scapegoat of my own desperate muddledom, asked him again and again what good he was to the world, ended by poking a lighted cigarette in his face and saying, 'Let me put this in your eye and see if it's blue.' Then well pleased with myself and having ruined the lunch party I laid my head on the table and went to sleep among the dishes.

The next morning I had a harsh hangover, sat looking at the

Annunciation lilies feeling I could drink them. Before leaving I arranged to make a trip to Spain with Anthony in the Easter vacation. In the afternoon I drove back to Birmingham, giving a lift in my little car to three oddly assorted young men. One was one of those Birmingham students who wanted to be Oxford aesthetes of the nineteen-twenties vintage; one was one of the new Cambridge undergraduates who were clever and careerist and Leftist and bristling with statistics; the third was John Cornford, also a Cambridge undergraduate, clever and communist and bristling with statistics, but for him the conception of career was completely drowned in the Cause; he was going to Birmingham to stand trial for causing an obstruction while distributing communist pamphlets in the Bull Ring (where the Chartist Movement had been launched in 1838). John Cornford was the first inspiring communist I had met; he was the first who combined an unselfish devotion to his faith with a really first-class intelligence.

He and the other Cambridge undergraduate sat in the back seat and talked about Trade Unions; the Birmingham aesthete sat beside me and talked about literary values. The Would-be Twenties and the Hard-Fact Thirties cross-patterned in my mind as my forehead throbbed and the car swung wildly on the road; when we reached the Birmingham suburbs we found we had been driving for miles with a puncture. The Thirties at once jumped out, were cheerfully efficient; the Would-be Twenties stood listlessly by, composing his face to a deliberate disdain. This was the first and the last I saw of John Cornford. Later that year the war broke out in Spain and, being no careerist, he went out to fight there and was killed.

XXXII

Anthony and I went to Spain while it was still peace there.[1] It was the first time I had been out of the British Isles since I had married Mariette, who was now, so I was told, in Canada; our respective solicitors had forbidden us to write to each other. As I was so much in debt Anthony had made me a present of my return ticket to Gibraltar. This was to be a gala holiday; we played piquet on our P. & O. boat and occasionally talked about the Popular Front; what with Blum and all, Europe was looking up. Landing at Gibraltar we went straight to Ronda where we met a little perky Cambridge don who told us that Spain would soon have her spot of trouble—not just yet (it was March at the time) but soon. He made this prophecy with a sly pride as if he were doing a card-trick.

From that visit I retain the usual jumble of impressions—the face of a legless beggar sprouting from the floor of a train and jingling a tin of coins; a vulture seen below us from the cliffs of Ronda, his shadow peacefully drifting on a chequerboard of olive and ilex; a gay bootblack in a street café in Madrid who took me unawares, tore the heels off my shoes and nailed on new ones; two little boys playing pelota against a sixteenth-century church on a quiet morning, a morning that belonged to no century at all; the face of a sucking pig looking up into ours from the lunch table; an indignant young American saying he'd been in some pretty tough dives but he'd never seen anything so disgusting; a double-chinned obese old man like a Pontius Pilate by Bosch who was drinking cassis as if in eternal silence—what I have written I have written.

As Anthony was covering the architecture we spent our time walking and gaping. There was a street in Toledo called the Calle de los Niños Hermosos. There were the huge walls of the Escorial enclosing a positive nothing, a nothing that is deadly cold, while its dome is like the cosmos of Parmenides, a solid sphere that pre-

[1] Easter 1936. Cf. *Autumn Journal*, vi.

cludes all chance of change or progress. There was the paradox and the pride of the cathedral at Segovia—a dome imposed upon Gothic. There were many tortured saints whose death was almost an orgasm; there were flights of candles upon Holy Thursday before altars not yet looted. There were omelettes at every meal and a cup of coffee every other hour. At Aranjuez I looked up from a café table and there crossing a bridge in the middle distance just as if they belonged there (but the middle distance itself belonged in a primitive painting) were two camels.

Nearly every day was rainy and cold; we kept indoors when we could—in churches, hotels and picture-galleries. The one thing we liked in Madrid was the Prado. Greco, Goya and Zurbaran, these were the three great artists and the weather did not affect them. Whenever in the Prado I came to Greco's *Descent of the Holy Ghost* I was reminded of Yeats's poem *Byzantium*—'flames begotten of flame'. And that is what Greco's pictures are. Their subject hardly matters; what matters is the incandescence of Greco himself, the Pentecost of his fingers, the counterpoint of aspiring brush-strokes. Those elongated saints of his are built for speed, their limbs lick upwards, the bellows is always blowing them. Thus his huge picture in the Church of San Tomé in Toledo, the *Burial of Count Orgaz*, is split in two by a horizontal division—two worlds, two methods, the static below, the dynamic above. In the world below the Count is laid out in armour, a mitred Saint Augustine bends over him and behind them is a wall of ruffed and bearded heads, of grave but griefless faces, all is staid and frozen. But above the wall of heads all is upsurge.

Our new revelation was the painting of Zurbaran. In the Museum at Seville are two pictures of his which require the word 'inevitable' —bread become God but still bread. In one the Virgin Mary in a great blue robe held up like a tent by cherubs is laying her hands in blessing—and it is a blessing you believe in—on the heads of kneeling Carthusians. The other is a picture of a Carthusian refectory (those white robes were a godsend to Zurbaran), a design mainly of parallels, crockery and loaves on the table as precise as in a still-life by Chardin, and the monks in still-life too; the whole is as clean as an operating chamber where no one will ever operate; a lyrical intense placidity; a haunting matter-of-factness.

As for Goya. To look only at the Goyas in the Prado is to journey through every climate—satire, realism *Walpurgisnacht* fantasy, the rococo picnic, the horrors of war, the passions carnal and spiritual. Goya always hits hard; his *Maja* has not only more sex-appeal but more finality than Manet's *Olympia* which was inspired by it; his *Shooting Party* explodes so with agony that you feel your arms shoot up like the arms of the murderee. And how could Maria Luisa pay him to put her soul in the killing-pot and pin it out for ever on a board like a gorgeous and horrible moth?

Some Left Wing critics, babbling about 'integrity' and 'social consciousness' and 'realism', have claimed Goya as a great revolutionary. On their own Ruskin-like premises only a revolutionary in life can be a revolutionary artist, and artistic integrity presupposes an integrity of ethics, that is politics. Very well; take Goya's life.

Born in 1746 of peasant parents; to Madrid when aged nineteen, got a dagger in the back, a roysterer; off to Rome a playboy, climbed the lantern of St. Peter's dome, whored and drank, was deported to Spain disgraced; kept low company still, was idle still till given a commission; the tapestry cartoons—gypsies and dandies—more delicate and stronger than Watteau; began to be a name, went hunting with the brother of the king; dipped into the French Encyclopedists, picked up one or two notions of progress, but his paintbrush rose on its own, needed no aphrodisiac; Charles being crowned the Fourth, was received at court with a salary, painted his master to the life—as a fool, a glutton, a cuckold, fatuous, gross; painted Maria Luisa also to the more than life—ruthless harridan aged with rancour and lust in a beautiful black mantilla; had become yet more of a name, could refuse to paint grandees, could have the courage of his whims; went to bed with the Duchess of Alba, her hair a mythical cloud and her name was Doña Maria Theresa Cayetana de Silva y Alvarez de Toledo; around his fiftieth year the guitars died, became quite deaf, had eye-trouble too, general bad health; but his blood was alive and venomous, bubbled up into *Los Caprichos*; and in 1799 became First Painter of the Court; but in 1807 was Napoleon's invasion and next year fighting in the streets, mass executions; so dipped his handkerchief in mud, sketched a battle on the wall of a street, the *Dos de Mayo*; salaaming to Joseph Bonaparte who entered Madrid with trumpets drew on the side *Los Desastres de la Guerra*; Joseph went out and Wellington came in, so salaams again, painted the Duke on commission; Wellington went out and Ferdinand came back, so went into hiding, was pardoned of course and restored First Painter of the Court; in decrepit old age frescoed his home with witches, but when nearly eighty shook off the dust of Castile, moved to Bordeaux, became a patron of circuses; nearly blind still caught at tags of colour, and drinking cups of chocolate through the day and still taking interest—in the human tragedy, the human farce—aged eighty-two he died.

But so many of the great have been opportunist; even Luther and Mazzini sold out, double-crossed at moments. Not that this sanctions opportunism, but who are the Marxists to sit in the opposite corner and preach the Categorical Imperative? The beam is in their own eye. The great danger of Marxist doctrine is that it allows and even encourages opportunism. All their talk about strategy. After a bit the Marxist, who is only human, finds it such fun practising strategy—i.e. hypocrisy, lying, graft, political pimping, tergiversation, allegedly necessary murder—that he forgets the end in the means, the evil of the means drowns the good of the end, power corrupts, the living gospel withers, Siberia fills with ghosts. Fills with the victims of idealists trying to be pragmatic—or of pragmatists pretending to ideals. And the present master of the Kremlin, being infallible, has scrubbed the walls to get rid of the echo of the voice of Lenin who admitted he made mistakes.

The Hammer and Sickle was scrawled over Spain that Easter. The walls were still plastered with posters from the recent elections, ingenious cartoons showing the top-hatted banker in rout or political prisoners peering out from behind a grill in the gaping mouth of the capitalist. If Spain goes communist, Anthony said, France is bound to follow. And then Britain, and then there'll be jam for all. Which incidentally will mean new blood in the arts—in every parish a Diego Rivera. And easel-painting at last will admit it is dead and all the town-halls and factories will bloom with murals and bas-reliefs in concrete. For concrete is the new medium, concrete is vital.

We went to Seville in Holy Week, watched in the rain the processions of Penitentes. We had not of course expected a religious atmosphere but we did hope for a good show, a high-class carnival;

we got neither, the show was shoddy and desultory. So was the army parade that we watched on Easter morning. The soldiers draggling along in the rain out of step reminded us of the new boys in the Marlborough O.T.C., puny bored little creatures anxious for the word 'Dismiss'. Half an hour later there were truckloads of young communists going off to a mass meeting, red shirts, red blouses, a coppice of clenched fists. After the soldiers they looked very human and alive. And that afternoon, to round our Easter off, we went to our first bull-fight.

The rain was so heavy that at first the bull-fighters would not come on; the spectators began to murmur and hoot, the ring became littered with their hard leather cushions. These cushions were then gathered up and the show began; the grey rain fell on the old be-mattressed dobbins and the men in Christmas-cracker fancy dress and the silly mooching bulls. The many accounts which I had read of bull-fights had failed to convey to me their irony–on one side the skill and grace of the matador, on the other side the clumsy ineptitude of his victim, and the tawdry trumpery accessories and the tiers of connoisseurs and vulgar *voyeurs*. The bull with banderillas like Christmas candles nodding in his back looks too much of a fool for pathos, but he recovers his dignity as he dies when after his futile lurchings, stoppings-short and bewilderment, he decides to lie down as if from sheer boredom; you think he might be going to sleep and then he is dead. The next moment all again is trumpery; while the seats are pullulating with waving handkerchiefs and grins, a jingle of bells announces the mule team which collects the bull and tows him around the ring, the spectators applaud wildly– something has been accomplished–but the bull himself is now just a sack of matter, of dead meat nobody wants.

We returned to Gibraltar by way of Algeciras and there we heard shouting. Mob of clenched fists outside the great west door of a church. We waited a long time and the door opened, a young man drove out in a sports car. The crowd howled, threw a few stones very wide, then gadarened into the church. Anthony and I went off for a drink; when we returned we looked into the church and the walls were dripping with fresh red slogans, with hammers and sickles; high up over the altar stood a man in an empty niche– looking, Anthony said, like a figure in a Toller play–who was trying to fix a red flag. But he was short of nails, the flag would not stay put.

We spent that night in La Linea at the backdoor of Gibraltar; Gibraltar shuts its gates at nine like an Oxford college. About three in the morning we were woken by a burst of oratory – '*Muera Lerroux! Muera Inglaterra! Muera . . . Muera . . . Muera . . .*' Thinking it was a political meeting but what an odd time to hold it, we went to the window. Walking very slowly down the middle of the street was one drunk man, dignified, superhuman, a procession all to himself. His palms were held out to the stars and the phrases of his bronze invective flowed without check and broke on the sleeping walls. A deprecatory shadow ran out from a wall, caught at his elbow; one ought not to make a fool of oneself in public, in the presence of the whole town's dreams. But the drunk man paid no attention to his friend, his triumphal march was his own. *Muera Gil Robles! Muera* everyone! *Muera . . . Muera . . .*[1]

[1] Manuscript B ends here. The remainder of the text is transcribed from manuscript A, a rough draft: see Editor's Preface.

XXXIII

Birmingham had now begun to irk me. I had some wonderful pointless nights walking through back streets with Reggie Smith, dropping into his father's house at two in the morning and there would be his father playing chess in the kitchen with his brother. But when I got back to my own house I was oppressed by Mariette's colour-schemes which she would not call colour-schemes and by her gadgets which were intended to make the home permanent. I accepted a post at Bedford College for Women in London, then went off to Iceland to join Wystan and collaborate with him in a travel book.

Our travel book was a hodge-podge, thrown together in gaiety. There is one moment I remember that I did not mention, on a boat coming down the west coast from the Isafjord, a coast split up by fjords. The setting sun in the cold sea made a super-de-luxe picture postcard and we all were crowded on the side of the boat looking at it. Suddenly an old German nun, wrinkled, plump and timid, who obviously normally kept herself to herself within the Chinese wall of her faith, suddenly turned to me with the face of a young mother when the nurse brings in the first of all her babies, and exclaimed in ecstasy '*Wunderschön! Wunderschön!*' and I, conscious of a moment of communion, smiled and said '*Ja.*'

The Doddses also left Birmingham; Dodds had been appointed Regius Professor of Greek in succession to Gilbert Murray. There was a lot of silly opposition to the appointment; it was argued that they ought to have had someone from the spot who had been tutoring in Mods. for decades, that Dodds, who had been editing Proclus, must have forgotten the authors of the syllabus, that Dodds was a radical, a spiritualist, an alien. . . . And so on and so on. Randolph Churchill wrote in the *Daily Mail* saying it was a disgrace that someone who had been a pacifist in the last war should be appointed a *Regius* Professor. I had rarely felt so ashamed of my Alma Mater.

I was delighted to move to London where there would be so many people to talk to and I would take the *News Chronicle* every day and the *New Statesman* every week. While looking for a flat I stayed with my sister in Highgate, dreamed that a bomb was falling plumb on the bed. Crossing my arms tightly I threw myself out of bed, fell like a log on the floor, triumphantly thought 'It has missed me.' But no, it was a time bomb, there it was on the bed and about to go off. Hastily, I seized the rubber hot-water bottle by the neck, threw it with all my force through the open window, went to sleep self-satisfied. In the morning there was no hot-water bottle, I had to go down to breakfast, say to my sister, 'I'm awfully sorry but I've thrown your hot-water bottle into the neighbour's garden.'

I took a flat in Keats Grove in Hampstead and imported my child and his Scottish nanny and my dog. I omitted to order the *News Chronicle* and the *Statesman*, began a life which was a whirl of narcotic engagements–meetings for a drink, political meetings, private views, flirtations, the experimental theatre, the question of my overdraft, the question of Spain. In November my divorce became final after an eleventh-hour flutter with detectives.

Literary London as I met it fell in two categories; there was the old gang who were just literary and there was the new gang who were all Left. I met the old gang at the house next door in Keats Grove which belonged to Robert and Sylvia Lynd who gave frequent literary dinner parties. Hugh W.,[1] J. B. Priestley, Oliver St. J. Gogarty, Rose Macaulay. . . . They all of them had charm but, with the exception of Rose Macaulay, they talked as if the world were static. Sylvia Lynd was a brilliant hostess with a whimsical brand of wit and a way of flattering anyone she was talking to, her voice very clear and silver–drops of hard clear water. Robert Lynd on the other hand had a husky voice, as if his cigarette ash had got into it–he was always dropping it, chain-smoking–and a North of Ireland accent, and there was a Siamese cat, very spoiled, temperamental. Both the Lynds in earlier days had been fervent supporters of the Irish revolution; now they were politically pink in a mellow

[1] Hugh Walpole?

gentlemanly way, whereas their two daughters were red, got themselves injured by the mounted police in East End communist meetings.

The new gang was much more middle-aged in its behaviour, was addicted to committees. Committees to save democracy, to protect writers, to assist refugees, to pass, when everything failed, a measure of protest. The great subject was Spain. The English press both of the Right and the Left over-simplified this subject. The *Daily Worker* (then a very fashionable paper with the intelligentsia) naïvely assumed (1) that communism in Spain was the same brand as the *Daily Worker*'s, (2) that Republican Spain was wholeheartedly communist, (3) that therefore Republican Spain would win. The *News Chronicle* naïvely assumed that the cause of Republican Spain was the cause of democracy and English liberalism. The *Daily Telegraph* naïvely assumed that Republican Spain was completely red and that Franco was a gentleman and fighting for the English Upper Ten and the City of London. And all the time David Low went on drawing his brilliant cartoons, riddling Franco and the Chamberlain Government with ridicule, and having them published in the *Evening Standard* which was owned by Lord Beaverbrook who staunchly supported Chamberlain and regarded the Spanish Republic as part of the Moscow Menace.

There was a great deal of talk at this time about realism which was now almost equated with propaganda. Various poets who had formerly written personal—i.e. unrealistic—poetry of a sophisticated somewhat symbolist type, had now gone realistic, trumpeting readymade slogans and asserting over and over their conviction that the Right (equals the Left) would triumph. Sylvia Townsend Warner, Edgell Rickword, Randall Swingler, filled the *Left Review* with poems about barricades. What did you say? (Almost in the shadow of the Stukas.) Oh! *barricades*—I'm sorry, I didn't quite catch you. Realism. . . .

Take the case of Stephen Spender who was now living in a chic apartment with a colour scheme out of *Vogue*, a huge vulcanite writing-desk and over the fireplace an abstract picture by Wyndham Lewis. Very comfortable and elegant but not quite big enough for Stephen; his enormous craggy apostolic flaring face seemed liable to burst the walls. Stephen in the early thirties had written a book of literary criticism, *The Destructive Element*, the text for the sermon being taken from Henry James: 'In the destructive element immerse; that is the way.' The thesis of the book was that James, like Pt.,[1] was a herald of the Revolution; not being born at the right moment, all such writers could do was immerse in the destructive element. But now the right moment had come. Stephen followed this up with a book called *Forward from Liberalism*, chosen by the Left Book Club, and so under the aegis of Mr. Gollancz dumped upon thousands and thousands of men of good will for whom the Left Book Club was Church. Yes, S. argued (accepting the dialectic), liberalism had played its part; once the vanguard, was now reaction; the man of good will today must acknowledge the Third International. His book, however, offended many in all parties. The Right did not like it, the Liberals did not like it, and the Comrades— many of them—could not help noticing that S., who wanted to be at home with Stalin, was much more at his ease with J. S. Mill.

Then, after he had joined the Party, came S.'s play *Trial of a Judge*, hailed by Christopher Isherwood (this mutual admiration was only too understandable) as the greatest play of our time, but written in a verse too intricate and clogged for the stage. The intended moral of the play was that liberalism today was weak and wrong, communism was strong and right. But this moral was sabotaged by S.'s unconscious integrity; the Liberal Judge, his example of what-not-to-be, walked away with one's sympathy. The Comrades observed this and, at a meeting arranged by the Group Theatre to discuss the play, a squad of them turned up to reprove S. for his heresies. It was an exhilarating evening. There was a blonde girl, pretty and ice-cold, who got up and said that the play had been a great disappointment to herself and others in the Party; they had gone to the play expecting a message and the message had not been delivered; and *yet*, she said, there *was* a message to be given and they all knew what it was. She spoke precisely and quietly, never muffing a phrase (you could see her signing death-warrants). Certainly, S. answered, there was a message and they all knew what it was; an artist had something else to do than to tell people merely what they knew and give them just what they expected. The heckling went on. One after one the Comrades rose

[1] Proust?

167

and shot their bolts. Marx, Marx and Marx. S. began to trail his coat; Marx, he said, was not necessarily what Marxists thought he was and anyhow you can't feed Marx to an artist as you feed grass to a cow. And another thing—the Comrades went on—this play gives expression to feelings of anxiety, fear and depression; which is wrong because . . . S. said if they felt no anxiety themselves, well he felt sorry for them. Lastly, an old man got up, very sincere, very earnest, toilworn. There was one thing about the play, he said, which especially worried him; of course he knew S. could not have meant it, there must have been a mistake, but the writing seemed to imply an acceptance of Abstract Justice, a thing which we know is non-existent. S. deliberately towered into blasphemy. Abstract Justice, he said, of course he meant it; and what was more it existed.

After that S. gradually fell away from the Party; he had not been born for dogma.

Then there was the strange—but typical—case of Goronwy Rees. Goronwy's father was a Welsh minister; Goronwy was academically brilliant, a Fellow of All Souls, a novelist, an editor of the *Spectator*, a playboy. He was short and wiry, had curly black hair and that Welsh charm which takes an ell if you give it a millimetre, would have made a wonderful travelling salesman. One evening there was a gathering of some fifty people—mainly writers—to oppose Fascism. Day-Lewis and Goronwy were the speakers. Day-Lewis spoke first, in his tired Oxford accent, qualifying everything, nonplussed, questioning. Then Goronwy, who was just as Oxonian as Day-Lewis, took over and spoke like a revivalist, flashed his eyes, quivered with emotion, led with his Left and followed with his Left, punch on punch, dogma on dogma, over and over-statement, washed in the blood of—well, nobody asked of whom, but it certainly made you stop thinking. Writers today, Goronwy said, had a function. But no initiative, they must not have initiative, they must not think for themselves, they were only there to take orders, orders from the only progressive class in society, orders from the Proletariat, no writer today could do anything at all of value unless he laid down his personality, made himself a mouthpiece and nothing more than a mouthpiece, made himself a living trumpet for the Working Classes to blow through; the truth was not in *us*— not *qua* writers, the truth was in the Proletariat, the truth and also the victory. After the meeting Goronwy suggested that one or two of us should go to P.'s; he said he felt like oysters. Oysters at P.'s are very expensive.

While there were many motives driving the intelligentsia towards the C.P., there was one great paradox nearly always present; intellectuals turned to communism as an escape from materialism. Materialism, that is, in the popular sense–that materialism which in more easy and archaic pockets of the country bolsters up the physical comfort of individuals and which, in places where people think, had for so long acknowledged the principle of enlightened self-interest, of mere utilitarianism, as man's only ideal in a mechanistic universe. Marx too postulated (and aggressively) a mechanistic universe but with the aid of the dialectic he stood it on its head, brought back teleology. Tennyson's 'one increasing purpose', discredited because it was founded on a world of *laissez-faire* liberalism, free trade, nationalist democracy, where wild competition between individuals and groups and nations was assumed somehow to work out for the best, gave way to the Marxian purpose which, like early Christianity, promised self-fulfilment through self-abnegation, freedom through discipline. Young men flocked to this new creed just because it made demands on them and because, while it attacked human individualism, it simultaneously made the cosmos once more anthropocentric; it exploded the idea of purpose in Nature (Nature was blind) but asserted purpose in the world. Because the world was *ours*. Marx was to the poets of the thirties what Rousseau was to the poets of the Romantic Revival. This in spite of Marx's own warning against the romantic revolutionary.

I continued dreaming about bombs and the fascists, was worried over women, was mortifying my aesthetic sense by trying to write as Wystan[1] did, without bothering too much with finesse (witness *Out of the Picture*[2]), was bothering not to bother. Shortly after seeing the film of Dr. Mabuse I had the following dream. I had been invited to a houseparty. The party was given on a little peninsula in a marshy lagoon at the end of nowhere; the other side of the lagoon was invisible. The peninsula consisted of a long neglected garden in the centre of which was a knoll on top of which was a house. This house was a skeleton; the boards of the walls and

[1] W. H. Auden.   [2] A play by MacNeice, published 1937.

169

floors had gone, there remained only the structural beams and the staircase. There were many people—everyone I knew—being social in the garden, but I, having arrived late, went straight through them up to the house where I unpacked my suitcase and laid out my spongebag and brush and comb and—I think—some books upon the floor, i.e. upon the ground. Then instead of joining the other guests, I went up the staircase and picked my way over the joists which had supported the upper floor (I have always liked climbing over ruined houses). While I was perched up there it happened. The alarm. Like sirens or bells but you could not hear it, it was more like the shiver on a pond when a breeze comes on it out of nothing. At once the people in the garden began flooding down towards the entrance in the narrow neck of the peninsula, like beasts fleeing from a forest fire.[1] For They were coming. I hurriedly climbed down, ran after my friends who were by now nearly all at the entrance. The sky was getting darker and the air itself denser and breathing like an animal asleep. But as I caught them up I remembered my suitcase, I knew it was unimportant, what was of vital, of final importance was escape. All the same I went back up the knoll to the house, collected my belongings, put them in my suitcase, and carried it down the garden which by now was empty of people. I found myself walking along an overgrown path and in the flower borders on either side there was growing, instead of flowers, a regular row of swords planted with the point up as regularly as tulips, curving shining swords. I hurried on to the neck of the peninsula and there was a wall of rough stones, in it a little Gothic gateway such as you find in Victorian rockeries. In this gateway there stood a soldier in khaki with a fixed bayonet. I stopped in front of him. He remained fixed with a fixed bayonet. A terrifying imbecile cackle made me look behind and there at my left shoulder stood Dr. Mabuse from the film, cackling and leering; he had a great bush of orange-red hair. On sight of him I awoke.

1937 for me was a year of wild sensations. At the beginning of the year I knew a girl called Leonora who was a musical actress, very tall, very blonde, all eye-veils, furs and egotism; dabbled in religion and poetry, mixed her conversation with French and German, and was painted by Royal Academicians. My relationship

[1] Text uncertain.

with her was make-believe on both sides and it ended with her throwing a teatable at me. The cups bounced about the room and the walls were spattered with tea-leaves. We both exploded into laughter – perhaps our one real moment of communion. After that I went about with — of whom I cannot write, but who was for me what is called an education – or rather illumination; so feminine that I sometimes felt like leaving the country at once;[1] and so easily hurt that to be with her could be agony. She could be so gloomy as to black-out London and again she could be so gay that I would ask myself where I had been before I knew her and was I not colour-blind then. Of all the people I have known she could be most radiant. Which is why I do not regret the hours and hours of argument and melancholy, the unanswerable lamentations of someone who wanted to be happy in a way that was just not practical.

Dodds would sometimes deplore the importance that our generation attached to personal relationships. We were asking, he thought, the impossible, were side-tracking the human genius. Of course one needs personal relationships, but not as the end of existence; and looking at the lives of my friends I had to agree that this side-tracking was continuous, unfruitful, appalling. Once you decide that X is all you want, you ruin X and yourself. Whoso saveth his life shall lose it. And even the psychoanalysts, whose job it is to put such relationships in a right perspective, are on a long-term view destroyers because they are only concerned with saving your life for you. It is better to be like Rilke and capitalise your own loneliness and neuroses, regard Death as the mainspring. Or it is better – if you can do it – to become the servant of an idea. But if you take either of these courses, you have got to commit yourself utterly; if you give yourself to Loneliness or Otherness it must not be a negative thing – a mere avoiding of other troubles, mere sublimation – but it must be positive, an End. Thus people have become monks sometimes in order to avoid the trouble of sex, sometimes out of perverse sexuality, but that is not how people become saints. Not real saints. In spite of analytical researches into the pathology of sainthood, the saint, like the mathematician, has got hold of something positive. And so have the real hero and the real artist.

Think how we get bogged in our personal intrigues, *ignis fatuus*

[1] Text uncertain.

171

after *ignis fatuus*; modern sexual life is a hangover from the mixed drinks of an obsolete romanticism and the Christian ideal of monogamy. In respect of sex I see England in the thirties as a chaos of unhappy or dreary marriages, banal or agonised affairs. The pattern of every night shot through with the pounding and jingling of bedsteads but somewhere in the hearts of the couples on the beds is a reedy little voice of query: Is this enough? or Is it what I really want? or Can this possibly go on?—When will it end? When will it begin?

Freud having taught[1] my generation that sex repression is immoral, fornication had become a virtue. It remained to discover that neither fornication nor chastity is an end in itself, that it all depends on how and why you fornicate or how and why you are chaste. The myth of chastity having been exploded, we discovered that some of the substitutes for it were equally chimerical. If it was a pathetic mistake to think that chastity in itself has spiritual value, it is also a pathetic mistake to think that acts of fornication piled up indiscriminately will somehow give value to life. As for that *hygienic* view of lovemaking advocated by so many alleged experts, that should be left to people who like everything in cellophane, who believe in a mechanical Progress and expect that technique alone will bring in the millennium.

This obsession with sex means that many people who take up other activities do so out of pique because sex has disappointed them. But nothing undertaken out of pique is likely to be very successful. This may partly explain the failure in our time of so many movements both in the arts and in public life. We were a nation of sexual frustrates.

Sexual promiscuity in our England was a legacy from nineteenth-century Enlightenment. The Emancipation of Women, Every Girl her own Harlot. The resulting paradox is like the paradox of Free Trade—there is nothing free about it. Those whose ship comes home have probably bankrupted others, if not by breaking up a marriage or making the future uncertain, at least—less directly—by encouraging others to gamble in a field where the majority must lose.

The modern Don Juan is the counterpart of the nineteenth-century self-made Captain of Industry. Winning through against

[1] This is of course incorrect though widely believed.

odds he assumes that the world is his oyster, and always will be for those who have the requisite courage, technique, imagination. Which of course is a black lie. Man cannot live by courage, technique, imagination–alone. He has to have a sanction from outside himself. Otherwise his technical achievements, his empires of stocks and shares, his exploitation of power, his sexual conquests, all his apparent inroads on the world outside, are merely the self-assertion, the self-indulgence, of a limited self that whimpers behind the curtains, a spiritual masturbation.

It was this world that tended to force creative writers into journalism. Not so much for money as because money remained a symbol of energy. To beat them on their own ground. To show these commercial bastards that one knows the ropes as well as they do.

In 1937–8 I gave way to this impulse, accepted commissions for prose books for which I had no vocation but which, I thought to myself, I could do as well as the next man. It flattered me that publishers should ask me to do something unsuitable. The more unsuitable, the more it was a sign of power. Many of us were still reacting over-much against Art for Art's Sake, against the concept of the solitary pure-minded genius saving his soul in a tower without doors. Our reaction drove us to compete with the Next Man. But once you come up against the Next Man you begin to lose sight of the sky. The Next Man swells to a giant, you find your face buried in his paunch and on his paunch is a watch ticking louder and louder, urging you to hurry, get on with the job–when the job is finished there will always be another. In commercial writing, in 'bookmaking', one comes to think of carelessness and speed as virtues.

XXXIV

Nineteen thirty-eight was like my dream of the skeleton house. The alarm came in the autumn. Perched on the very joists I scrambled down quickly, began shrieking for solidarity. The terror that seized London during the Munich crisis was that dumb, chattering terror of beasts in a forest fire. In Piccadilly Circus at midnight hand after hand shot out as if from robots, grabbed the Extra Editions. The intelligentsia sat in the Café Royal moaning about their careers—there would be no more picture shows, no more publishing of books, no more (and how Marx would have laughed) free speech. At about 2.0 one morning I dropped into a cabmen's shelter. Taxi-drivers in London have a very small vocabulary—xxxxxxx, xxxx, xxxx, bloody. 'Them xxxxxxx Germans, it xxxxxxx well makes me xxxxxxx sore.' Inarticulate but perhaps no more so than the press, the politicians, the intellectuals.

I found the Territorials hastily, inefficiently, cutting down the grove on the top of Primrose Hill. In the darkness a little hardjawed man addressed me, cavilling; 'and if they want a good gun-emplace-ment,' he ended, 'I know a place in Ireland . . .' (He was Irish.) The next morning Primrose Hill looked so forlorn that I took the train to Birmingham, stayed with John Waterhouse. We spent the day listening to the radio. The faces in the street were just as lost as in London. Overheard remarks were all on the one topic: 'England and France is like brother and sister. Always has been.' In the evening we went to the Birmingham Hippodrome which was featuring George Formby and Florrie Forde. The house was packed and uproarious. George Formby took his ukulele, ran through his famous repertoire—'Cleaning Windows', 'Chinese Laundry Blues'. His pawky Lancashire charm was just what we wanted. Waves of nostalgia for the *status quo* broke on the balcony in hoots of laughter. And Florrie Forde, now in her sixties, enormous, mammose, steatopygous, appeared each turn in a different dress, equally loud, equally bulging, a good sort essentially, once a chorus girl, once a principal boy, now with her voice gone still a music-hall sweetheart, sentimental as honeysuckle, vulgar as artificial violets, two hundred pounds of walking bonhomie and game to the last ounce of wobbling flesh.

Then Chamberlain signed on the line and we all relapsed. Back in London Primrose Hill was embarrassingly naked, as if one's grandfather had shaved his beard off. Propped on treetrunks on the top of it were two or three little museum-piece guns, ingenuously gaping at the sky. Newsreels featured the life of Chamberlain – the Man of Peace after 2,000 years.

XXXV[1]

In December 1938 I accepted a suggestion that I should visit Barcelona in company with some other English writers. The other writers falling out or ill, I decided to go by myself, got a visa for Spain from the Spanish Consulate in London. — was very disapproving, said I only wanted to go to Spain to show off. I answered that it was rather late in the day to show off in this way, as nearly all literary London had long ago done the rounds of the trenches in Madrid and hobnobbed with the Republican celebrities. I admitted, however, that my motives were egotistical; I was sensation-hunting, testing myself, eager to add a notch to my own history.

Before leaving London I was called up by a Mrs. B. who said the Spanish Embassy had told her I was going to Barcelona, and as she and her husband were going the same time, let us meet on the train to Perpignan. 'You will recognise me,' she said, 'because I am very stout.'

— and Ernst and I had a fabulous dinner at P.'s, and Ernst and I went on to spend Christmas in Paris. Paris was under snow and very beautiful. We ate and drank a great deal and before leaving for Perpignan I bought a long piece of salami, a small bottle of cognac, some biscuits, lump sugar and two tins of condensed milk.

I caught the Perpignan train with five minutes to spare and met the B.'s in the corridor. Mrs. B. was Russian, large and gushing, double-chinned and with the movements of a stranded sea lion, a brilliant linguist only her accent was cockney. Mr. B. was smaller, worried, precisely querulous. Mrs. B. seemed to be a more or less orthodox Stalinist, carried so many proper sentiments around with her that she got tangled and flustered with them like a lady pushing through Oxford Street after a day's Christmas shopping. She and her husband took their Spanish prospects very seriously, were going to meet all the right people, and had both been inoculated for typhoid.

[1] With this chapter cf *Autumn Journal*, xxiii.

We had coffee and rolls in Perpignan and waited for the diplomatic car which was to take us to the frontier and on to Barcelona. There was a hitch of course. Mrs. B. lolloped with vexation; Mr. B. testily, fussily, told her not to fuss. After an hour's delay two Spaniards arrived with a car and drove us to Le Perthus; Mrs. B. delightedly poured out her Spanish on the driver. The road wound uphill between prickly vineyards of winter; the Pyrenees, pure and indifferent snowpeaks, looked at us, or rather not-looked at us, as fish not-look at you in aquariums. As we got near Le Perthus the B.'s became volubly tense, afraid of complications at the frontier. Le Perthus has only one street running downhill straight into Spain. Several ropes were drawn across it. When we got out to show our passports they told me 'Yours is not in order'; I needed a French visa for exit from France into Spain, must go back to Perpignan to get it. The car of the B.'s sailed downhill towards the war and I waited for a bus back northwards.

It took me a whole afternoon to get a visa from the French who gabbled about Non-intervention and were bureaucratically obtuse. After that I looked up an address I had of a wine-merchant. He was elderly, plump and affable, sitting in his office ten thousand miles from Spain. When I told him I was going there he opened his eyes and laughed, said, 'Are you not afraid of being violated'?

I hated Perpignan with its little canal-like river running between stunted trees, was glad to leave again next morning, a beautiful candid day. At Le Perthus this time they approved my passport and allowed me a little further downhill, into actually Spanish territory. I was told to wait in a shed where a number of Basque soldiers were gathered round a small iron stove. A tall man with a widebrimmed hat and side-whiskers, pretentiously friendly, came up to me, asked was I a journalist because he was a journalist, one of the most leading journalists in Uruguay. I thought him rather phoney and remembered vaguely that Uruguay was known for its sympathy with fascism. Escaping from his bonhomie I walked around the shed looking at the political posters—Negrin's Thirteen Points, warnings against spies—a man with an enormous ear or an enormous eye, a man with swastika eyes and fasces for a nose. The Basque soldiers seemed to have little to do with these posters, seemed to move in a world of fatigue lit up only by humour; some of them had some time or other been wounded, all looked hungry and one felt were much younger than they looked. They made way for me at the stove, said I must be cold. A dirty old man, a civilian, took an old crust of bread from his pocket, laid it on the stove and sat watching it.

The Uruguayan journalist was nervous, wanted to move on, but no one knew when we should move. We waited a couple of hours and an official appeared behind a counter, ready, but not too ready, to examine passports. A rather mousy young man in a mackintosh came in and took out his passport as if he had done this hundreds of times before; his passport being blue, I went up, asked was he British. He said yes he was, was taking a car to Barcelona. I asked would he give me a lift and he looked at me aloofly, said 'Are your papers in order?' I said yes. He said, 'I won't give anyone a lift unless their papers are in order.'

My papers were in order and he agreed to take me in his car. We drove downhill, the day lifting and fresh as a salad, long bamboo grasses on either side of the road dancing in the breeze from the mountains. The young man was attached to the Quaker unit in Barcelona, was bringing in a new car for them. He was tired and efficient and had the backseat full of new books–detective novels and *Charles Laughton and I* by Elsa Lanchester; had been in Spain since early on in the war, in the early stages drove trucks of oranges from Valencia. 'Those were the days,' he said. His name was D. O'D.

After a few miles there was another rope over the road and we stopped for a customs examination. Asked why I was going to Spain I said Propaganda. The Spaniard examining my bag chuckled at the salami and cognac. We drove on into La Junquera and stopped for a meal. La Junquera was like a stage set before the actors come on– a double row of bone-white leafless plane trees, blank-faced houses, some of them a faded pink, rubble here and there in the streets, a blistered poster on a wall, no one to be seen but one or two staring children. We went into a place for a meal, got chickpeas with little hunks of meat in them, even some wine. O'D. said we were lucky, both meat and wine were unheard of through most of the rest of Catalonia. After our meal we tried four or five cafés for coffee, the proprietors looked at us with a weary astonishment, said 'Nada,

nada,' coffee was something prehistoric. O'D. offered a child a piece of chocolate; the child backed away from him like a frightened kitten. An old man reading an ancient newspaper looked over the top of it, said 'Take it; the señor means you to have it.'

The drive to Barcelona was magnificent, mountains in the distance both to right and to left, blue sky, white clouds, bamboo groves ten feet high, plane trees along the road, one or two cactuses; every so often a woman carrying a sack on her head; women gathering firewood. They all wanted lifts, signalled to us to stop, but there was no room in the car. I was a little shy with O'D., felt myself a parasite. And, just as when I had first come to England, I could not believe where I was. 'This is Spain,' I said to myself. 'This is where war is.' The signposts at the crossroads said so many kilos to Madrid.

At the towns we were stopped by controls who checked the car. Whenever we came to a control we hid our cigarettes, for tobacco could no longer be bought. O'D. talked about Charles Laughton. We passed through Gerona which charmed me; charming of course was what Spain was for in the old times.

It was getting dark when O'D. and I reached the outskirts of Barcelona, the industrial district. It was dark when he dropped me at the Majestic. The reception clerk in the Majestic told me there was no room, I must go elsewhere. I went out, feeling lost, down the Paseo de Gracia, down a black street with trees and men as trees walking. No lights, no traffic, nothing but people, great numbers of faceless people flowing up and down the street and speaking low and little, like the spirits on the banks of the Styx. The city, I had been told, had doubled its population. Before the war at this time of day men and women would turn out to walk, the classic occasion for badinage, courtship, gossip; Barcelona had once been the city of tarts and taxis, individuals picked out clear; which now was a circulation of limbo crowds, nowhere to go, nothing to eat, moving perhaps to kill time or to keep themselves warm. I turned left along the Cortes and tried another hotel. Full; they apologised in French. Then I found myself in the revolving doors of the Ritz and the entrance hall full of the B.'s and the B.'s full of themselves.

The Ritz was still very Ritzy, a great staircase snaking from the hall, thick-carpeted, mirrors, Corinthian capitals, waiters in white coats and bow ties. You could even get aperitifs of sorts—vermouth or an insipid pink drink called a Combinacion. The great lounge was full of shady- or seedy-looking persons, shabby little generals, foreign journalists, harpy-faced women with dyed hair and prominent breasts, and a dirty-faced, pompous immature little Moor in a turban, whose job was propaganda broadcasting to the Moors on the other side; he kept delving into his pocket and popping sweetmeats into his mouth. On the tables in the centre were copies of the *Mercantile Guardian* and the *Liverpool Trade Review*.

I had dinner at a table with the B's. The waiter served us with the rhythm of cosmopolis, served us vermicelli soup and a slice of cardboard toast. Mrs. B. said Barcelona was wonderful, she would never have believed it, Negrin was wonderful, del Vayo was wonderful, the spirit of the people was wonderful, she had been on her feet all day. Two young Englishmen came up as we were finishing—Richard Rees who was working for the Quaker unit, and D. Darling who had lived ten years in Spain, had come to hate England and seemed to know all Barcelona. They talked about the Non-Intervention Bombing Committee whose members were accustomed to staying in this hotel: the British representatives had been a joke straight out of *Punch*, unbelievably ignorant and unqualified; a British colonel had thought Madrid was in Catalonia and there was a general who demanded a through train from Barcelona to Cartagena—only six months after Franco had cut the country in two. They hadn't of course known there was any food shortage, were astonished and indignant, said it was not humanitarian. But the real joy of it was that Franco nearly hit them with bombs on their first visit, broke the windows in the Ritz; the old generals were furious, said that he knew they were there, couldn't be a gentleman.

I had a beautiful room high up, with a bathroom of my own and hot water; the Ritz had the only hot water in Barcelona and the Majestic had the only central heating. I hid my food stores in the wardrobe, laid an overcoat on my bed, turned on a reading-lamp in a baby-pink silken shade, kept my socks on in bed and read Franz Borkenau's book, *The Spanish Cockpit*. Borkenau's point is that you must not see Spain through foreign glasses, that communism and fascism in Spain are not the communism and fascism we know. I was woken up in the night by people singing the 'Lambeth Walk.' In the morning there was the crowing of cocks, one of the distinctive sounds of the city. Those who could kept hens – sometimes rabbits – on their window balconies.

The next morning I took an aimless walk by myself. In the Paseo de Gracia the plane trees were still covered with leaves, russet, dried and rustling. At intervals ribbons of canvas were hung across the streets – propaganda in Spanish, Catalan, Basque. The shops were open but empty – tiers of empty pigeonholes, empty shelves, maybe one hat in the window. In the Plaza de Cataluña there was a series of big posters illustrating the career of Col. Macia, also propaganda posters urging civilians to back up the fighting forces – pictures of grimfaced steelhelmeted soldiers entrenched in the Catalan mountains and mottled with Christmas-card snowflakes. Many of these posters were handpainted, executed with a beautiful fluency. Outside the Banco de Viscaya on the south side of the square there was a list of the stock-market prices for 17th July 1936.

From the Plaza de Cataluña the famous street the Ramblas flows downhill towards the port. Like the Paseo de Gracia the centre of this street is a promenade where you can walk between two rows of trees, a one-way passage for cars on either side of you. The Ramblas are full of cafés; before the war, Darling told me, you could stroll down here and take your pick – each café had its habitués, you could find any sort of company you wanted; in any case music and drink. These cafés were now bleak caves, no bottles to be seen, dry marble, empty beer-pumps. But the book-booths on the promenade were still doing business – copies of the 15 daily newspapers, books on political and economic theory, children's picture books, highly coloured period calendars – ladies in picture hats dreaming in boats among swans. And there were one or two old women selling mimosa or gardenias, a relic of the days when the Ramblas were a riot of flowers. People moved up and down slowly as if time were infinite, all of them pinched with hunger. The girls had their hair carefully waved, in many cases dyed, had high heels, lipstick. A woman sat on a doorstep holding her child like a monkey, cutting its nails. Another woman, emaciated, leaned against the wall, spat blood into a handkerchief. Soldiers, some of them wounded, walked unsoldierly about, grimy, in home-made cloaks. A chemist's shop, all but empty of goods, had one or two bottles in the window; one was a cure for obesity.

The next day, Saturday, was beautiful with sunshine. To justify my presence, I drove to see various sights with a girl from the Propaganda Ministry. We visited two schools in the upper part of the town, unscathed by air-raids and gay with bougainvillaea; both were converted convents. The master of the first school apologised, could not show us over it; the day before had been a feastday, the chairs were in all the wrong places. The second school was north of the Diagonal, very clean and spruce, the floors of speckless tiles (a perfect school for propaganda). The chapel had been turned into a playroom, fitted up for pingpong. A young woman schoolteacher, lipsticked, with hornrimmed spectacles, very efficient, self-possessed, told us the state of affairs: there were 400 children but only fourteen teachers and a tiresome lack of books. She showed us the school theatre; they had just been doing a play by Lorca, had painted the backcloth themselves—a Castilian plaza. They had also painted the walls of the room—Mickey Mouse, Donald Duck. There was a laboratory and a carpenter's shop and, for the smaller ones, a collection of butterflies. She took us into a class of small children busy decorating the margins of their exercise books. They were all very clean but one little girl had chilblains which made each finger a great sausage. While we were in this class there was a deep and pleasant thudding and the children stampeded to the window—'four aeroplanes, I saw four aeroplanes'. The teacher scolded them back. When we went out into the courtyard the planes had gone but the blue sky was spangled with balls of white cottonwool where the anti-aircraft shells had exploded.

We went on to a colony for refugee children from Madrid—more bougainvillaea, more spruceness. The girls were sitting sewing in the sun. We were shown their dormitories—pretty little rooms with spotted coverlets, pictures of Ginger Rogers. The woman in charge, like many in such positions whom I met, was abundantly cheerful and winning, said the children's clothes were sent from Switzerland but their real problem was the medicine chest—nothing but cottonwool and oxygen water. She brought us the smallest child, a little boy of about two but no one knew his age for certain—his father was killed at the Front and his mother was in an asylum. Then she took us to watch the girls dancing or rather doing eurhythmics – they evidently thought that this mathematical arid eurhythmics would impress us more than the traditional folk stuff. The piano was out of tune but the girls enjoyed themselves, placing their bare feet carefully and all according to the book.

We went on to a military hospital on the outskirts under Mount Tibidabo. In the courtyard two one-legged men, trussed up in contrivances of steel, were gibing at each other for their clumsiness. The sun shone down on comics with plaster limbs. Inside a reek of sweat that choked you, disinfectants and chloroform, through every open door bearded men lying on beds; they had 1,500 beds but were about to make a clearance of patients, for a new batch was due from the Front. A young man took off his shirt to be examined by a doctor; I had never seen anyone so wasted away, his arms matchsticks, his chest hollowed like a soup plate.

After a lunch of chickpeas I visited the Casa la Pasionaria, a colony of refugees from Bilbao. This was a privileged colony with special funds. The children in their dining-room were having cocoa and rolls of white bread (also on occasions had fish, an item which holders of ration tickets had not been able to get for two months); the walls were gay with Popeye the Sailor, knocking down Mussolini, Franco, or riding the José Luis Diaz with his pipe and his spinach, the José Luis Diaz smoking a pipe itself, and fishing over a warship called *Fascismo* .The old women had their dormitory high up in a Gothic chapel. Families were encamped together. In one room a group of women massed round us chattering gaily like an aviary, one of them was feeding a baby; an old woman with some terrible eye disease was the wit of the party, bantered the nursing mother, asked me was I Russian. No, English. She smiled through the corruption of her eyes and made a wisecrack about Mr. Chamberlain.

When I had finished my propaganda tour I went for a walk by myself to Barceloneta, finding my way through the narrow streets to the north of the Ramblas. More and more houses had been hit as I got near the port, some of them evidently by high explosive – presumably in the famous raids of March 1938. One house of five or six storeys had had the whole of its innards torn out; the back wall and one side wall remained; high up on the topmost storey two shelves were attached to the side wall; on the lower shelf was a plate-rack full of plates and on the upper two bottles unbroken. When I reached the port the street was full of great holes and heaps of debris. No one came down now to the port who could help it; Richard Rees had told me of his drives down there to collect packages for the Quakers, said 'I don't mind risking my life for something useful but when it comes to boxes of old tennis balls . . .'

Barceloneta is a peninsula to the side of the port, small houses arranged in rectangular blocks, narrow straight streets, a working-class district. Everyone had long ago left it, it was a stinking, be-rubbled desolation, all the streets blocked with fallen masonry and powdered mortar, most of the houses smashed in, the old wallpaper showing indecently, the doors removed for firewood. It had the fascination of obscenity, of chalky dog-dung on a wharf, of old dried bandages, of bones. The houses were like skulls without eyes, without jaws, there was no more flesh in the world.

I walked back quickly because raids were more likely after dusk, slackened my pace when I reached the Plaza Cataluña which could normally be taken as the upper limit for bombs. I reached the Ritz about seven, went up to my room, dinner was due at 7.30. It was New Year's Eve. Just at 7.30 the siren went, wailing like a lost soul; I at once felt excited and afraid. The lights in my room dimmed, were dim for a few seconds and went out. I went to my open window. The night was chilly and clear with a brilliant half-moon and Orion lolled over the city. From either side of him the searchlights went up, six from the left and two from the right, moved easily and quickly but indolently, fingering the stars like a blind man playing with jewels. There was a silence as if before a thunderstorm; only a cock crew. For a long time there was nothing but silence, nothing alive except the antennae of the searchlights, impotently, indifferently probing; long sprays of bluish silver; firemen's hoses but no fire visible to play on.

Then suddenly the tempo changed, the anti-aircraft opened like hounds baying a burglar, the searchlights moved more quickly, tracer bullets floated up in strings—red stars from a funfair. Then the bombs—red bursts from the ground. Red bombs on the ground, white bursts of shells in the sky. More strings of tracer bullets, rising slowly like bubbles, gentle, amusing, ineffectual. Then it was over but the room stayed dark, the all-clear was not sounded. I waited in the window, but there was only silence and chill and Orion still commanding the sky with all his stars intact. I suddenly felt very hungry; fetched the salami from the wardrobe, cut off slices with a razor-blade, peeled off the skin with my thumbnail, feeling in peeling it off a sense of exhilaration, achievement, as when one peels off a scab. Then it started again—anti-aircraft deep and beautiful, shattering bomb-fall, funfair. And after the bombs there was suddenly something in a searchlight—a particle of shining matter. The searchlights on either side came together like closing fingers till there were only two bars of light, a cross on the sky and a plane in the middle of the cross. I expected the anti-aircraft to go on firing but they were silent. The speck in the cross grew smaller but kept in the lights, smaller and smaller, a speck, mere speck, the merest and then a non-speck. The searchlights vanished.

When the all-clear had sounded and the lights went on, I went out of my room, met the wry-faced camarera whose face was for once relaxed. '*Las bombas! boum! boum!*' she said with a broad grin, as if showing the local sights to the children. I went down to dinner, shrimps cost 65 pesetas but I took temera and lentils. It turned out the bombs had fallen very near, just round the corner in the Paseo de Gracia, first raid on the centre for months. There had been eight minutes between the siren and the bombs, unusually long, plenty of time to take shelter but people had remained in the street thinking it was a raid on the port; the number of dead was not certain.

After dinner I went with Darling to a light operetta—all about lovers and irrigation problems. As we came home through the darkness we heard young men singing rather drunkenly; God knows where they had found drink. Darling told me it was a Basque song popular in the music halls—'The Englishman who went to Bilbao'. I asked what he did there. Oh, he said, the girls were so lovely, he never wanted to go back to England.

Next morning I went to look at the damage. The pavements in the Paseo de Gracia were powdered with glass, there were several shallow bomb holes in the street, a stone seat had been blown off its legs, there was blood on a wall to the height of fifteen feet; a few Sunday morning strollers were standing, quizzical connoisseurs, looking at the dirty brown stains. The bombs had been very small, about 30 lb., no use upon buildings but with plenty of blast.

I turned along the Cortes and came upon a milling crowd, thought it was a food queue, a riot, a political meeting, but no it was only the stamp collectors doing their Sunday morning swapping. I walked almost out of the town as far as the bullring; it was a beautiful morning. Outside the bullring they were selling locust beans. In an open space beyond a colonnade gypsies were encamped, cooking in malodorous cans; boys were playing pelota against a wall. I passed the Museum, which still advertised a Spring exhibition of Modern Art–the Spring of 1936–and climbed the long steps to the Montjuich gardens, got a magnificent view of the city. All very peaceful, Sunday morning. I could distinguish the fantastic church of the Holy Family–a dream by Hans Andersen when his temperature was high. I descended the hill into the Paralelo.

The Paralelo used to be what tourists like, squalidly picturesque with more than a hint of vice. The streets are narrow and steep, the houses overhanging. Many of the downhill streets were now blocked up with earth where they were making new shelters. In a little plaza a one-legged man sat contentedly on a doorstep in the sun, his one leg out before him, hens around him had dust baths, a black and white cat, as lean as if created by Daumier or Steinlen, prowled meaningfully after nothing, and a white dandified dog with a spitzy face looked out of a window high up. In the next street I was watching some children playing with marbles when I heard an imbecile laugh. I looked all around for the laughter, thinking that that was what war did, but there was no one in the street but the children. The crazy laughter going on, I realised it came from above me. High up on a balcony was a green parrot among ferns.

The window balconies were nearly all green with ferns or aspidistras, making the streets like gullies, the people like cliff-dwellers; some were wired over for hens, some gay with washing. The rooms seemed full of people.

That afternoon I was taken to tea with Antonio Machado in a grand house in the suburbs. The ground floor was full of hens and nondescript refugees, Machado and his family were in a great white room on the first floor, all mirrors and gilt and an ornamental cornice, but chilly without a fire and white dustcovers over the furniture–a museum, a mausoleum, a box of dried cowries. There

186

were many relations, all apologetic because they had so little to offer us, all refugees from Andalusia. His mother was 90, abstracted. Machado himself, the most famous poet in Spain, who wrote propaganda for the Government, was ill, tired, rolled his own cigarettes, dropped ash on his waistcoat, smiled and made conversation; asked about English communists,[1] English literature. One of his friends there, a musician, was doing research into Spanish fifteenth-century dance tunes, preparing a book on the subject; he played us some tunes on the piano.

That night there was another air-raid as we were waiting in the lounge for dinner. The siren went, the lights went out, but no one in the room even paused in his sentence. A little pageboy went out and stood in the street, told the passers-by that they could use the hotel refuge—come quietly, no need to hurry.

On Monday I went round some canteens with members of the Quaker unit. The first was a dingy restaurant which fed 900 children —forty grammes of bread and a cup of cocoa for each. In the kitchen sink there was a tiny black and white puppy who lived by licking up spillings. The second was a room in the Hotel Colón which looks on the Plaza Cataluña; it was no longer used as a hotel. The room had chandeliers, was smartly panelled, but the panels were pocked with shrapnel. While I was watching the children filing in, noticing that several, even a ginger-haired baby carried by its mother, wore earrings, I was addressed by a Spaniard who worked there, very thin and worn, in a shirt without a collar, but nonchalantly humorous. As I could not talk to him in Spanish, he spoke dog-French—*Quelle guerre! Quelle guerre!* the Italians had killed his two brothers. I asked about the Italians in the new offensive, how many of them were there. All, he said; all were Italians, no Spaniards at all, Spaniards would not do these things, yes all were Italians, about 80,000 of them. *Quelle guerre!* the bombs fell. 'The bombs fall,' he repeated, philosophically droning, drowsing, 'the bombs fall'; but then as it were woke up, his face lit into a smile, 'but the Italians,' he added, 'they fall too.' Revitalised, he turned dramatic, pointed to one of the windows. 'See that window? I was standing here one day and they dropped bombs in the square. A man came in through that window without his head.'

[1] Text uncertain.

187

The third canteen was much gayer; the men who had been told to paint the walls had of their own accord put in all sorts of floral decorations. They had a feeding list of 500 children but 200 of them were ill—mainly scabies and whooping cough.

We drove on to look at the market which was attended by those who have ration tickets; 'there won't be any food there of course'. This was nearly true but to my friends' astonishment there was a new supply of chickpeas. They told me some facts about rationing: one ticket would get you 150 grammes of bread, every day except Sundays; one ticket would get you 100 grammes of chickpeas plus 50 grammes of peas but you could only get those once a week, maybe once a month; the ration of oil was a quarter of a litre but there had been none now for three months and then it had been bad, just machine oil; the ration of meat was 100 grammes of meat plus 20 of bone but there had been none now for a month; and there had been no fish for two months. Returning to the question of oil, a Spanish woman told us a joke; a household of eight having at last obtained half a litre, the purveyor threw in a packet of magnesia. Against indigestion.

We went on to see a children's *comedor* where a peseta a day was charged per head. 2,500 were fed here, got lentils and little bits of meat, pear jam for dessert. After that I saw a refugee colony—not one of those shown off by the propaganda people. The smell was as thick as peasoup, a fog of inveterate filth. The rooms were arranged round a patio, greasy whitewashed walls scrawled all over with aeroplanes; one girl whose bed almost filled her dim little cell had covered the walls with photographs of film-stars—Gary Cooper several times. Others had their beds in the gallery of the chapel. The boys' dormitory was also scrawled with aeroplanes and a little rebellious poem beginning '*In esta cochina casa . . .*' the gist of which was that nowhere dirtier was possible, we have rice every day but no oil or grease to make it eatable.

It was nearly time for the midday meal, the refugees were queuing in the patio, each one holding a tin. Thinking of Goya I wondered if history moved; their faces were classic with haggardness. In the kitchen were three enormous pans of lentils and some women, themselves refugees, ready to ladle them—one ladleful of lentils per head and a small piece of bread; one ladle without bread in the evening; no breakfast. A pretty gypsy-like girl with a ladle in her hand was voluble, embittered–not, so far as I could make out, against any officials or government or even the war (those were invisible) but against the great drums full of lentils and the lack of cleanliness and oil. The figures from Goya filed in and held out their tins, then retreated like dogs with a bone. As I left the patio, an old woman had crept away by herself, was holding her bread in both hands, gnawing it completely absorbed.

That evening I went to a news theatre off the Ramblas. There was a cartoon called *Juquetes Olvidados* and a newsreel of a dogshow in Moscow; the dogs looked very luxurious.

On Tuesday morning I visited the cathedral; it had been hit once by a bomb which came through the roof over a side aisle. Much of the stained glass had been broken, lay in crumpled unrecognisable fragments. The images of the saints had been parked in the cloisters from which the famous geese had now vanished. We went up on the roof, picked up pieces of shrapnel and two stone fingers of a saint.

In the afternoon I watched a pelota game, there was much applause, some betting. The four young men in white looked curiously like English cricketers, especially when doing their backhands–a movement like a left-handed batsman doing a full-blooded drive. The noisy repartee of the ball, the jokes and cheers of the spectators, seemed to exorcise the war. I went on to the Catalan Ministry of Propaganda where they showed me atrocity photographs–a sprawled woman with her upper half intact, great marble breasts, her stomach open to the air and her legs vanished, endless coils of entrails. 'We have others,' they said, 'but we are not allowed to give them to you. It is a pity, we are sorry, they are filed away. Many much better than these. *Beaucoup plus jolis.*' '*Plus* jolis?' I said. They shrugged their shoulders: '*Plus forts.*'

There was an air-raid next morning at a quarter to ten–more cottonwool in the sky, two planes disappearing to the east like naughty birds leaving an orchard; naughty was the most they looked, not evil, not destructive; flying so easily back to their nests in Majorca. On my way to visit the University I talked with a Spaniard in the Cortes who was standing against the wall in the sun. 'You see?' he said. 'Here we have the war but we also have the fine weather.' There was another air-raid during lunch; I was already so acclimatised to the mood of the city that I took it like everyone else, as a matter of course, that is callously. They said that the New Year's raid had killed about 60.

In the afternoon I wandered down towards the port, came on a narrow street where they were bartering food—sprats, locust beans, pumpkins, mussels, nuts. Barter was now the best way of getting things; a cigarette would buy almost anything.

Diverging into the Citadel Gardens which were bleak, with dead leaves running, I suddenly saw a reindeer, realised there must be a zoo. It cost me 50 centimos to enter—a long narrow strip of desolation, dead leaves, a smell of corruption. A mangy brown hyena; a brown bear, mere skin and bone, with green eyes, lying in a corner; other bears lying about, the remnants of the kingdom of flesh, licking the bars of the cages or slipping their tongues into their nostrils; a shattered kiosk; some incongruous pots of geraniums on an island in a pool in a bird-run; a jackal which in Catalan is *xacal;* a tangle of wire, smashed roofs, where once had been apes; Osa Polar, an old ragbag with hard knobs in him, his neck very long, very thin, his whiteness no more white—he lay stretched out, his neck as scraggy as a fowl's waiting for the chopper, no movement at all but a twitch of the nose or a blink of doom-dimmed eyes; some rhesus monkeys accepting sprays of privet from little girls; a kangaroo catching the skipping dead leaves, nonchalantly eating them.

The B.'s at dinner told me they had been investigating prices—fountain pen 2,000 pesetas, chicken for Christmas 500, oil 100 a litre, shoes 500, eggs 130 a dozen. That is, prices which had been given; it didn't mean the things were there to buy.

Thursday was a wonderful morning of wind and sun, the dead leaves gadding in circles. Darling told me I really should see some of the architecture, took me to the townhall and the Generalidad; in the latter, in the patio of the orange trees, there were fat fish swimming in a pool, very cool, very peaceful, but why had nobody eaten them? We went up to the Propaganda Ministry; Darling and his Catalan friends slapped each other's faces playfully, he obtained from them a dozen eggs he had specially ordered; they were for one of the waiters in the Ritz, a wounded ex-soldier whose wife was ill and family starving (the waiters were not fed by the hotel). We hid the eggs in our pockets. 'Take care the girls don't slap your flanks,' they said as we left.

We went into a News Theatre—the usual pro-Stalin propaganda, several Disney cartoons, an idyllic film of the Crimea—the evolution of attar of roses. When we came out a stage moon was shining down the Diagonal—a marvellous night, just the sort of night for a raid. At dinner in the hotel we gave the eggs to the waiter. He smiled like a seraph, gave Darling a light slap on the side of the head, but insisted on paying for them. 130 pesetas. 'What are you to do with these people?' Darling said.

A dapper little ex-grandee, a friend of Darling's, appeared after dinner in the lounge, said a wonderful thing had happened, he had just got some coffee from Cuba, would we care to come down and accept some of this coffee? Yes of course we would. He was very pleased but, suddenly remembering, explained. His coffee was in his flat near the cathedral, a very dangerous district. So dangerous he no longer slept there. But that was where the coffee was. He would quite understand if we should care not to come, especially seeing that the moon . . .

The street outside was narrow, be-rubbled, deserted, a stage set for villains in cloaks. But the flat itself was a bijou piece, small, very daintily arranged, bachelor comfort and good taste. The walls were covered with drawings by Spanish imitators of Picasso. The low bookshelves contained Edgar Wallace in English and Cocteau in French. The coffee was Cuban. There was a tiny radio set; he turned it on while we waited for the bombs, got an Italian station broadcasting pro-Franco propaganda in Spanish. At 11.15 we got our own war news—Borjas Blancas had fallen but the offensive on the Estremadura front was making good progress. Darling and the Spaniard shook their heads; the fall of Borjas Blancas was bad. The Spaniard turned the knob, got an Irish pot-pourri from Radio Lyons, comic or sentimental blarney-go-blackthorn songs in a faked and sugary brogue.

The siren went next morning about breakfast time. Again as before a thunderstorm there was a hush but here, unlike a thunderstorm, the birds went on unabashed. Cock after cock over the city and futile palaver of sparrows. Nothing happened and they sounded the all-clear. Coming down into the hall I met a crowd of women coming up from the refuge in the cellar, the Ritz's ladies of fortune in quilted dressing-gowns jostling the poor from the street.

The concert in the afternoon was Bach, Sarana, Ravel. After dinner I talked for a few minutes with André Malraux. He was jittery, hard to follow, switching from English to Spanish to French, his words broken up by a queer nervous noise out of his lungs. Very depressed about the war, still more about the social situation. Some statistics about the farms and the factories, some observations on barter—soap for rabbits. But the chief trouble was spiritual, the bloom was off the revolution. 'This Spanish war,' he said, 'once it was a bride and now . . .' (with disgust) 'it is a wife.'

I went down to the Plaza Cataluña to see the people sleeping in the Metro. During the day they took away their blankets and mattresses, brought them back at night. The great dim station was the real underworld of dreams, in dreams I had seen it all before—the long lines of sleepers with their heads against the wall, five children under one blanket, the resigned faces that were lost to the sun. Most of them were asleep, one or two old women sat up looking into the gloom, their children ranged along the wall like toys—a limbo of weakening tissue. *Juquetes Olvidados*.

The next morning I drove round with members of the Quaker unit visiting schools and *comedores*. The Catalans have always been devoted to printing; one of these schools had its own printing press but could no longer operate it owing to lack of material. The children, however, combined to produce watercolours—scenes of air-raids, bodies on stretchers, blood, flames, the figures neatly distinct tripping down steps to a shelter, *cuidados* coming out of their mouths, limpid colour, dainty line.

We visited a new children's *comedor* in the industrial district to the east, which was being constructed out of an old cinema and theatre next door to each other. Already they were feeding 2,500 a day. Yes, but we expect to feed *six* thousand—will take some time of course. Here is the new dining-room, they said, standing in a roofless barn. And here, in a filthy backyard full of rubble, here we shall have a patio—flowering trees; and *that* will be a children's club, they will run it all by themselves.

One ladle of lentils at noon, a ladle of lentils at night. An old woman, black under the eyes, tilted her bowl, drank off the hot water, then ate the lentils dry. One acquires a technique. Some *comedores* got more, some less; one received surplus flour from America, the passage paid by the American Red Cross. Near the University was a five-pesetas *comedor* for workers only where they got two courses–two. Chickpeas, doled from huge pans like golden cartwheels; then rice and a few beans; in the evening even a little endive salad. They had just begun rationing acorns.

In the Ministry of Propaganda the flags were moving east on the map. It was not good at all but of course they would never get here. Tarragona yes, he would probably take Tarragona; that was really all to the good, though it would be a pity if he destroyed the cathedral. And meanwhile there was the Estremadura–so highly featured in the papers.

On Sunday I was taken down by Audrey Russell to Tarragona. We had three lorries full of provisions, mainly great sacks of powdered milk, and there were two of us in each lorry–Audrey Russell and Richard Rees and Robert Morley and myself and a Spaniard who worked for the Quakers with his wife. It was a beautiful day and we picnicked over the Mediterranean on a rocky hillside. On the road we had met several refugees, presumably from Borjas Blancas. In carts piled high with belongings or riding donkeys or leading a goat by a rope, bearded old men and women with shawls over their heads, a flavour of the Flight into Egypt. We took our lorries into the main square of Tarragona and asked where we were to put the provisions. No one knew. An aldermanlike person came up and said while we were waiting we really ought to see their air-raid shelter, it was something quite out of the ordinary, had so many different exits. To oblige him Richard Rees and I went down under the square by the light of Richard's cigarette lighter; as this burned his fingers he only put it on spasmodically. It was certainly a very fine shelter and we could not find our way out of it; every passage seemed to lead into a little blind cell. When we did get out we were at the far end of the square. Almost immediately an air-raid warning went. Women and children began trooping down into the shelter as a matter of course, their faces unperturbed, rather bored. Richard and I stood in a doorway and watched the sky. People appeared at the upper windows along the square, rested their elbows on the balconies and watched the sky also. Three or four minutes after the warning had gone four bouncing girls of about sixteen came rollicking arm in arm down the centre of the square laughing hilariously. No planes appeared and after a short time they gave the all-clear. The indifferent faces reappeared out of the ground.

Unloading the lorries was very hard work as the sacks of powdered milk weighed 100 kilos each. Rees and Morley had the knack of handling them but I felt they would kill me. One sack fell off the end of the lorry and some of the powder spilt over the street. Children clustered round, scooping it up into their mouths with their hands. I had not sweated so much for years and found it wonderfully comforting. When we had finished our work an official gave us some Spanish brandy, now a fabulous rarity. I found myself in the mood of a schoolboy's O.T.C. rag. We sent one lorry home with the Spanish couple and drove on into the military zone to Reus, where we arrived just too late to see a dogfight over the town.

On our way home, at dusk, we got hungry. Audrey Russell said she would find us a really safe place to stop, she still had some chocolate and some wilting little pastries like mince-pies. When the stars were out we arrived at the Roman arch which the road goes around in a roundabout. Audrey Russell said this was just the place, Franco would never drop bombs within miles of it because it was such an antiquity and there was nothing here anyway to bomb. The four of us got out and sat by the side of the road, Audrey Russell portioned out the chocolate, explaining that it seemed to have been gnawed by rats. I had my first mouthful of pie in my mouth and was gazing at the very serene night when a bomb fell from nowhere just beyond us. We lay down in the stony ditch and before our eyes a chain of bombs, six or eight, fell parallel with the road, so rapidly that I had no time to be frightened, merely thought what a wonderful show. First a big red flower and then another; then where the flowers had been, a powdery blue effulgence spreading upwards and outwards with scalloped edges, joining up with the next. When the last had fallen we got up shakily, climbed into the lorries, turned off their lights and drove on slowly; a hundred yards further on there were two shallow bombholes in the road with a crowd of figures standing by. We stopped and Audrey Russell got out to see if anyone was hurt. No one was hurt but they all wanted lifts to Barcelona; they climbed into the backs of the lorries. Several more people stopped us on the way back, dark unknowns out of a dark unknown hitchhiking to further darkness.

The next day I had to go home, for Mr. B. had told me that the London University term was beginning. I could only get transport by air and when I got to the Air-France office I found I had not quite enough pesetas; they refused to take French money or English. I sprinted back through the streets to the hotel where I had just paid my bill and said, 'Give me back 50 pesetas and get it out of Mr. Darling.' They did so willingly; money was not much use anyway.

In the Air-France office I got talking with an American, short, very broad, very tough, with the face of an amiable gangster. On the lapel of his overcoat he wore the little metal badges of all the different Government parties – Communist, Anarchist, Catalan Nationalist, all of them. 'You see,' he said, 'I wear the lot; it creates good feeling.' He was an able seaman, had been in the International Brigade till eight months ago and, his ship happening to call at Barcelona, had got off to see how things were; was now going to fly to Marseilles. When I had admired his insignia he pulled out a large silver watch and his face became seraphic. 'See this watch?' he said and turned it round so that I could read on the back his name – Charles A. Scarpello – with a date; 'I got this off a lieutenant-colonel I had the pleasure of killing at 400 metres.'

He told me there was no doubt that the Government would win and everything then would be wonderful. I asked him what about the dissensions between the parties. That was nothing, he said. 'I'll tell you what they must do,' he said, his childlike gangster face beaming with sheer conviction, 'when they've won this war they must take all these parties and take the — out of each of them and put them together into one big party for the good of the country.'

He went on to tell me about the machine-gun nest he and his buddy had made on the Madrid front. It was the best machine-gun nest on the front, they had been specially congratulated on it by the colonel; he gave me the exact measurements of it, the number of railroad sleepers and sandbags they had used. There was only one snag though, he said; they had to have a hole in it to fire out of—well there was a sniper on the other side was so good he could put a bullet through that hole whenever he wanted to. 'But that was all right,' he said, 'we knew about him. We used to put our cans up there for him to open them.'

He was very enthusiastic about Spain, the Spaniards were bloody good fighters, it was a bloody lie to say they were not, the Spanish women were wonderful, you couldn't do better for a wife. He had seen a lot of the French in the International Brigade, recited to me the dog-French doggerel verses he used to make up at their expense; they were good fighters too. 'If you get into any trouble at the customs,' he said, 'you call on me. I speak the lingo pretty good.'

At the customs at the Barcelona airport I had to turn out my pockets. The officials were puzzled by a little notebook full of illegible English verses in pencil. 'What is this?' they said. '*Poesia*,' I said. They handed it around to each other frowning. Then Scarpello appeared. 'What is that?' he said. 'Just a few verses I wrote,' I said, feeling foolishly out of place. Scarpello jerked his thumb at me. '*Propagandista!*' he said to the officials. They handed back the notebook and I flew over the Pyrenees. Scarpello had to take another plane, would join another boat at Marseilles, would look me up in London sometime, he said. I think he was perhaps the last person I met who felt that he knew all the answers.

Toulouse was astonishing. I had only been ten days in Spain but Toulouse was a new world. The shops were bulging with goods, there were pyramids of fruit upon stalls, you could order what you liked in the cafés. The people looked plump and complacent, smoking cigarettes and cigars; when you smoked you aroused no envy and the stubs lay ungathered in the ashtrays. I sat having a drink in a café and felt more lonely than I had felt for months. These French were really alien, there was no danger or hunger to unite us, they were busy making money for here money still made sense, they were family men for their families were still intact, they were self-centred for what else was there to be? It was all only too understandable but I still found myself hating them. And I began to hate the English too who had passed by on the other side. Passed by under an umbrella. And then, very logically, I found myself hating myself.

XXXVI

By the time I was back in London the Republican defence was crumbling. The Left held a last meeting in the Queen's Hall, speaker after speaker denouncing the Non-Intervention Committee, Ellen Wilkinson, redhaired, tiny, huskily screaming against Chamberlain, her anger flaring up through her hair, an incendiary bomb. A young man who had fought in the International Brigade told very simply and movingly how the Brigade had held for months a position considered untenable and prophesied that this would be repeated—'Our front line tonight is in the suburbs of Barcelona.' Barcelona fell.

The Conservative Press were already pandering to Franco. The morale of the Catalans, they said, had always been shockingly bad. The wilful obstinacy of the Republican government had reaped its own reward. And when the question of recognising Franco became acute the *Daily Telegraph* proclaimed in an editorial that not to recognise Franco now would be an act of intervention.

The Spanish tragedy ended in fiasco. Miaja, who had long been the hero of the *Daily Worker*, whose statuette was bestowed by the Spanish Ministry of Propaganda on every visitor to Spain, was suddenly covered with pitch as a counter-revolutionary. The young men for whom the Spanish war had been a crusade in white armour, a Quest of the Grail open only to the pure in heart, felt as if their world had burst; there was nothing left but a handful of limp rubber rag; it was no good trying any more. Books such as that by Martin Blazquez, *I Helped to Build an Army*, made only too clear the self-deception which the Civil War had occasioned in nine minds out of ten. There is no such thing as a snow-white cause. The Spanish refugees who began trickling into London surprised Londoners by their retrospective lack of unanimity.

I borrowed my sister's ancient Lea-Francis and drove to Twickenham with Goronwy Rees and — a half-bottle of whisky. Once more to see England play Ireland at rugby football—the sort of conflict one could really understand. In which what is important is the technique and not the end (sport, like art, has its ivory towers). Technically, it was a fine exhibition, George Morgan, now a veteran, loping through the English with arrogant indolence, selling the dummy and they always bought it. Goronwy, who was a football fan, forgot his ideology, forgot her private perplexities, cold air and whisky were tonic, the Lea-Francis taking us home chugged like a faithful beast through the inhuman suburbs. But it is not every day you can watch a rugger international. And you cannot read James Joyce all the time. And the globe keeps rolling towards a pocket without a bottom although on the way the green cloth field is smooth.

I had a dream at this time that I was caught by the Nazis. They took me to an enormous wall built of Pelasgian blocks. In this wall was a great wrought-iron gate of eighteenth-century workmanship. They unlocked this gate and thrust me through it, locked it behind me. I found myself in the Alps with a narrow pass before me, began to ascend the rough and desolate track. Plodding upwards, looking straight ahead of me or hardly looking at all, I was conscious suddenly of something on either side, looked to the right and the left. On the right and the left of my track, padding along in parallel silence, were bears. Bears of every size and colour, going inexorably forward, but looking at me sometimes sideways. I had the feeling they were 'not quite right', steeled myself to go on, careful not to annoy them. Then ahead of me, higher up the pass, I saw a woman, with a stab of joy in my diaphragm hurried to overtake her. Overtook her; she looked straight out of Bond Street, tall and blonde, the height of elegance. She too had been caught by the Nazis, I walked along beside her and the bears walked on each side of us. But everything was all right now. 'Who are you?' I said at last. 'Oh,' she said suavely, 'I am the Czar's governess.'

XXXVII

For Easter 1939 I visited the Great Unvisited. America, which for people in the British Isles is a legend until they go there, is one big pumpkin-pie fairy story. The *Queen Mary* going west was packed with refugees, mainly Jews from Central Europe who covered their basic sorrow with volubility, fuss; only for a moment or two when they stopped troubling the water could you see the wreckage on the floor of their mind.

The *Queen Mary* did not seem like a boat at all, you were hardly conscious of the sea, enclosed within shell upon shell of satinwood walls and sunk in clubroom chairs. The atmosphere was ultra-British: in the evening the Purser in the Tourist Class organised spelling bees; in the First Class lounge, business men were losing and winning hundreds of pounds nightly at bridge and poker. Meanwhile, the radio announced the Albanian crisis but international crises by now were a case of 'Wolf, Wolf'.

The second night out I was sitting at the Tourist bar, isolated, insulated from others, when an American offered me a drink. He was a little man in his early forties, going bald down the middle, with deep lines on his face from the struggle for commercial existence and eyes that did not care very much but cared enough to be comfortable and friendly; the sort of little man the English would call common. 'What's your sport?' he said to me. 'Well,' I said, 'I used to play a bit of tennis.' 'I knew it,' he said, 'I knew you were a sportsman the moment I saw you.' 'That shirt,' he added. He himself was a golf professional.

It was a hard life being a golf professional, you had all these girls coming to you for lessons–real gorgeous–and you could not seduce them because you would lose your job. Of course you can hold their wrists and all that, rub up close to them correcting their stance. But that only made it harder. Yes, sir; in his job you needed some self-control.

He and I sat one evening after dinner drinking whiskies and sodas with a couple of middle-aged American spinsters (one was a school-marm who had blown her savings in Europe) and a tall old man with dirty white hair sweeping back from his forehead, the profile of a corrupt bird of prey, the leer of a satyr and a steel clamp on his leg (an American flyer, he had been wounded in the last war). After a round or two of drinks the spinsters began to giggle, then went anti-Semite. The school-marm who came from Chicago explained to me, as if teaching me the ABC, that once a Jew moves into a street everyone else has to move out of it. 'Why?' I said. Because, she said gently, pitying my innocence, because they are so filthy in their habits; you should see what they throw out of the windows. But I had known a lot of Jews, I said. . . . 'Oh yes,' she said, 'you have quite a different *class* of Jews in England.'

Not that she was intolerant, she said, now what Hitler did to the Jews, she couldn't agree with that. But there was no doubt . . . The tall old man, who was getting drunk, interrupted her, took the conversation to his bosom. 'I'll tell you something,' he said, 'and it's God's truth. You may not know it but I know it and I'm glad of it. One day soon the lid's going to blow off this country and every damn Jew's going to get what's coming to him. And will I be glad to see it!' He pictured with gusto the burnings and lynchings, the purification of the States. Half an hour later he drew himself up, dramatic. 'I'll tell you something,' he said portentously, 'I'll tell you something I wasn't going to tell to anybody.' But he told us nothing, he merely swept back the lapel of his coat showing a large metal badge that said 'British Columbia Police'.

An hour later, maudlin drunk, he was telling the golf professional how he seriously thought of getting married, a funny thing he had never been married, well there comes a time when a man gets lonely and did we know what he had spent on his house, on central heating, refrigerators, gadgets of all kinds–so many dollars, so many dollars–well when you've done all that you need somebody to share it–and there's plenty of girls, he added, *young* girls would be glad to.

The *Queen Mary* docked early in the morning and we were already past the Statue of Liberty when I got out on deck; Lower Manhattan was bang up against me, a phallic gaiety of steel and concrete, something one knew so well one could not believe it. A silver carillon starting in the back of the mind; the tinkle of cubes of ice in a million highballs, the brittle xylophone of the wishful heart.

My first walk was up Second Avenue, unshaven down-and-outs stopped me to beg; there were two cities in this city, two cosmopolises, poor and rich. Glass and marble and banks like cathedrals on one hand; endless grimy streets on the other, with their iron fire-escapes showing, with bone and iron showing.

Cataracts of peanuts, winding-sheets of cellophane, oceans of milk in cardboard containers. (He drank it in with his mother's milk. What? A sense of necessity. Which equals necessity of accident. Which equals madness. Which equals in the long run nought—the indifferent frigid sky that no skyscraper can dent.)

The windows of the shops in Fifth Avenue were full of stream-lined dryads. For spring was on the way. The long sophisticated fingers of the dummies snaked their way up to flower in magenta nails. Here and there was a window with only a flowering tree and among its blossoms a hat with a trailing veil; a placard below it—'We thought we heard a robin.'

Mariette and Tsalic came up from the country to see me. They both looked unreal in the city; or perhaps too real for the city. Mariette, whom I had not seen since 1935, seemed oddly different and the same. Larger than I had known her and with the shade of an American accent, but the same torrent of talk, the same school-girl's vivacity, the same absolute assurance that what she knew she knew. She told me in detail of their life in Elizabeth, that dreary industrial limbo outside New York City. Tsalic and she had run this children's recreation ground—several thousand children in relays, problem children, dead-end kids, all colours and sizes, all diseases and vices. The recreation ground was close to the railway line, in the shadow of the Singers Works. Most of the parents who were employed were employed in Singers but most of them were not employed. Tsalic and she had solved the problem of the real bad lots—Polish and Irish toughs—by putting them in charge of the others. In the end they had started a library; it grew very fast; the bad boys used to come along with bundles of books inside their coats, say 'There's plenty more where these came from'—thefts from the public libraries. Oh my, Mariette said, you learnt a lot from those kids.

However, they gave it up for the farm; Mariette had wanted to farm and live with animals. Tsalic had farmed too though he still was a ballet fan. Now they never came to New York. You get so you lose the taste for it, Mariette said. Besides, she never could find her way about in New York, she couldn't understand these streets that were only numbers. Of course there were nice things in New York–the neon lights on Broadway; and the Automats; and you could get lovely things to eat in places called Chock Full O'Nuts.

The first lecture I gave in America was at State College, Pennsylvania.[1] My host who was large and slow of speech spent an hour or two preparing me for my audience, alarming me. He guessed I'd never met this kind of audience. Kind of difficult. Not what I'd been used to in England. And not what I'd meet at Harvard. After the event he congratulated me. 'They gave you a big hand,' he said, 'they usually only do that for an orchestra.'

In New York I went one night to a night club with some semigilded youths who spent their time explaining that there were other night clubs better. In a circle surrounded by tables naked girls with scarlet feathers or sequins stuck on their breasts and groins gave an exhibition of not very good dancing and stereotyped sex appeal to tired business men with pouches under their eyes and heavy jowls. Some of these business men were like obsolete babies; their mouths were compressed into a lipless line but seemed, none the less, to crave for a rubber dummy, a comforter. But someone has dropped the comforter under the table. Better not give it him, Sis, it may have germs.

Owing to central heating the American house seems like a Turkish bath to people fresh from England, and in this bath the radio is always on–news of crisis, of earthquake, of apocalypse over the mountains but you lie easy in your towel, perspire, call for a drink. The assassination, says the announcer, took place at a quarter of eight (his voice is dry and impersonal). The event is considered likely to have international repercussions. And then his voice changes, becomes, as the case may be, unctuous, wheedling,

[1] Now the Pennsylvania State University.

parsonical, or hail-fellow-well-met. And now, folks, I would like to remind you for a moment that in spite of Dr. Gugg's assassination, you are still alive. Yes, indeed. Now being alive, folks, you will want to make the most of it and I am happy to be able to tell you that for one dollar twenty . . .

I visited an elderly magnate 50 or 60 floors up in the Rockefeller Centre. He was sitting at a huge desk, everything beautifully slick, and making believe he was busy. Out of the window was miles of glittering city–city to end all cities, perpetual motion, towers going up and towers coming down, systole diastole systole diastole, deglutition, digestion, excretion of traffic, arrows and arrows of the sun hitting the body of the saint, the young body that never grows old or dies, merely feels pain, Sebastian. The magnate was affable but very self-assured, showed me his view with pride. Then as I was putting on my coat his manner changed, he became hesitant, shy. You know about poetry, don't you? he said. Well, I'm supposed to. 'Er,' he said, 'er, well there's something I'd like to show you. Of course I'm not a professional.' He opened the kind of drawer that was meant for government archives and handed me a menu card–menu of the annual dinner of his firm's employees; down one side was the list of dishes, down the other was a poem in blank verse. This firm, the poem said, was not like some firms, was a noble cause, a crusade. While I read the poem–the verse was technically competent–the magnate stood by me, coyly smiling, expectant. A life spent dodging arrows but glad in a way when they hit him.

One evening I went to a party with some Trotskyites. My host stood under a photo of Trotsky, to whom he had acquired an outward superficial resemblance, shook hands with me and said, 'Of course we think that the trouble with you literary people in England is that you're all so Stalinist.' Taken by surprise, Stalinist being a word I had hardly heard in London, I demurred mildly. 'Well,' he went on, 'can you tell me why the Spanish government lost the war in Spain?' I thought. 'I suppose the main reason,' I said, 'was disparity of armaments.' He was genuinely shocked. '*That*,' he said, 'is a very materialistic way of looking at it.' Not at all, he went on; there was a Stalinist conspiracy to lose it between the Negrin government and Franco. Next day I passed a C.P. bookshop in uptown New York. The window was full of a pamphlet – *Why the Spanish War was Lost. The Trotskyite Conspiracy*.

At this time I met someone whom according to fairy story logic I was bound to meet but according to common sense never. A woman who was not a destroyer. Something inside me changed gear, began to run easily in top.

Once upon a time there was the seventh son of a seventh son. He lived with his father in a house where everything was always the same. One day he said to his father, 'Father, I want something different.' 'Right,' said his father and gave him a nickel, a dime and a quarter. 'Whenever you want something different throw one over your shoulder.' The seventh son walked to the turn of the road, took out the nickel and threw it over his shoulder, found himself floating in fog, no land or sky but somewhere beneath him sea; he heard the foghorns. He floated a long long time; sometimes the foghorns were nearer, sometimes further. Then the fog suddenly vanished and ceased to support him and he fell on the deck of a ship; the sun was shining on brass and paint. The sailors were busy; they said nothing to him but they grinned. He felt himself happy because they were busy. In the captain's cabin was a chart of the third hemisphere; the mast had a halo of gulls; after a week flying fish appeared and after another week were singing. Nobody spoke to the seventh son; they grinned only, went on with their jobs, gave him three meals a day. He wanted to work too, offered his assistance aft and forward, in the cook's galley and the stokehole. But they merely grinned, put him gently aside. He stood in the stern and watched the churn of the water, felt unhappy because everyone else was busy. Slowly and hesitantly he took the dime from his pocket – they were good companions, he was sorry to leave them – and threw it over his shoulder. Then there was no more sea.

The asphalt plain that stretched to the horizon was marked out in numbered squares. He found he had a dicebox in his hand, had to throw the dice in order to move. Sometimes they took him forward, sometimes back. Within the horizon's circle the rattle of the dice was the only noise, the dun-coloured air was as empty as the mind of the Last Man. The Last Man, who has watched the ebb of history, knows that the tide will never return to the shore.

The seventh son put little hope in the dice. If they threw him

7 seven times running, then maybe . . . But the law of chances gave one to doubt . . . He prayed to the God whom nobody knew about, threw a 3 and a 4–makes seven. Threw a 2 and a 5–makes seven. Threw a 1 and a 6–makes seven. Threw a 6 and a 1–makes seven. Threw a 4 and a 3–makes seven. Threw a 3 and a 4–makes seven. He prayed to the God he could not believe in, rattled the dice in the box and threw them like shooting stars. They fell on the asphalt and began to roll. 'Stop,' he shouted, 'stop. Make seven.' But the rolling dice went faster. He followed them over the plain.

O God who ledst me out of my father's house, through the timeless fog and the sea of singing fishes, who hast brought me into this purgatory of squares, stretch down Thy hand, O God, out of the dead sky, and stop the dice, dear God, make them stop, make seven.

They continued rolling–so fast that they left him behind. As he ran choking in pursuit he noticed the dice were getting larger. The more they outstripped him the larger they became. Unable to run any more he sat on the asphalt, put his head on his knees and closed his eyes. His mind was as empty as the dun-coloured air.

Then somebody's finger–maybe his own–pushed up his eyelids. The dice had come to rest on the horizon, two mountainous altars of ivory but he could not read the numbers. If I can only get there, he thought, I can read the numbers. With the effort of the Last Man who wants once more to *begin*, he began the trek to the horizon.

It was long afterwards he passed through the gates. The ivory gateposts reached to the sky, one bore the number 6 and one the number 1. And once you are through you are through. In the country of prisms and fountains in the middle of which there is a lake of ice and a figure skating in the middle of the lake. This figure may be a man or a woman or a child–you cannot tell, for the lake is so big– but such is the grace of its movements around the unseen axis that you know there is nothing you have ever wanted so much as to meet this figure and talk with it. But you dare not go on the ice.

The seventh son sat on the edge of the lake and thought 'If I wait long enough this being will leave the ice. At least when it starts to get dark.' But the hours passed and the night would not come and the dance, the skating, went on. 'If only,' he thought, 'if only things were different', and he took out the quarter and weighed it in his hand. This, he thought, was the greatest gamble of all; all he wanted was to put an end to the skating, to meet the skater.

The quarter in his hands became as heavy as a discus but he threw it, shutting his eyes. There was a swish of curtains, a meter ticking, warmth on his shins. He opened his eyes; the frozen lake and the skater, the prisms and fountains were gone; he was back in his father's house where everything had always been the same. But now everything was different.

XXXVIII

I found myself back in London with renewed vitality but afraid of imminent disaster. I felt immediate nostalgia for America.

Some Labourite members of the staff at Bedford College asked me to speak to the girls on the significance of May Day, rally them to cut their lectures, go marching the streets. I did so reluctantly, told the girls that they need not think that by marching on May Day they were saving the world but they might as well march all the same. The progressives up till now had lost every battle, but their functions were not yet quite atrophied and if they kept talking it would at least be harder to gag them. The Labourites were disappointed, said America seemed to have had a gloomy effect on me. The girls turned out for their march buoyant enough.

A few days after my return I was called up by an official of television who asked me to take part in a television programme; about eight authorities were speaking on different aspects of American life and they wanted someone to speak at the end and strike a more general note, had thought of me because I was fresh from the scene. How did they mean, I asked, a more general note? Oh, you know, they said, just give your own ideas of the significance of America. I wrote down a few notes and sent them along. At the eleventh hour they called me up again, disappointed, even a little piqued. This won't do, they said, it's too impressionistic; we wanted something bigger, more comprehensive. I asked them to be more precise and at last discovered that what they wanted me to say was that America was the only true democracy and the white hope of civilisation. Even if that were so, I said, I shouldn't say it; I didn't see what good it was to a British audience, who were stuck in these islands, to be told that Europe is lost but that there is a wonderful utopia away there over the Atlantic. And anyway America wasn't a utopia. Did the television people, I asked, know of America's fascist potentialities, of her alarming trend towards anti-semitism? Yes, they said, they knew that but perhaps they had better get someone else to take my part on the programme. Perhaps they had, I said.

This argument merely brought to the surface a debate going on within myself: was America today preferable to England and, if so, why? The blah about democracy could be discounted. Neither of the countries was a true democracy but England, being less hysterical, could at least be less undemocratic in an emergency. Even this American hysteria, however, was perhaps the vice of a virtue, connoted vitality. The English man-in-the-street was possibly a *better* man, i.e. more virtuous, more enlightened, more civilised, than the American man-in-the-street, but his virtues were static, the seeds of growth were dead in him. His tradition itself had become a liability, whereas the corresponding lack of tradition in America was an asset. America's mixed population kept the country plastic, one could move one way or the other, evade the rigours of caste. It had been bad for England to live so long off her Empire. An over-populated island, she was like fifth-century Athens, able to maintain free speech and a comparatively high standard of living, but only on a basis of gagged and impoverished subject peoples.

The fact which swayed me most was the overcrowding; England was becoming one big suburb. She was at her prime when her population was around ten million. Whatever the political pros and cons of America and England, America at least scored on geography. Sooner or later, I thought, I will get on the quota and quit.

The summer of 1939 was a steady delirium, the caterpillar wheels of enormous tractors rearing on every horizon. As individuals there was nothing we could do – just mark time or kill it. Reggie Smith came back on leave from Bucharest and stayed in my flat, refusing to sleep in a bed but using the sofa in the sitting-room, scattering his clothes over the room. His irrepressible cheerfulness was just what I wanted. Even when he met someone new and decided to get married, his volubility, wit and animal spirits remained unimpaired. He had taken it into his head to write a thesis on the poetry of D. H. Lawrence, so in July, when my term was over, he and I (who was writing a book on Yeats) used to go every day to the British Museum and read in the reading room, being searched for I.R.A. bombs when we entered the gate.

The British Museum became a sort of club for us. Ernst and Reggie and Walter Allen and several others and myself were all attending it. When any of us arrived in the reading room he would walk around under the fantastic dome to find someone else and they would go out and have a coffee or a beer. The day was broken up by coffees and beers and I would also go out frequently and sit in the colonnade for a cigarette. The colonnade of the British Museum is the quintessence of peace. Many people come in from the streets to eat their lunch upon the steps and the pigeons pick up the crumbs. There are many refugees already beginning to hibernate.[1] Though the sun shone most of July, and one afternoon a fleet of French airplanes flew over us, a demonstration of our ally's invincibility.

It was outside the British Museum that I met Mulk Raj Anand, a young Indian novelist. Mulk was small and lithe and very hand-some, wore shirts, ties and scarves of scarlet or coral, talked very fast and all the time, was a crusader for the Indian Left. A conversa-tion I had with him about Yeats brought up the subject of spiritual India. It was all a mistake, Mulk said, India was *not* spiritual, no Indian had even thought so until fifty years ago. India was earthy, matter-of-fact; it was the Anglo-Indians who had loudpedalled her alleged mysticism. These Anglo-Indians, Mulk said, used to spend most of their lives in India and never even look at the Indians, conscious of themselves as English, superior, a race apart; then they would retire, go back to England and find they had lost touch, were a race apart there too; it was then that they began to romanticise India – in order to bolster up themselves. And the oddest thing was that they had put this over on some Indians. Even Rabindranath Tagore, a very fine poet, Mulk said, in the original, had got a lot of his mystical stuff from retired English officials. Mulk himself would have none of it. I asked him about yoga. Oh yoga, he said, that's not mysticism. His father, who was a craftsman, did yoga for an hour every morning, it merely increased his efficiency.

Mulk was one of the few people in London who still had public enthusiasms. The books of the Left Book Club, which by now were mainly of academic interest for the English, were for him more functional, alive, because he could make them applicable to India. No doubt he oversimplified the Indian question; but contemporary

[1] Cf. 'The British Museum Reading Room' (*Plant and Phantom*, p. 22).

India, like Czarist Russia and unlike contemporary England or France, was a place where the thought of a vital minority had a chance of being realised in action, where you could be *simpliste* and get away with it. His country was so old it had become young again; ours was merely puffy and short of breath like Hamlet. Like Hamlet ourselves, we amused ourselves commenting on others, enjoyed distractions of sport and spectacle. On the August bank holiday a troop of us went to the Holborn Empire to see Marie —. Every other joke in the show was about dandruff.

Everyone told me that if I was going to America, I had better go quickly; war would break out within a month. I had however planned to go to the west of Ireland with Ernst and the fatalist within me said, 'War or no war, you have got to go back to the West. If only for a week. Because you may never again.' And Ernst was the perfect companion for this; you could be sure he would like the landscape and the people and laugh when the car broke down.

On the day Ernst and I were to leave for Ireland, Reggie Smith got married. We were all too late for the registrar and filled in time before he returned, drinking in the bar of the Ritz. Reggie and his girl and Walter Allen and Ernst and myself and Stevie Smith. None of us had been in the Ritz before and we felt like Tamburlaine— 'Holla, ye pampered jades . . .' We were alone in the bar except for Jim Mollison, silent and sullen in a corner, the glory that was the twenties, who had landed dead beat at the Cape in a jungle of clapping hands. Whereas now it was we who were on top of the world. Or so we thought on the strength of our mint juleps, the harsh leaves of the mint brushing against our lips, the titillation of a male kiss, the eternal vegetable world.

Ernst and I landed in Dublin,[1] went up the Nelson Column like any trippers, bathed our eyes in the hills of Wicklow. And then to the north to join my family who had taken a beautiful house at the end of Cushendun bay. It was the house where Moira O'Neill had lived, the popular sentimental poetess who wrote 'Songs of the Glens of Antrim'. Ernst and I used to walk across the bay every night; the reflection of Jupiter was a strong stain on the sea. Every

[1] With the remainder of this chapter cf. 'The Coming of War' (*Plant and Phantom*, pp. 33 ff.).

morning we drove to Ballycastle to play golf, buying a daily paper before our game. One morning the paper announced the Russo-German pact. 'Ought we to go back?' Ernst said. 'Certainly not,' I said. We went out on the course, sliced and hooked into the river, into the sea, into a ruined abbey, returned home with a crazy appetite, crazy.

In the last week of August we drove west, in Elizabeth's old Lea-Francis, so noisy, so sympathetic. Slept the first night to the sound of running water. Under Croagh Patrick met an old ragged drunkard who took me by the arm: 'Now, me dear boy, answer me this. What would be the reason for this war?' (The war had not yet started.) 'I suppose,' I said, 'there are a lot of reasons.' 'Listen to me, me dear boy, I'll tell you why it is. Suppose now, suppose you was eating dried potatoes and another fellow was eating beef. You'd want to take it off him, wouldn't you? If you had the strength. Well, that's all it is. You'd want to take it off him.'

We arrived in the town of Galway on a Thursday. Galway is the strangest town in Ireland—austerely grey, half the houses ruins, the skull and crossbones, emblem of the Lynch family, carved in relief on the walls. To the side of the harbour is the Claddagh, once a mecca for tourists, it was so picturesque, so unbelievably haphazard, so dirty. But De Valera has changed all that. A few of the old thatched cabins remain, none in line with its neighbour, humping themselves a little above the mud like a brooding hen whose eggs are never to hatch. But most of the Claddagh now consists of municipal houses, two storeys high, the same as anywhere else.

Galway, though for years forgotten and decayed, still has hopes of a renaissance. They were dredging the harbour to make it fit for ocean liners. All that night we heard the dredger grumbling and wheezing. To make Ireland safe for plutocracy.

After breakfast on Friday Ernst and I went up to look at the salmon weir. We leant over the bridge and there were the salmon in the Corrib, facing upstream, oscillating slightly but keeping their places. Why they wanted to do that we couldn't imagine, but it looked very pleasant; let the Corrib do what it likes but you can defy it. Defy it by staying where you are. 'It is nearly time for the news,' Ernst said. I let him go back to the hotel, stayed watching the salmon. They stayed where they were. Walking back later I met Ernst who looked upset and at the same time relieved. 'It's started,' he said, 'they invaded Poland last night.'

The little chambermaid in the hotel said, 'If Hitler comes after me I'll run.' Ernst and I got in the car to drive to Dublin, stopping at pubs to hear the latest broadcast. A young man in sports clothes said to us: 'Eire of course will stay neutral. But I hope the English knock hell out of Hitler.' Ernst wanted to catch a boat that night but we thought we had time to visit Clonmacnois which lies on the east side of the Shannon. The Shannon in Ireland is a division between two worlds. Once you have crossed it to the east you have left behind the world of second sight, re-entered the world of common or commercial sense. The Shannon itself is unlike the rivers of the mountains. Today it was a broad dull silver band, placid in drizzling rain. The tombs and broken towers of Clonmacnois were grey and placid too. Expecting nothing again.

When Ernst had left I was alone with the catastrophe, spent Saturday drinking in a bar with the Dublin literati; they hardly mentioned the war but debated the correct versions of Dublin street songs. Sunday morning the hotel man woke me (I was sleeping late and sodden), said, 'England has declared war.' Chamberlain's speech on a record was broadcast over and over again during the day. I went to Croke Park in the afternoon to watch the All-Ireland hurling final – Cork in crimson against Kerry in orange and black. Talk of escapism, I thought . . . There was a huge crowd of Gaelic Leaguers, all wearing their *fáine*, one-minded partisans. Hurling is a beautiful game, very fast, both violent and graceful. The ball which is small and brown soars like a bird, is hard to follow with the eye. Towards the end of the game there was a violent thunderstorm. Water poured down the tiers, lapping around our ankles. I put a newspaper over my head and it was pulp within a minute. An old shawlie was still offering bananas for sale; I bought one from her and it also was pulp in my hands.

Next day I drove north; the north was already blacked out. My family were still at Cushendun, Miss Popper[1] was still bathing and doing her exercises, the night was still lathered with stars. I had

---

[1] The Poppers, father and daughter, were Austrian refugees whom Bishop MacNeice had befriended, giving them a home in his house.

never felt so unhappy, and there were no words for it. Just as our capacity for satire had already been outstripped by the lunacies of the dictators, so now this calamity was beyond and below our vocabulary. Only Mr. Popper was cheerful. He had foretold all this months ago—the Russo-German pact, everything; everything was going to plan and the war would be over by Christmas. He was looking forward to Belfast where he hoped to have access to the libraries, to continue his notes on etymology.

I spent the rest of the year alternately in Belfast and Dublin. Belfast, gloomy at all times, was gloomier now, full of patriotic placards and soldiers; at night the tramcars moved slowly along like catafalques, glimmers of spectral blue. My family still had family prayers in the morning but the god of the house was the radio. 'And that is the end of the news.' But it never was. The favourite song both over the air and in the streets, where it was sung by truckloads of soldiers, was 'Run, Rabbit, Run'.

Going to Dublin was changing worlds—a dance of lights in the Liffey, bacon and eggs and Guinness, laughter in the slums and salons, gossip sufficient to the day. Dublin was hardly worried by the war; her old preoccupations were still preoccupations. The intelligentsia continued their parties, their mutual malice was as effervescent as ever. There was still a pot of flowers in front of Matt Talbot's shrine. The potboy priests and the birds of prey were still the dominant caste; the petty bureaucracy continued powerful and petty.

I remember from this Dublin of the Fall a number of hilarities, of happigoluckinesses, of tangents away from reality. One afternoon I went round to Jack Yeats's studio—the tidiest studio possible, a high eighteenth-century room with elaborate mouldings on the cornice. Yes, Jack Yeats said, he found them a great standby; when he had nothing to do he just watched those mouldings, all of them were animate. See there, he said, that is the Pompadour, that is Elizabeth Barrett's little dog, and these are some little men having a walking race. He gave us Malaga and with a deft oldmaidish precision squeezed some drops of orange into each glass. An old lady present, who collected modern French paintings, was talking about her childhood in Ireland—how many carriage-horses they had, how many carriage-horses the neighbours had, how many hunters, etc. 'But now,' she concluded sadly, 'now there are no neighbourhoods.'

Ernie O'Malley was there too, sipping his Malaga quietly. A legendary figure from the Irish Revolution, who had run Michael Collins's intelligence service, who had been riddled with machine-gun bullets, he was now, while still young, living in retirement in Co. Mayo with an American wife and growing his own vegetables. He had a great deal of charm but, unlike most Irish who have charm, was neither flamboyant nor noisy. A Gaelic scholar, he was sceptical about the use of Gaelic. And sceptical about Irish politics. But not embittered; he liked it out there in Mayo; during the summer people kept dropping in and during the winter no one. He and Jack Yeats and I went out into the street together, a great wide Regency street bathed in a warm grey and ending in a mountain vista. An old woman offered us violets. Jack Yeats bought us each a bunch. As we walked away he told us the old woman's history. He knew the history of all the beggars in Dublin.

Keats said that he could subsist for ever writing poems and burning them. There is something of this about Jack Yeats. Far more human than his brother, he has never bothered with publicity, has gone his own way developing a manner of painting which seemed very *outré* to Dublin, slashing the paint on thick but with subtle precision, building up obscure phantasmagorias, combining an impressionist technique with a melodramatic fancy.

Back in the North there was a painter too whom I saw, George MacCann who had done surrealist work but thought most surrealists were phoney. George, like George the electrician in Birmingham, was a man who suited the name—you could not imagine him having any other. He had the rich earthy quality, shot with grains of humour, that every George should have. I used to spend weekends in his cottage in Co. Armagh, drinking whiskey and exchanging our memories of the ludicrous, then sleeping on the floor by a turf fire. George's family had always lived in this district, so he took a clannish pride in its geography; every other hill was a link with some ancestor—several of which ancestors, as George described them, were rogues. George's great virtue, and the one he most admired, was vitality.

In Belfast for Christmas the household was still gloomy. Mr.

Popper, however, was bubbling with his etymological theories. Language, he explained to me, standing in front of the drawing-room fire and making the appropriate gestures, all language began with a kind of onomatopoeia. Now there are certain words which always begin with P. Take the German word '*pochen*'—what the miner does in the mine, what the baby does inside its mother, what . . . My stepmother was unable to hear any of this analysis which became more and more anatomical. But Mr. Popper was not in the least salacious about it; his interest was that of the pure scholar. Like Jack Yeats going on painting and George MacCann reciting stories of drunks and vagrants, Mr. Popper riding his hobby made me feel that perhaps after all the Dark Ages might miss us.

At the New Year I crossed to London, then went on to America. I wanted to see if the fountains were still working and the skater still skating on the lake.

APPENDIX A

Landscapes of Childhood and Youth

(Pages from an unwritten book)

In the beginning was the Irish rain and, marshalled by a pious woman described as a 'mother's help',[1] I pressed my nose against the streaming nursery window for a glimpse of the funeral procession on its way to the cemetery the other side of the hawthorn hedge. Our life was bounded by this hedge; a granite obelisk would look over it here, and there across the field of corncrakes could be seen a Norman castle, and trains would pass as if to the ends of Ireland (in fact ten miles to Belfast or twelve to Larne), but, by and narrow, our damp cramped acre was our world. The human elements of this world need not be detailed: guilt, hell fire, Good Friday, the doctor's cough, hurried lamps in the night, melancholia, mongolism, violent sectarian voices. All this sadness and conflict and attrition and frustration were set in this one acre near the smoky town within sound not only of the tolling bell, but of the smithy that seemed to defy it. The soil in the kitchen garden was black and littered with flints, but in easy digging distance beneath it lay a stratum of thick red clay sticky as plasticine. At times everything outside seemed clammy and everything inside stuffy (I am not denying the moments of glory—of apple blossom, dew, haymaking, or those April showers which in Ireland persist for twelve months), so that from a very early age I began to long for something different, to construct various dream worlds which I took it were on the map.

The first of these dream worlds was 'The West of Ireland', a phrase which still stirs me, if not like a trumpet, like a fiddle half heard through a cattle fair. My parents came from that West or, more precisely, from Connemara, and it was obvious that both of them vastly preferred it to Ulster. The very name Connemara seemed too

[1] 'Miss Craig' in *The Strings are False*.

rich for any ordinary place. It appeared to be a country of windswept open spaces and mountains blazing with whins and seas that were never quiet, with drowned palaces beneath them, and seals and eagles and turf smoke and cottagers who were always laughing and who gave you milk when you asked for a glass of water. And the people's voices were different there, soft and rich like my father's (who made one syllable of 'heron' or 'orange') and not like the pious woman's or the ferocious mill-girls' whom I always expected to pelt us with rotten eggs. All this was hearsay, spindrift, but we had a little visual evidence—two photographs of Achill Island, framed in plush. One of these, as I remember it, showed a conical mountain, plainly Slievemore, which seemed to be all of stones in a landscape all of stones—a refreshing contrast to our own landscape of unkempt hedges, thigh-soaking grass and factory chimneys. Still, it was the plush frames that beatified this vision. But I was not to visit Achill or Connemara until I had left school. So for many years I lived on a nostalgia for somewhere I had never been.

Instead, my first travelling was to Wales to visit an uncle, when I was little more than an infant. I do not remember if this implemented or destroyed any myths;[1] in fact I remember very little of it. Nothing of my uncle's face or of his wife's. Only a great shining vista of well-scrubbed boards, which might have been a pier or a deck, and the ventilator cowls on the steamer, the purpose of which I did not guess but which both delighted and frightened me. And sharing a cabin with my mother and admiring a little red pad on the wall with a hook for her gold watch. And thick buttered toast in the same cabin in the morning. And some gaudy seaside buckets outside a shop on a promenade. And sitting in a train trying to knock an old man's newspaper out of his hands. That is all, and it seems an age before I was again released from our hedged-in acre and our lamplit house where the wicks always needed trimming. Really, I suppose, it was a couple of years later when, vastly more conscious, I suddenly met the Atlantic. We got out of the train at what seemed an inland station. There were flowering currants on the platform—disappointingly familiar because we had them at home—but somebody redeemed this by giving me a bag of dried ginger. Ginger was new to me and, before I had got over the tang and surprise of

[1] See Editor's Preface, p. 14.

it, walking slightly up hill and round a corner I ran head on into a yet tangier surprise, one which is with me still when the open sea catches me unawares. That first time it hit me with everything it had—a sting of salt, a gust of herring, a concert of gulls, a circus of white horses, a dazzle of distance.

The name of this undreamt-of place was Portstewart, a minor seaside resort next door to the better known Portrush; I was taken by the identity of the prefix which seemed to imply a close relationship between them. Place names were pregnant things then. My sister had been born in a poor district of Belfast called Ballymacarrett, a name which I found both comic and savage. Belfast itself sounded hard and unrelenting but this may have been due to its associations. Our own town Carrickfergus was a name to be proud of—we knew that it meant the Rock of Fergus who had been some great man in the dim past—but I disliked its abbreviation Carrick which in the local voice sounded like a slap in the face. And within our parish, radiating from our house, were a number of attractive names. Going up the North Road—our usual walk because all others meant going through the town and the pious woman feared epidemics—we first passed the Busky Burn, a dim little stream full of rusty tins but glorified by its name, then Love's Loney (a dialect improvement on the English Lovers' Lane) and so to Mile Bush where our choices were three: north up the Red Brae (there was nothing red about it but the name seemed to suit its steepness, the carthorses had to take it zigzag), or right along the Sullatober Road, a musical purplish name, or left along the 'Ballymena Road', equally musical though, as we found out later, it went nowhere near Ballymena. Also within walking distance were Bonnybefore, Woodburn, Trooper's Lane and Eden, the last conducive to a split mind, for I always thought of the Garden as I approached it only to find some dour cement houses and a shop labelled Drugs, which sounded wicked. Of the many names which cropped up in the grownups' conversation, pure names because I had never seen the places they were attached to or which had attached themselves to them, I was elated by Magheramorne and Donaghadee, as I was later by the more exotic names in the geography book—Valparaiso, Montenegro, Mississippi, Constantinople, Madagascar, Antananarivo, Copenhagen, Rio de Janeiro, the Zuyder Zee, the Limpopo,

Mesopotamia, and, above all, Yucatan, which my sister and I were to use as a war cry.

We came to Portstewart two years running but the two visits have became one for me. My memories of it range from the sea, which has never grown smaller, through a low cliff, which then seemed huge and vertiginous, to very small things indeed–shells, grains of sand, or tiny blue beads which on wet days my sister strung together in our poky lodgings where I shared a bed with my mother and, because of what someone had said, was afraid she might 'overlay' me. There were also open-topped trams, jellyfish, a porpoise at a fishmonger's, and (this I hated) dead gulls in the fishing nets. But out of it all three visual experiences were the sharpest. First, a golf course beside the river Bann with red flags on the greens and strange red objects (maybe buoys but they seemed too tall) sticking up out of the river; the former I liked but the latter made me uneasy. Second, a road in the evening between high blind walls with long grass blowing on top of them; the road seemed to stretch for ever and we did not feel the wind in it, so were led to imagine on either side of us a forbidden endless prairie ruled by the wind that blew the grasses (I felt like this again at the far end of the Khyber Pass looking over farflung and not-to-be-visited Afghanistan). The fascination of this corridor-like road is something I have met, but with a difference, often since. In the approach to the old gate of New College, Oxford, or between the warehouses in St. Katharine's Way east of the Tower of London, but with such the appeal is more to being closed in (wombful thinking, I suppose), whereas the point of the walls at Portstewart was not the enclosedness but the vast spaces they cut us off from.

The third and greatest experience was also a matter of space and distance, but distance cut on a curve and outlined in white. The Atlantic was already for me the biggest thing this side of God but so far I had only appreciated its size head on, my back to the land and nothing but water in sight. Now I found it even more revealing suddenly to perceive the shore outlining and underlining the ocean till both disappeared simultaneously as one's eyes strained to stretch after them. Magilligan Strand–not that I then knew its name–is one of the longest and smoothest strands in Ireland and at one time was used for motor racing. No one of course had told us where we were going, but we suddenly came round a corner and there it was, unbelievable but palpably there. Once again, as with my first sight of the Atlantic or the unfelt wind beyond the wall, I had the sense of infinite possibility, which implied, I think, a sense of eternity. And once again it met me over a brow and round a corner.[1]

This explains perhaps why I have never steered myself much. An American friend once said to me rebukingly: 'You never seem to make any positive choice; you just let things happen to you.' But the things that happen to one often seem better than the things one chooses. Even in writing poetry, which is something I did early choose to do, the few poems or passages which I find wear well have something of accident about them (the poems I did not intend to write) or, to put it more pretentiously, seem 'given'. So Magilligan Strand was like falling in love. For such occasions the word 'falling' is right; one does not step into love any more than one steps asleep – or awake. For awake, like asleep, is what one falls, and to keep falling awake seems to me the salt of life much more than existentialist defiance. We cannot of course live by Keats's Negative Sensibility alone, we must all, in E. M. Forster's phrase, use 'telegrams and anger'; all the same what I feel makes life worth living is not the clever scores but the surrenders – it may be to the life-quickening urge of an air-raid, to nonsense talked by one's friends, to a girl on top of the Empire State building, to the silence of a ruined Byzantine church, to woods, or weirs, or to heat dancing on a gravelled path, to music, drink or the smell of turf smoke, to the first view of the Atlantic or to the curve of a strand which seems to stretch to nowhere or everywhere and to ages before and after the combustion engine which defiled it.

So home we went with our hair and shoes full of sand, and the first World War came and my mother's death, and I did not travel again till 1917 when I went to a prep school in England. At the beginning of the War, not being sure which side we were on, I had tended to confuse England with Germany (the two names sounded much alike to me), and even now England was beyond my imagination. Transported across the Irish Sea and seated in an English train, a very strange train which had a corridor (my sister had told

[1] Cf. 'Round the Corner' (*The Burning Perch*, p. 13).

me of these; 'good for running races', she said), I kept saying to myself 'This is England' but I did not really believe it and, as it was night, could not see those differences which stamp a thing as real. But, though full of disbelief, I was vastly excited, and when daylight came I perceived that England was not just an imitation of Ireland; the fields and hedges and houses were different, and as for London when we got there . . . it was not Belfast, it was foreign. And foreign it has remained to me.

Euston, Waterloo, then Dorset. County Down had been different from Co. Antrim, the drumlins of the former seeming to me highly exotic and it being also the county where I had eaten a turkey's egg in a farm near my mother's grave, but Dorset was most unlike either. Woods, yellow stone houses, and fossils for the picking. I was not used to buildings with style nor to such a variety of landscape, though I missed the Irish light for the lack of which my father condemned all English landscape as 'stodgy'. I came to Sherborne with no preconceptions about it, but before my four years there were up I was reading into this country of the Dorset-Somerset border a wealth of legend, mainly drawn from Malory. From a point within walking distance we could see Glastonbury Tor which someone, possibly our headmaster Littleton Powys, told us was the site of Camelot. So I organised some of the boys into Knights of the Round Table, I myself being Sir Gawaine (we tactfully had no King Arthur), and we roamed the country with lances, once luckily finding a cave. This make-believe, which we might have been thought too old for, did, I think, enhance my feeling for the Arthurian legends. After all, nearly everyone who reads *Hamlet* is playing Hamlet in his head. But Hamlet is for adolescents (which we all to some extent remain) whereas Arthur's knights have few values or problems too old for a prep school. And their battles and joustings have the fascination of cricket averages, while the country they move through is, like Spenser's, so indeterminate or never-never that it can easily be superimposed even on the parklands and quarries and pinewoods of Dorset. This transposition was helped by the placards saying 'Trespassers Will Be Prosecuted'.

At Sherborne, though I had felt this already in Ireland crawling in our garden under the hairy potato plants or sinking up to my calves in the strange blue clay on the shore at Bonnybefore or stung in the face by sand or soothened by the soft rain, I realised that a country is not just there for the seeing but there too for the sense of touch. The seasonal differences were far more marked in Dorset than in Ireland, and here I met my first hot summer and my first big snow. But even on more neutral days Dorset impinged on me through the local yellow stone over which I ran my hands and the earth from which we scooped fossils and the hedges which stabbed us while we looked for caterpillars and the pines which whipped us while we climbed them for woodpigeons' eggs. Our headmaster's religion was natural history and he strode through the country like a walking belfry. Ding! a something-or-other fritillary. Dong! a this or that orchis. But I was lazy about learning the names of butterflies and wild flowers; I preferred to run my fingers along the bristles of a 'Woolly Bear' or around the smooth whorls of an ammonite. And one day we were caught in a deluge and our Eton collars turned to a clammy pulp, uncomfortable yet elating; I felt that the rain had not only put paid to my detested collar but was saturating both my body and my soul, thereby letting me into that miraculous circuit of water which we had learnt about in the geography class.

Sometimes from Sherborne I returned home via Dublin. Dublin was a glorious name in our family and had pleasurable associations of violence, but my first memory of it seems to consist of three things—the outside of a Vegetarian Café, now understandably vanished, the taste of some very black, very salt chocolate, and some little black bog-oak pigs in a window of knick-knacks. Whether I was impressed by the spaciousness of the streets, the generous grace of Stephen's Green or the vistas ending in the mountains of Wicklow, I now could not possibly say. Today I am so at home in Dublin, more than in any other city, that I feel it has always been familiar to me. But, as with Belfast it took me years to penetrate its outer ugliness and dourness, so with Dublin it took me years to see through its soft charm to its bitter prickly kernel—which I quite like too. At school of course I had begun by playing the Wild Irish Boy, although handicapped by the lack of the usual W.I.B. boasting matter; I could not ride a horse, I had never poached salmon, my background was pathetically suburban. But a boy at my prep school who lived in Dublin claimed to have been shot at by Countess

Markiewicz, and I once travelled home in company with her daughters; at least I thought they were her daughters, at any rate they smoked. My father was one of the very few Church of Ireland clergymen to be a Home Ruler. This was another reason for despising Co. Antrim and regarding myself as a displaced person. Sometimes this feeling caused an inner conflict in me. Shortly after World War I, I was sent from Belfast to Dublin in the charge of a dear old gentleman who was pestered on the way by a drunken American soldier, fresh from the Front and full of hatred for kings; they were all, he said, including King George, Germans. The dear old gentleman, being a loyal Orangeman, was outraged, so the American appealed to me and I, as an Irish nationalist, sided with him. 'This little boy,' said the American, 'has more sense than you.' I felt guilty. But at Amiens Street station I envied the American as he walked into the bar full of glittering bottles.

About this time I decided to be a missionary when I grew up. Our house was full of missionary literature and it seemed the simplest way to visit foreign parts. Especially Darkest Africa (I was fond of Rider Haggard and of a book by Ballantyne about a whole shipwrecked family who trekked across Africa on foot and *en route* shot all the wild animals) and India, which had tigers and turbans. South America I was not so keen on nor yet Ungava, though we had periodic visits from a native of our town, the son of a fisherman, who was a missionary to the Eskimos and blinked all the time from snow blindness. As for the Muslim countries, I ruled them out after looking through a book of my father's called *Islam*; I had no interest in being a missionary to people who did not have idols. Idols and big game and exotic costume were then my chief requirements in a foreign country. I cannot remember, while at my prep school, having any wish to visit the Continent. We had one boy at the school who had been brought up in Belgium and we thought him a fool.

From Sherborne I went to Marlborough, another entirely new landscape (there are no chalk downs in Ireland). I was disappointed in the fossils, if that is the right name for the flint rind of what was once a sponge but now is powder. But the slow line of the North Wiltshire downs, with occasional copses sitting plump on the skyline like hippopotami, gave me once more the winged Mercury feeling, while on the other side Savernake Forest countered that austerity with its beeches and deers' rumps and bracken. Both downs and forest then gave me aesthetic satisfaction, but both were also the scene of compulsory runs (sweats they were called). We ran against the clock and, to start with, this was torture; I loathed the conveyor belt of trees which I had to force behind me through my own leg power and lung power, and the ever-receding grey brow of the downs with their aristocratic indifference to our rainsoaked wasplike jerseys. But after a year or two of this lungs and legs became free and in pounding over the elastic turf one felt attuned to this country, of its earth earthy but also free of its air. And the more wind the better, I thought, as I had thought when a small child in Ireland, holding my mouth open, trying to drink it. Physical discomfort, it dawned on me, my hair one river of sweat, could be a bond between myself and my context. Or rather could help to make me a context. Dry throat and aching legs and bursting chest, such things made me feel I belonged to the landscape. And before I left Marlborough my friends and I used to get permission to go midnight runs for pleasure. But on these we had time to stop and lie on the curving earth and feel it revolve under the stars.

During these five years of my 'teens my family took their summer holidays in September, which made my transitions from summer to winter uncomfortably abrupt: I would leave my sister bathing or playing tennis in Anglesey or Perthshire or Donegal and find myself next day in the shadow of the goalposts. So I set out for such holidays feeling I was on bail (as I now feel on nearly all holidays). Going to a church service in Welsh where a woman in the pew behind was suckling her child, I would feel 'Any day now I shall be back in that neo-Gothic chapel with its languid frescoes where none of the wives of the beaks would dream of suckling a child and the service is all in dull English.' I was still—or pretended to be—anti-English, a feeling which in a few years' time was to be intensified when I fell into Marlborough's equivalent of Bloomsbury.

My next holiday after Anglesey was in Perthshire around my fifteenth birthday, for which I received a pocket Kodak; with this I spent hours trying to achieve as romantic a view of Highland cattle as one we had in a large engraving at home. Highland cattle were right up my glen at that time—along with bagpipes and ruined castles and spinning-wheels and mountain rivers and loneliness. One day I climbed alone a small mountain which turned out not so small. From the top I tried to draw Loch Tay in my pocket book and then, realising it was late, bounded down the mountain, slithering, tumbling, all scratches and bruises, only to find my family were out, visiting the Burial Place of the Clan MacNab. As a result I never got into this burial place and felt cheated, for the Clan MacNab were also up my glen. Was their name not rather like my own (all my life I have been addressed as MacNeill, MacNish, etc.) and were we not born allies against the barbarian English? To set the seal on this holiday I rescued–or thought I rescued–my sister from drowning, though I was not so pleased when my stepmother that night attributed this achievement to the goodness of God who had taught me to swim so well (not that I did swim well or do). Anyhow, God or no God, it had been a dangerous episode, and danger now became one of the objects of travel, though my father and stepmother both tried to nip its red flowers in the bud.

A year or two later we were all nearly drowned and I enjoyed this thoroughly, which I should not do now. We had been for the day to Rathlin Island off the north coast of Co. Antrim and had eaten boiled eggs with dirty eggspoons which called forth complaints from my father, who thereby, I felt, lost face. Rathlin, where Bruce had watched the spider, was cut off from the mainland by a notorious sea and its people were entitled to be primitive; I felt that my father's dog collar was strangling more than his neck, so it was partly pique that made me pleased when, a gale having suddenly sprung up, the boatmen refused to take us back to Ballycastle. My father, however, in spite of his fears for his family, could not face a night with dirty spoons and eventually bribed a boat to risk it.

The crossing took a very long time and was like the Giant Dipper. We had hardly put out from Rathlin when the great cliff of Fair Head disappeared under the sea. And a good thing too, I thought, but we climbed our own cliff of water and there was Fair Head again, riding a briny chaos and preparing another disappearance act. And so it went on; a wave would carry us up till we seemed higher than the cliff and then we went down in the lift, feeling like Pharaoh before the waters engulfed him. My father and stepmother were both looking like Pharaoh, which added to my exhilaration, as the salt water poured down my neck and I hummed to myself, inaudible in the storm, 'A policeman's life is not a happy one'. But, thinking it over afterwards, I exonerated my father; he must only have been worrying about us, for had he not told us how in the 'West' (to which Rathlin after all could be no more than a poor approximation) he had often pulled his oar in a curragh, commenting that that was the sort of oar for a man, not the little flimsy paddles they used in the North? Later I was to see him in Achill Sound, in his shirt sleeves and without his unheroic collar, bending over one of those great oars against a roaring current, while my stepmother gazed from the shore, half frightened and half ashamed for him.

It was in Ballycastle – but I think on a later visit – that I learned to play golf. To me there was nothing incompatible between this most bourgeois of games and my romantic feelings for the desolate, the primitive, the antiquated. I enjoyed driving; from the start, once in half a dozen attempts I could drive two hundred yards which made me feel like a bird, for I did not just follow the flight of the ball but felt myself soar inside it. I also loved using a mashie – the higher the shot the better – but could never control it, so I often went over the green. The greens themselves bored me; I would have liked to delegate the putting to someone else. And highgrade professional golf, which I have never watched, must, I imagine, be boring all the way. Select the right club and hit the ball correctly and you're there? Not on my life. I liked forcing.

In a later September (for my seventeenth birthday) we went to Donegal, my first holiday in the 'South' though it contains the most northerly cape in Ireland. We should have gone south earlier had it not been for the Troubles; my father, in spite of his nationalism, had said, 'How can you mix with people who might be murderers without you knowing it?' And sure enough, on almost our first drive through the mountains, a little man rose up from a ditch and threw a heavy sack through the glass window of the car. The sack turned out to contain boots and the little man to be the local drunk, but this confirmed both my father and my stepmother in their forebodings and once more, in my eyes, they lost face. I was only afraid they might curtail our holiday – the Donegal mountains were fulfilling my ancient hankering – and I resented their disparagement of southern 'lawlessness'. I knew very well that the little man was not a criminal and, though I had never yet had an alcoholic drink, I already suspected that my father's teetotalism was cutting him off from people. As a small child in my home town, walking as the night fell with the pious woman through a slum street called Irish Quarter West, I used to pass a pub with an opaque but gaily lit window which gave forth laughter and a strange rich smell; it attracted me like the house across the street in Hans Andersen's story 'The Shadow'.

But during the next weeks in Donegal my father redeemed himself. Not only did he seem to know half the population by name but he cheerfully greeted the other half, confidently waving his walking-stick, and the other half replied 'Good day, Father.' I was pleased that he did not repudiate the 'Father', though I did not know then that both sides of my family had not so long ago been Catholics.[1] The only Catholic I had known well up till then had been a cook of ours called Annie who was very much warmer and gayer than the pious woman and who knew tricks and riddles and legends and had made a crochet cover of shamrocks and wheels for the altar in her chapel. This 'altar' added to her glamour; we had only a communion table.

It was in Donegal that my travelling got seriously mixed up with my reading. Coming in from the wet heather and wallowing in the turf smoke I read and reread Yeats's 'Land of Heart's Desire' and also some of his early lyrics. 'The wind blows out of the gates of the day' seemed to me just what the wind did in these parts, and 'the lonely of heart', of course, seemed to me just what *I* was. I am sorry to say that at the same time I read and reread a long sentimental fairy-storyish poem by Alfred Noyes, which, apart from its sentimentality, could not have been more out of key with the bogs and rocks around me. Since then I have found that even some authors whom I greatly admire are unreadable in certain countries. I took Dante to India but he did not wear there, and in most parts of Ireland Tennyson is out of the question. On the other hand in Iceland I read the whole of *The Mill on the Floss*, but that was perhaps because Iceland did not really get under my skin. I cannot understand now how after sitting for hours on a rock in Sheephaven with yellow pancakes of foam flying round my head like a

[1] This is true only of the family of Louis's mother. (E.N.)

merman's custard-pie fantasy I could go back to the farmhouse and stomach Mr. Noyes's butterflies and Little Boy Blues.

The next year I accompanied my father and stepmother on a tour of Scotland in an Austin saloon. This I found boring and exasperating; under the influence of Anthony Blunt, who ran at Marlborough something called the Anonymous Society, I had just discovered Van Gogh and was in no mood for either the Lowlands or the Highlands. I was annoyed when my father compared his own countrymen unfavourably with the hardworking, well-informed, clean and thrifty Scots, and I felt like screaming when my stepmother pointed out the beauties of the scenery. Sitting beside the chauffeur I slept through much of this scenery and was asleep when on our return journey we arrived in the centre of Edinburgh. In Edinburgh I bought a copy of Plato's *Phaedo* and turned a blind eye on the Scots. Within a year, my first year in the Classical Upper Sixth under G. M. Sargeaunt, I had become reorientated. Sargeaunt, who was Graeco-Roman rather than Christian, a somewhat languid *arbiter elegantiarum*, had instilled into many of his pupils, without appearing ever to press, a code of aesthetic values which excluded bagpipes, Kipling, and most forms of gush and art-as-the-bird-sings; we also tended to imitate his drawling delivery and the slow grace of his movements. At the same time Blunt was lending me art books which made me think that all art came from the Continent; he lent me also three small coloured prints for my study, to the disgust of the boy with whom I shared it—a Duccio, a Patinir, and an El Greco. So the Scottish heather now stank in my nostrils; I wanted a landscape as in my Patinir or as in the Italian painters or the French Impressionists. My great discovery in Edinburgh was an original Gauguin; Edinburgh itself passed me by, remained to be discovered later when the Devil's Advocate revived in me.[1]

For I did not yet pay much attention to the people in the places I visited. Blunt gave out that things were more interesting than persons, and anyhow, after years of isolation in the Carrickfergus Rectory, I was shy with strangers even when they interested me; besides, I felt the presence of my family an obstacle to communion with others. In Donegal I assumed that all the natives, being more to the West, were superior to those of Co. Antrim—

[1] See above, pp. 152f.

more warmth, more charm, more humour—but usually I noticed only rare individuals. A centenarian woman in Donegal who had gone too small even for her smallest of cottages and who offered us snuff with an age-old quaking courtesy. And a petite blonde film star in jodhpurs (worn, I think, only for the picture she was making) who aroused a pre-puberty lust in me in Perthshire. And, going further back, the Welshwoman suckling her child. At school it was only individuals whom I liked; and in strange places, from now and for several years to come, I was not really wanting to know, say, the Scots or the French but only to meet a few persons, or preferably just one person, who might fulfil some of my romantic wants. Yet all the time the others were waiting to be known, not nomads like the film star nor freaks like the centenarian but more typical members of their own special societies—the diffident gentle Americans one meets in America, the hearty yet formal Norwegians who suddenly switch to neurosis and embarrassing self-revelation, the Indians whose poise and rhythm make nonsense of Mayfair and Long Island, or the shepherds of Crete who are Homer's heroes come to life again, as quick on the draw, as self-contained, as generous.

I had not yet crossed the English Channel, for which I was laughed at at school, but during my last year there I looked more and more south in imagination. Just after my seventeenth birthday I had read a long paper to the Anonymous Society on Norse mythology and had thought that Iceland and Norway would be wonderful countries to visit; such wishes had now become philistine (though here again the Devil's Advocate was only sleeping). Neither Sargeaunt nor Blunt had much use for the battle-axe, and my reading predisposed me to the Latin countries—with one exception, Russia. Russia seemed a quite different but even more powerful antidote to a world that I now was describing as parochial. This Russia, of course, was not the never-never land of the Soviets but the never-never land of Dostoievsky as imagined by a boy who had no experience of poverty or violence. In Russia enthusiasm was allowable and Sargeaunt's writ did not run. But elsewhere in my dream travels Sargeaunt and Blunt were at my elbow, also Anatole France, Aldous Huxley and Sacheverell Sitwell (whose *Southern Baroque Art* was one of our bibles, the word 'baroque' itself becoming almost a synonym for 'excellent'). Of the Mediterranean countries

Greece, on paper, came first. But only on paper; I was tired of being told how the Ancient Greeks were so well ordered, so rational, so immune to the vulgar craze for size, while secretly I thought that their architecture—which of course I knew only from photographs—suffered from the lack of arches. What I really wanted was the Mediterranean proper—or improper—where people lay about all day under magnolia trees or something, drinking Lacrima Christi and Calabrian wines, being witty at the world's expense and waiting for a night of love. I was then still a virgin and had not drunk wine, but by the time I left school in the summer of 1926 I had decided, or at any rate pretended, that Oxford, where I was going, was not worth going to.

I had visited it for the first time in December 1925 to sit for a scholarship: this unknown to my father who was still toying with the idea of sending me to some serious university like Glasgow; Trinity College, Dublin, where he had been himself, was ruled out, I assumed, because of the doings in that city. The glamour of Oxford had been dinned into me—no, that is the wrong word, sprinkled over me with a scent spray—since my time at prep school where the headmaster's brother, Llewellyn Powys, had come and lectured us on Oxford's distinctive atmosphere, something, it seemed, which gave you a pleasant disease from which you never recovered. At Marlborough we had rumours of its decadent goings-on (this was the era described by Evelyn Waugh in his novels) which, though in themselves attractive, seemed unduly to depend on money which I knew I should not have much of; this perhaps was the real reason why I said I didn't care if I got a scholarship or not. We were all very clothes-conscious at that time, and I came up for the examination in my first tailormade suit (it had cost less than £6), having up to then failed to convince my parents that readymade clothes were a stigma—though even here I tried to have it both ways, explaining in a long letter to my stepmother that while clothes made to measure were necessary to my career I really saw through such affectations. Anyhow, arriving in Oxford, I was probably as much concerned with my own appearance as with Oxford's, just as my packet of ten Gold Flakes, brassily blazing in my pocket, meant as much to me as the colours of Oxford stone, honey or oatcake or burnt toast.

All the same, though against what I thought my will, Oxford at first sight—and also at first hearing (innumerable bells and clocks and the clatter of pewter dishcovers) and also at first smell (frowsty College bedrooms, dregs of beer, a lavatory with the inscription Πάντα ῥεῖ, οὐδὲν μένει)—struck me (no, that is the wrong word, stroked me) as something unique which I yet, at the back of my eyes, had foreseen. The examination took place in Christ Church Hall, and as I was staying in Merton my morning trek to a table too near a gargantuan fire ran me the gauntlet of much decay and felicity. Leaving Fellows' Quad in Merton where, as I think I already knew, Charles the First's Queen had stayed during the Civil War, I passed along Merton Street under its mellow tower (which I still prefer, as being more solid, to Magdalen's), and so, after a glimpse of Corpus's pelican, came head on to Wyatt's great Doric gateway, black and flaking and hoary and leading to more hoariness beyond; Peckwater quadrangle had not yet been refaced. From Peck I swung round the corner into Tom Quad, which on the first morning astonished me by its sheer spaciousness, spreading like the belly and corruption of its founder, Cardinal Wolsey. Next came the fan-vaulted staircase round the single column soaring, soaring, till we found ourselves in the enormous hall, cluttered with little tables which creaked under anxious elbows. Here, roasting by the fire which all the same I admired for its old-fashioned extravagance, I drew on my store of examination tricks and admitted to myself half guiltily, 'I should really rather like to come up here.'

The life I expected for myself at this time was a Pateresque affair of hard gemlike flames, a sequence of purely aesthetic sensations, except of course for the erotic ones. But adolescence is self-contradictory, and I was hurt when Blunt denounced politics as beneath the attention of a civilised person. Most politics, yes, but not Irish politics. If I had one foot poised over untrodden asphodel, the other was still clamped to the ankle in the bogs. Thinking myself back to eighteen and looking still further back from there, I can see these places I have mentioned whizzing past like telegraph posts seen from a train; and, oddly enough, the earlier ones seem more real. Magilligan Strand had been unexpected and so had been the ventilator cowls, but once one starts expecting things one's own self-consciousness intervenes and perverts.

Oxford gave me the freedom not of the Middle Ages but of the Eighteenth Century or of the Regency. Austerity had not yet reared its ugly face, and to have two rooms of one's own and breakfast and luncheon served in them and a toppling coal fire and no sense of time seemed to me, after Marlborough, a delectable reprieve from the elbowing and shoving, the nagging and dragooning, the compulsory this and that, which so far had constituted life for me. The staircase system of the colleges is conducive to individualism, with your own name over the door, your own oak to make your rooms impregnable, and, above all, your own scout. My scout had never compromised with the twentieth century. He was a tiny man designed by George Cruickshank, with a long ratlike moustache, a perky yet portentous manner, and a greasy bowler hat which he kept in the sink on the staircase. He was full of aphorisms, 'Brains runs in a family like wooden legs, sir'; of snobbery, 'The old Warden, now, he was a gentleman, I remember him riding his horse into the porter's lodge' or 'I could always tell when Lord Birkenhead had been drunk because then he would hang his trousers over a certain picture'; and of a certain romanticism—he had seen the moon under an arch at Tintern Abbey. When he was reproaching me, for my taste in pictures or for not entertaining enough, he would edge to the door for his curtain line and then slam it behind him. Period.

Oxford in October 1926 was entering a transitional phase. The master decadents had just gone down and their acolytes were soon to follow them. One still heard the word 'Aesthete!' venomously hissed in the streets, but W. H. Auden was already in his rooms in Peck, dressed like an untidy bank clerk and reading in a self-imposed blackout all sorts of technical unaesthetic matter or flapping his hands while he denounced the wearing of bright colours or the cultivation of flowers. All the same, the first Oxford party I was taken to, by a heavily powdered Old Marlburian, seemed as happily unaware of the General Strike just past as of the Slump soon to come. There was nothing to drink but champagne—and nothing but tumblers to drink it from—and all through the evening one pretty young man sat in the same armchair talking to no one except a stuffed spotted dog which he joggled up and down on its lead. This, I thought, was the life, but it was my first and last party of that kind. There were other such parties for a year or two, but I had not the money for those circles and I was not, and could not pretend to be, homosexual.

I withdrew to a group of less fashionable intellectuals, including two unpowdered Old Marlburians, Graham and John.[1] Graham had a hankering for the smart world, but he too was not rich; also he was industrious. He had small rooms in the roof in Lincoln, with a cuckoo clock and blue beer glasses, where we would read John Donne's sermons to each other, relishing words like 'vermiculation'. Our first summer term we shared a hired canoe and, partly because of *The Waste Land*, spent whole afternoons or even mornings paddling beneath the gas works, a fine place, we decided, for reading Webster. This obsession with *The Waste Land* and Webster, which we shared with many of our contemporaries, was not, I think, merely due to a wish to be 'modern', though that certainly was something we did wish. I honestly believe that, though we were fresh from school, we had absorbed that sense of futility, of belonging to a society without values, which the ebbing of World War I had left behind it.[2]

Thus both Graham and I used the word 'middle-class' as a term of condemnation, though or perhaps because we knew we belonged to that class ourselves. In the same way the word 'moral' became derogatory, while as for religion—and here we would raise our voices if there was a clergyman in hearing—everyone knew that all religion was nonsense. Even as I would say this, I would feel rather hypocritical, for, greatly though he now exasperated me, I would remember how my father would come in to breakfast on Easter Day beaming as though he had just received a legacy; and I realised that his life, though not by any stretch of imagination a life for me, was more all of a piece, more purposeful, more satisfactory to himself and perhaps to others than the lives of most people I knew. But Graham and I went back to Donne's sermons, pretending they had nothing to do with religion; it was just all style—and death. When Graham's mother died, unexpectedly under an anaesthetic, he went round for weeks murmuring a Latin line from Skelton, 'Et ecce nunc in pulvere dormio.' Which certainly was not affectation.

Religion, then, being ruled out, along with morals and politics—

[1] Graham Shepard and John Hilton.   [2] Text uncertain.

and indeed with scholarship, value, not fact, being what mattered and value meaning mainly aesthetic value—what we really hoped for was 'experience'. Pater once more, but backed up by Roger Fry. Even before leaving Marlborough we had swallowed Significant Form and were strenuously trying to dissociate paintings from their representational content. (Blunt had set up an easel in the bathing place to paint a corrugated-iron shed for its abstract virtue's sake but had been turned out by the bathing master, a zoologist, who thought he was going to slip in some nudes.) Cézanne, of course, was the touchstone. I had seen one exhibition of original Cézannes, where I found a satisfaction which I had precalculated. This, though probably largely wishful seeing, was still, I believe, an illuminating experience; there was something about Cézanne, I thought (and I still think so), which fills you like a steak and kidney pudding—only you've got to be hungry. But I no longer think that his 'subjects' do not count; whatever his own theories, his card-players to me remain people and his apples the essence of appledom. I feel the same about Chardin's dull brown loaves. We may have asked him for an abstract, but by God he gives us bread. Still, at that time we wanted to be purists, at least with Cézanne and the painters after him; with some earlier works of art our reactions were adulterated by history or xenophily. 'Baroque' was still a magic word, though all we could find in Oxford was the porch of St. Mary's with its barley-sugar pillars (a good chance here for the mystique of the Spiral) and the 'scandalous image' above it which had so outraged Cromwell's puritans. Perhaps the chief reason why we praised the baroque was that it was so scarce in England.

For the foreign was calling strongly. I sat in my canoe and watched a goods train lumbering over the railway bridge and marked the names on the vans to insert in a disillusioned sketch: 'Hickleton –Lunt–Hickleton–Lunt–Hickleton–Longbottom–the placid dotage of a great industrial country.' For I did not want placidity, or dotage, or industry; I wanted certain new worlds which really meant old worlds, the Mexico of D. H. Lawrence or the Capri of Norman Douglas. Having just read Virginia Woolf, whose impressionism seemed more sympathetic than Pater's hard gemlike flames, I would spend hours dawdling in 'Mesopotamia' devising phrases for the skeining of water in the little weirs and waterfalls. But though there was obviously enough and to spare of sensuous delight in England (Mrs. Woolf's own writings were very English), I felt that cross-Channel impressions would be even more vivid – apart from having greater snob value. Travel! Travel must be 'experience' at its highest.

But I had to contend with my very untravelled family: my father had never been out of the British Isles, while it was many a year since my stepmother had painted watercolours of the Pyramids, and neither of them thought the Continent was suitable for people under twenty; my father also thought the French a disgusting race because they used toothpicks. It was only after I had written several letters of pompous and dishonest argument that I obtained the money from them to pay for my first visit to France. I crossed the Channel with John – it was his first visit too – about the end of June 1927. We stayed in the Rue Vavin, in a cheap hotel recommended by Blunt, who, though he was at Cambridge, was still in some ways our oracle. This hotel pleased us both greatly, because it was in Montparnasse (one of the names to juggle with – six French novels in the air and a life-sized nude out of a hat), so that from our bedroom every night we could hear the racket of the Dôme which we did not know had had its day.

John was a very silent young man and uncomfortably full of common sense, but I had admitted him as also among the prophets because he could write nonsense verses and even paint a still-life; also he was a good listener and would mop up when people had been sick. I do not know if he expected all the same things from Paris that I did: we both wanted to look at paintings – we had been commissioned by a friend at Oxford to buy for him any 'modern painting' we might choose that did not cost more than £30, which we found to our surprise a very limiting figure – and we both wanted to taste French food and drink French wine and smell French smells (we spent an hour one day trying to analyse the 'typical' smell of Paris); but I, at least, also wanted adventures with people, preferably strange people such as women. Because of this I was very reluctant to move out of the cafés where I was always hoping that, in spite of our lack of French, we should get into conversation with some of the young men with drawing books or some of the girls with blue make-up; but our contact with the latter was nil, and our only contact with the former was when John noticed one of them drawing me, which flattered me but was not enough. Still, I did have one petty and naïve adventure when in the small hours sitting by my little pile of saucers representing a string of benedictines, and John having gone away to sleep on a bench, I was picked up by a fat old man in a broad-brimmed black hat; it was the hat that got me, I assumed he must be a painter or a poet. Sure enough he said he was a poet and I said '*Moi aussi*' and he asked me home to stay with him. I did not guess what this implied, so I went along with him willingly, thinking 'This is the beginning; the next thing I know he will introduce me to Picasso.' But the next thing I knew I was in a very bleak apartment with cane furniture and hardly a book or a picture and the old man was making fat-fingered ogling overtures. So I had to run away, feeling both alarmed and disappointed.

John, probably because of this episode, was beginning to get irritated both with the cafés and with my company—when I described a bridge over the Seine as 'significant', he said 'Significant of what?' —so we packed up our rucksacks and went to Fontainebleau. I had every intention, under the influence of such writers as the Sitwells, of reacting voluptuously to Fontainebleau; but my knowledge of the French kings was very deficient and my knowledge of furniture more so, and all I can remember now is a vague impression of gracious proportions and a lizard flickering on a wall. From Fontainebleau we set out to walk by night to Chartres, and enjoyed being frightened by an unseen Baskerville dog who paced us and bayed us through the forest on the far side of a fence. When the dog and the forest dropped out we got bored and tired and, abandoning the pretence of being Francophil, I talked to John about Ibsen whom he had not read; but when I tried to recount Ibsen's plots I found I had forgotten half the links. So by dawn we were both silent and, seeing an enticing heap of straw or hay by the roadside, lay down on it to sleep; when the hot sun woke us, we had been so bitten by insects that our bodies seemed covered with small molehills. But this discomfort, like the hail on the Marlborough Downs, appeared to revive my zest for the country through which we were passing. It may have been this same day that I got my strongest physical impression of Northern France: we were resting in a stubbly field much larger than the fields of England (let alone Ireland's green handkerchiefs), and the sun was vertical and the landscape flat and innumerable poppies made the heat seem hotter, as did the flapping straw hats of some passing peasants, and as did the chorus of insects, and as did the rumbling of a train which we could not see but which sounded as if it meant business—a business not ours, carrying unknown and unknowable Frenchmen through an endless plain where the insects would always murmur and the weather would never turn bad. This was far from being my sort of country and for this, at that moment, I liked it. I had come up against a landscape on which I could not impose myself.

The cathedral of Chartres, to me, was a nice breath of life—or was it death?—after Fontainebleau. I don't think I yet knew the phrase 'death-wish'; but that stone should run away from the earth where it belonged, to lose itself not in heaven but in its own inner darkness, stirred something in my own unquarried depths, something which if not a 'death-wish' was at least a wish to escape—the same desire to escape which, outside on the west front, had elongated and emaciated the saints. But a little later, at Versailles, I found the antidote to this, which I had failed to find at Fontainebleau. For Le Roi Soleil was at least something more than a name to me, and both the Galerie des Glaces and the formal gardens filled out a myth which had begun perhaps in Perrault and had been continued by works like *The Rape of the Lock*:

> Oh if to dance all night, and dress all day,
> Charm'd the small-pox, or chas'd old age away;
> Who would not scorn what housewife's cares produce,
> Or who would learn one earthly thing of use?

The word 'worldly' is always used pejoratively—which proves what hypocrites we are. For most of our best moments—though not all, and perhaps not the very best—are worldly, and we nearly all have the dream, found at its lowest in Hollywood success stories, of waking up millionaires as able to lay out gardens or orangeries as to make cat's cradles of string. On this visit to Versailles, when the signal was given for Closing Time, I loitered till the gates were locked on me. This annoyed a gendarme but set the seal on a fantasy; being the last man out I had, if only for ten minutes, taken the whole place over.

So back to Paris and yet more piles of priced saucers. Drinking in the street has always appealed to me since then, and this is the memory of that first short visit which links most closely with my present. French drink and French food had more than lived up to expectations, while I had smoked so many Gauloises that the smell hung round me for weeks; only the men and women had failed me, but then the French of both sexes had been badly miscast in my mind: we had been so conditioned to think of the French as exceptionally civilised and charming that we thought their civilisation and charm were something they would shower on strangers, even on callow ones like John and me. On our last evening in Paris, having paid our hotel bill and with hardly any money left, we missed our train, which pleased me: if a train is worth catching, I felt–which means that it's bound for one's proper destination–then just because of that destination it's also well worth missing. But our few francs only took us a drink or two into the night, and after one exciting glimpse of a row which involved some tarts and a negro we walked until we were footsore, then lay down and slept on a bench almost under the Eiffel Tower. We were woken roughly by two gendarmes, behind whom stood a little Indo-Chinese soldier with a rifle (you could hardly see him for the bandoliers); they asked me for my papers, and being half asleep I gave them a bookseller's bill. When they got angrier I gave them my passport, but they would not believe it and insisted that I was Spanish and John German. At last they let us go with a sour reprimand; in that morning's papers we read that two very young Spanish anarchists had just broken gaol in Paris. With this typically trivial bit of farce our great initiation ended.

APPENDIX B

Louis MacNeice at Marlborough and Oxford
by John Hilton

After trying to write down my memories of Louis I found most of the letters I had written to my parents from the time I–and Louis–went to Marlborough in September 1921 until I left Oxford in the summer of 1929. Apart from correcting one or two dates and cutting out some duplication I have left the statements from memory unaltered; and added excerpts from the letters at the end of the school and university sections. Contradictions of fact and discrepancies of evaluation have something of a stereoscopic effect; and he would not wish to be portrayed too tidily. As to further inconsistencies with his own autobiographic writings I can claim little more than to have been sometimes more accurate on trivial matters of fact which were apt to be transmuted by Louis's mythopoeic alembics. A person is more than a line in space-time. And how on earth do memories of a person–which, more than what he said and did, are changing expressions, half-conscious gestures, ranges of tone, exclamations, expressive silences–get turned into words?

The theme of this note, if it has a theme, might be called 'The POLDERGEIST and its exorcism'.

I once asked Louis whether he realised that, if the current beliefs of physicists and astronomers were true, then any movement of a finger or eyelid had repercussions throughout the stellar universe. This seemed to be a new thought to him and he gave it such attention as it deserved. It occurs to me now that it is as good an image as any of one of the great pleasures of being in his company. Before addressing him one had–or I usually felt I had–to choose with some caution a moment when he was not absorbed in some inner dialectic of his own; but if the timing were right one had the

239

sensation that any remark one dared to make would be weighed in the finest assay and, if not rejected as dross, would be taken into a whole universe of thought and sense without any barriers to whatever reverberations it was capable of setting up. His mind and sensorium formed a sounding board, an echo chamber, a court in constant session, a living touchstone, a presence, a force in being. As on a dark clear night, there was a sense of depth without bounds and communication without muffling, or 'noise' in the communication engineer's use of the word.

And at the heart of darkness a glow like Christmas. For the opposite pole of his attraction—which had me mesmerised, entranced and largely enslaved—was something like a non-stop variety show. The glow would bloom and broaden and show itself to have been the simmering lull of a volcanic spout of flying flares, explosive bombards, growlings, roarings, incandescent missiles, black-encrusted rosy lava, steam, smoke and ash; candle grease, barley sugar and coloured witchballs. There was a highly conscious showman in control of all this and, when the main fires had sunk beneath their vents and the air was only lightly traced with sparks and wisps and mutterings, however concentrated his meditation there was no curtain between him and the outside world whether as spectacle or audience; one's behaviour was still under scrutiny and one's attention somehow demanded.

In his later years—when I only saw him intermittently—his sympathies broadened and he became more concerned with the *vita activa* and the *res publica*. In the three years 1926-9 when I saw him constantly he was concerned largely with his own forces—and the aspects of the outer world that got reflected in or swept along with and transmogrified by their currents. He had little use for the vast majority of mankind or its interests and activities. And those he had use for he used (as he confessed later in one of his poems) for his own overwhelming necessities. To say this is to contradict the impression I have mentioned of the clearly perceiving, dispassionate and all-wise evaluator. This and other contradictions must be left to find their own syntheses. Only towards the end of those three years his love for Mariette began perhaps to lead him into a close human relationship, to some extent self-chosen, in which the other person was much more than spectacle or audience.

This is of course an exaggeration; among the rewards of friendship with him were the moments when he was concerned with one's own concerns. He recalled one such instance the last time I saw him when his character was being rather intemperately assailed by my brother Roger; and he reminded us in semi-comic protest with a touch of stage brogue how, when Roger as an unhappy schoolboy had spent a day in Oxford, Louis had gone to some trouble to amuse him, 'inventing all sorts of games'. And I still have the note he left in my room in Corpus wishing me luck when I was about to row in a race for the first time; I was surprised that he had noticed.

On the whole at that time he preferred to study mankind indirectly. He liked—or perhaps this came on a bit later—to read the 'small ads.' in the papers. Meeting people face to face he was apt to make too clear that he was treating them—head thrown slightly back, eyes quizzically narrowed—as specimens, bearers of the potentialities of the race, concrete universals perhaps. A remark ventured by the specimen would be visibly rolled around his mental palate and mental ear; and the response if any would be less than whole-hearted. He practised in this way a certain spiritual economy that I take to have been necessary to the protection of his inner world. He was afraid—as in the *Prayer before Birth*[1]—of being spilled. He did not mind at times appearing sly; and he did not always choose to recognise people he had met before (though his increasing short-sightedness was probably responsible for many imagined offences of this kind).

To read these surface tactics as signs of a chilly and callous being would have been a great mistake. The *vita activa* and the *res publica* got short shrift in any case from many or most of the aesthetic intellectuals of the twenties. The greater part of mankind seemed to have lent itself, or submitted, to modes of life productive of a great deal of ugliness and dreariness. We lived in an apolitical world of sense impressions, abstract thought and the arts; and thought that real kindness and understanding were only possible between persons who shared at least a fair slice of this world.

School had been a forcing frame for the efflorescence of this attitude. Marlborough in our time was fairly tough soil but grew a useful crop of, in their way, equally tough aesthetes. Our seniors,

---

[1] *Springboard*, p. 9.

John Betjeman, John Bowle, Ben Bonas and others, produced a rival to the school magazine called *The Heretick* with a picture on the cover of a lumpish hockey player being inveigled by fauns and the motto 'Upon Philistia will I Triumph'. The first (and only?) number contains a fantasy by Betjeman ending with the entry of a rout of PRODIGIES singing. Their song concludes 'We die a very pedantic don/A crusty college fellow.' It was alleged that Louis was one of the prodigies the author had in mind. (Betjeman was not altogether the suppressed and retiring character one might suppose from reading the Marlborough chapter in *Summoned by Bells*. He was to be seen bowling a hoop through the school court with a green feather behind his ear; and the adjustable sallies at the expense of the deaf bandmaster/invigilator of which he gives a sample were usually coined by him.)

Anthony Blunt was a link between the *Heretick* generation and our own, to which he belonged by age while far ahead of us in sophistication. His father had been chaplain to the British Embassy in Paris (Anthony's French was good enough for the master in the French set to hand over the class to him). The eldest brother Wilfred was then art master at Haileybury and, one gathered, moved easily in 'Bloomsbury' and similar circles. The second brother was in the City. Anthony pursued his scholarly study of the arts with the same dedicated, unswerving intensity that he has given it ever since and with the most infectious enthusiasm. Old for his years in knowledge of the world and knowledge of where he was going he was a dominating figure both in his assurance and incandescent spirit and in his imposing height and large, handsome, long-haired head. We traipsed along eagerly with him as well in his more special domains of passion for Blake, Breughel, El Greco, Poussin, Thomas Hardy, Beckford or baroque architecture as in the more common current walks of art theory—Bell, Fry, Jan Gordon—or general literature; or helped with the exhibitions he organised; posters (Jean Sylen, McKnight Kauffer) or non-art-master paintings by ourselves. And as eagerly we joined the Anonymous Society (so called because the art master, whose outlook was different, objected to its being called the Arts Society) which he formed, with the backing and unflagging hospitality of the Rev. Clifford Canning.

Anthony was also the link between Louis and myself, being in the same house with him and the same form with me; and for the last year or more at school Anthony and Louis shared a study while Anthony and I shared a double desk in the Mathematical VIth. They whitewashed the study–which seemed very daring amid the encircling gloom of grease-stained wallpapers–and it always seemed to smell of distemper and dying chrysanthemums. The desk relationship was–largely through force of circumstance–quieter than the one in the study; where one sometimes got the impression that the closing scene of the Mad Hatter's tea party was being performed, with Louis in the rôle of the dormouse being stuffed into the teapot.

For Anthony's and Louis's temperaments were strikingly different. If one had to attempt brief descriptive labels one might say that Anthony was then an austere hedonist living for disciplined gratification of the senses, with an eye for social esteem and seeking anchorage in system and scholarly detail. While Louis was a ribald seer, an anarchic and mocking seeker after the deep springs of action and faith or at least hope or at least a mythology which would keep hope alive in a world always transient and mostly trivial, sordid or brutal; though often ludicrous, sometimes brave and occasionally tender. He was not looking so much for anchorage; but his need for ballast was met by a rubble of fragments of ancient structures–Arthurian legends, Icelandic sagas, Norse and Greek myths, runes, chanted fragments of Pope ('O'er golden sands let rich Pactolus flow/While trees weep amber on the banks of Po'; 'Cause the loud winds through long arcades to roar/Proud to catch cold at a Venetian door'), Sir Thomas Browne ('Time that antiquates antiquity . . .'), nursery rhymes and songs ('I once had a beautiful doll dears . . .'), Latin ('*Animula vagula, blandula* . . .' and one day he brought out a wonderful, resonant hexameter mnemonic for the books of the New Testament after Acts– 'Romcorcor galephes philcol thes thesalo timtim . . .').

Other fragments of English verse that served as steady stand-bys were 'The lark that tirra-lirra chants . . .', 'Jog on jog on the footpath way . . .' and 'Fish dinners will make a man hop like a flea . . .'.

Louis and Anthony were both sons of clergymen but, looking back, it would seem that the father's faith had perhaps sunk more deeply towards the roots of the son in Louis's case, though this was not very apparent on the surface. There was a quiet, rugged grandeur about Archdeacon, later Bishop, MacNeice which could not fail to communicate itself; and perhaps its setting against the slums of Belfast and all the troubles of Ireland was more favourable to such communication than was the atmosphere of the Paris embassy. (Not that Louis's family background was all that unworldly; it ramified, chiefly I think from his stepmother, through the Irish gentry and their country houses and included distinguished soldiers.)

There was in fact much common ground; but it had something of the nature of a Dutch polder, won by collaborative effort against the harsh rigours of surrounding nature. It's difficult now to be sure who contributed what. Anthony was certainly the main stimulus to interest in visual things; Louis to the cult of James Stephens and Dunsany. Who added Edward Lear to this artificial island? Eliot and the Sitwells, Virginia Woolf, Forster, Huxley were inevitable, though Anthony had probably heard of them first. *The Principles of Literary Criticism* probably came in with a delightful American master, temporarily attached for our last term, J. Frederick Waring (what's become of him?). Louis introduced us to Apuleius, Anthony read a paper on Lucretius to the Astronomical Society.

The Anonymous Society enlarged the island (though the continuing identity of the nucleus was demonstrated, to my great pride, when a parody of a popular song gained currency with 'Yes, we are aesthetic' substituted for 'Yes, we are collegiate' and the names 'Blunt, MacNeice and Hilton' linked in the refrain. The author later became Governor of Jamaica; he was tone-deaf, shared a weekly bath with me and conceived it his duty to educate me in the current pop hits). This body usually met in the Cannings' pleasant house in the high street, with the garden running down to the Kennet. There were egg sandwiches, of which I ate more than my share. Papers were read, arguments were pursued (one of inordinate length between Anthony and a classics master about the rival merits of pictures by Picasso and Michelangelo whose reproductions lay on the floor at their feet), Dr. Goard, the new head science master, played Debussy, Ravel, Poulenc. There was a reading of vernal and amorous poetry when Louis declaimed the *Pervigilium Veneris* with harsh resonance and a percussive menace in the refrain that was almost a threat.

He read verse with a vibrant, plangent, scrannel, sometimes harsh, almost raucous, sometimes warmly rolling voice, the tone even, emphasis usually subdued, vowel sounds given enormous value, consonants such as final r's rescued from English negligence – the word 'iron' becoming practically two syllables. His expression would flicker from blazing pride to diffidence to cold disdain to mockery; the muscles beside his mouth would lengthen into something between comic despair and the sneer that might become a snarl on the faces of some jungle animals. One hand would be held out sideways, palm down, moving slightly up and down in a rhythm unconnected with the verse as though to quieten an invisible dog. In the middle of all this Canning would tiptoe out and come back to announce during a pause that the cat was 'having kittens like a machine-gun'.

Louis read two papers. Both I think were rather jumbled fantasies – or perhaps I was too slow, or too ignorant of their allusions, to see their shape. One was called 'Dreams' which gave scope for anything. Something rich, rare and exciting was happening, one did not quite know what; baroque, gleaming convolutions, darkness of old tombs, gods like trees walking, riot, reassurance, glory, doom.

The fact must be faced that my impressions of Louis at school are confused and fragmentary. We were in the same junior house for the first four terms. As new boys we were in the same dormitory, but my only memory is of a pallid, distracted creature being beaten by the dormitory captain for failing to fill his water jug. There is then a complete blank until the fourth term when as relative seniors we spent our leisure in 'Library' with dormitory captains and one or two other officials of the two 'houses' contained in the infamous building called 'A. House'. Here Louis and I established relationship at the ping-pong table. He was playing a lot of dab-cricket at this time with teams of classical authors against mythical heroes or Norse gods. (He was interested in all forms of cricket and had a backyard game at home which Graham Shepard entered into with zest and I didn't.) And I remember an occasion when he had his ears forcibly washed. From here we went different ways: he to a wing of the only humane piece of architecture in the place, the old coaching inn; and I to a modern block with no attractions. For the next two years I can scarcely have seen him except for glimpses in a muddy jersey on the rugger field or rain-soaked on runs.

But the last two years were full of accelerating excitement. The cramps of terror had relaxed without losing their bracing effect; the blood was singing; and here and there the walls of Philistia were beginning ever so slightly to crumble. The school magazine accepted our poems and prose. I see that its last issue before we left records a debate on the motion 'That the Youth of today is degenerate' in which Louis' was the second speaker for the opposition. 'Mr. MacNeice corrected a few errors of the previous speaker. By an adroit juggling of abstractions he proved him wrong. There followed a short attack on the enchanting delusion of the Good Old Days, and a simile about biscuits. We have developed our sense of humour which is a great advance. A little story about Adam and an Ape, a quotation from Cornford and another from Catullus completed this exciting oration.' It was followed by a less exciting one from Mr. Hilton on the other side.

Marlborough : letters

In my letters from school there is a reference in March 1922 to a game of chess with an unnamed boy who might well have been Louis; but his name – wrongly spelt as always – first appears in May of that year, last in a list of five names of people with whom I played a sort of rounders one evening. In the following term I record that he beat me at ping-pong when I had a stomachache and that we went for a walk one Sunday with a boy called (Basil) Barr. After this we were in separate houses and there is no reference to him until our last year except for two games of chess (each won one) and a statement in May 1925 that 'Blunt has also painted a picture and I find that MacNeice (the Irish genius) turns out about one a day, some of which, according to Blunt, are quite wonderful.'

Before this there are three references to Blunt, from which one can perhaps deduce room for growth in the writer:

Spring '23   [Having tea with a master.] 'A nice select little party only, just as we were beginning tea, that terrible boy Blunt came to ask for the key of classroom and of course had to stay to tea and monopolised the conversation.'

Autumn '23	'There is an exhibition of paintings by old Marlburians. Rather good on the whole. Blunt says half of them are coloured photographs and the other half black and white photographs. Poor old Blunt.'
March '24	'There's a new college paper coming out for the first time next Saturday called the "Heretick". It is a very high-brow sort of thing I believe. Blunt's got a lot to do with it. He says it is meant to form a focus for the literary talent in the school.'

Even the last year starts off with Anthony more to the fore, though Louis rapidly takes first place:

October '25	'I've been bullied by Blunt into joining his society . . .'
” ”	'Blunt's society isn't really eccentric. Its members include [the headmaster to be, the classical upper VIth master, Canning and two others] and a member of the school cricket XI.'
” ”	[School debate on Epstein's *Rima*. Blunt made secretary of the debating society though hardly ever having attended a debate before.] 'MacNeice spoke three times at tremendous length and annoyed most people considerably.'
November '25:	'The Anonymous Society includes two members of the XV one of them the head of the school' [Michael Robertson].
” ”	' . . . MacNeice is reading to the Anon. Soc. his famous paper on "The mailed fist of common sense and how to avoid it".'

15/11/25	*'Wooley Foster had a hen* *Cockle button, cockle ben* *She lays eggs for gentlemen* *But none for Wooley Foster*
	'That was one of the things MacNeice brought into his paper, which took place at last on Tuesday.

It really was simply astounding; an amazing and magnificent conglomeration of dreams, fables, parables, allegories, theories, quotations from Edward Lear and Edith Sitwell, the sort of thing that you want to howl with laughter at, but are afraid to for fear of missing a word. He spoke in a loud, clear, fast matter-of-fact voice going straight on without a pause from a long story about two ants who fell into a river and went floating down in company with two old sticks and a dead dog, until they met a fish to whom they said "stuff and nonsense; it's contrary to common sense to swim upstream; we won't believe it" and went on and were drowned in a whirlpool, while the fish swam on upstream until he met St. Francis of Assisi preaching to the fishes and gained eternal happiness. And the little boy's mother gave him an atlas with the British Empire painted red, saying all other countries were not respectable and especially the country of Xanadu, and a nicely bound edition of the shorter catechism, and sent him out into the world. And he met Coleridge riding on a golden unicorn who took him to Xanadu and so on.

'He started off with the mechanical vehicle of civilisation bowling down the long dusty road of commonsense full of people singing patriotic songs and chewing peppermints. On each side of the road were wonderful hedges and beyond were lovely fields and woods, but these they could hardly see for dust. Every now and then someone, like Blake, jumped out of the car into the fields and they said "poor fellow he's mad" and a few others leant out and picked things off the hedges like Wordsworth I think.

'He's all wrong of course and extraordinarily narrowminded, but I'm sure he's a great genius.

.   .   .   .   .

248

'The difficulty with Blunt is that when you suddenly find out that he's very narrowminded or something else which makes you feel thoroughly superior, and mention the fact in a tactful manner, you find that he's been perfectly aware of the fact for years and proud of it more than otherwise. He's infinitely more intelligent than MacNeice, but not nearly such a genius I should think. He stands for "sense" while MacNeice stands for "nonsense".'

7/2/26   'MacNeice has written his usual wonderfully brilliant and totally unconvincing speech.'

14/2/26   'Did I not tell you that MacNeice was proposing the motion? [The Victorians were greater than ourselves.] He was as sparkling as usual, though I think he went too fast for people to take things in properly: "rushing down the Gadarene slope of the 20th Century and disappearing with a clatter of hooves in a twilight of the gods". I found after I had made up a speech dealing entirely with their solidity and level-headedness that his was entirely emphasising their romanticism; so I stated definitely that there was no contradiction, and no one troubled to enquire further.'

21/2/26   'MacNeice came and read part of the Crock of Gold to S. and me with great effect.'

14/3/26   'MacNeice did write "The Spirit returns" [in *The Marlburian*] . . . and one of MacNeice's "Mr. Schinabel" series.' [Graham Shepard wrote a piece in the same number called 'The Andrograph'. He averred that the apparently exact description of Blunt at the end of it was unintentional.]

10/5/26   'MacNeice read me his poem for the Furneaux prize the other day and threw me into the blackest despair.'

'Yesterday Blunt, MacNeice and I bicycled to Avebury . . . back by East Kennet where

	MacNeice climbed up the church tower and rang the bell.'
16/5/26	'I have completed a poem for the Furneaux prize in spite of MacNeice. That is the spirit that made the British Empire.'
30/5/26	'I can't get the first lines of MacNeice's [Furneaux poem] out of my head.

> *But genius finds the commonplace a silver rhyme*
> *Others for beauty plumb the depths of time*
> *Inspired genius very genius saves*
> *Others inspired drown in the pearly waves*
> *Few are the instruments of golden tone*
> *That break not whom the gods do play upon.*

	And off about the confectioner's assistant and the city of Kinsay, Ding-dong, moon gong calls them out at evening song.'
21/6/26	'The Furneaux prize was won by a 100 to 1 outsider.' [I think the subject set was 'Inspiration'.]
June '26	'I did not write the moon-fishing poem – that was McNeice's [*sic*. This was the first time I had given him a capital N in the middle; but I never at school got everything right at once.]
25/7/26	'On Thursday night at the Anon. Soc. having stolen a punt with MacNeice I fell out owing to him and various other things and rolled about at the bottom of the river in the moonlight . . .'

Memory again

I have said that the last two years at Marlborough were a time of accelerating excitement. We expected – I did at any rate – that this upward-curving graph of the cultural living standard would become even steeper at Oxford. It did not. The uranium seemed to be more thinly spread, the blanketing medium more opaque. Perhaps the organising powers of an Anthony Blunt would have concentrated the available energies, as in fact seemed to happen in Cambridge. Certainly when in our third year a team of Oxford aesthetes was scraped together to play hockey against a similar Cambridge team, Cambridge captained by Anthony had more team spirit (and included a rugger blue); the Oxford captain, Stephen Spender, scored a goal against his own side. The succeeding tea-party was attended by E. M. Forster—he talked solely to the rugger blue— and it is difficult to think of an appropriate equivalent had the match taken place in Oxford.

Oxford surprised too in being not only uninterested in the arts but violent in defence of superficial conventions. People in Louis's college made a bonfire of some of his prettiest ties (one with small parrots among jungle flowers); and I was threatened with possible removal of my side-whiskers.

Part of what we were looking for was no doubt mutual admiration; but part also was that quality of compassionate consideration which can only be based on imagination that has fed in every available field and on a rage for understanding that plunders every storehouse and vineyard; and the gang spirit which multiplies the speed and voracity of such devouring and pillaging.

If we had both been absorbed in the rich new experiences and sympathetic companions we expected Louis and I might have gone more separate ways. As it was we were forced to rely on one another much more than had been the case at school. He saw a lot of Graham Shepard too. I was fond of Graham but we talked rather different languages and did not meet much at that time.

By a fortunate geographical accident my room for the first year was on the ground floor of an annex of Corpus looking on to the street opposite Merton Chapel. Louis would usually stop on his way to or from Merton and engage me in conversation through the window. This became such a habit that he was referred to—by Hamon Dickie, who later shared a sitting-room with Moore Cros-thwaite and later still lodgings with Moore and Louis and others— as my demon lover. He was certainly a romantic figure at this time with his dark hair parted in the middle and curling back on to his forehead over each temple, large dark eyes flashing and crackling with raging rhetoric, opening to enormous size in mimed astonish-ment at some banality or narrowing to slits to put him at an infinite distance of sardonic scrutiny. And his complexion, which I had not particularly noticed, seemed to be the only thing my parents, with whom he was very shy, found remarkable about him. I think they mentioned milk and roses.

About this time he acquired a large knobbed ash walking-stick which was sometimes a danger to passers-by. It became invested with the qualities of Stephen Dedalus's ashplant (*Ulysses* burst on us during this year), of Ygdrasil and other phallic objects. 'I hate the world,' he would chant (with full value for the vowels and the 'r') walking along one of Oxford's narrow lanes and swinging at the world's imaginary head; 'don't you hate the world?' I had no answer, having never thought of an attitude to such an unwieldy conglomeration and only hoping to make my corner tenable. (I was not good at seeing life whole; and was equally stuck for an answer on being introduced that summer to another contemporary poet, Vernon Watkins in Cardiff, who opened the conversation by asking 'And what do you think of the system?' meaning – it turned out – the public-school system. It had not struck me as something that might be altered; all my energies had gone to enduring it and forgetting it.)

We walked a lot about the city, not much in the country. It was between the rivers near Magdalen meadow that Louis's attention got fixed for a long time on the water tumbling down a slope below a sluice; this had a special meaning for him that never seems to come out altogether clearly from the various poems in which the image appears. In our first summer term we shared a hired canoe (the autobiography says he shared it with Graham Shepard; but this must have been in the second summer) and explored the waters in all their aspects, with particular attention to the stretches round the gasworks, but not excluding the small Berkshire streams. We had some splendid riverside picnic suppers with our growing circle of friends; also one in a summerhouse in Merton Fellows' Garden.

Louis's closest friend in Merton, Adrian Green-Armytage, was a charming, elegant, slender, gentle person who went about for a time in a cloak; a cousin of Graham Greene's. He and I later started ju-jitsu lessons together but only got as far as how to release your wrists from holds. Adrian's wrists were so thin that not even ju-jitsu could release them. In Corpus Moore Crosthwaite, heading decisively for the Foreign Office, played Mozart operas, Holst's 'Planets', 'Blackbirds' and Olshevska on his gramophone;

was keenly interested in architecture and interior decoration (and first swam Corbusier into my ken); and was a source of information on *savoir-faire* and *Salonfähigkeit*. He it was also who later introduced us to the mother of Mariette.

Over one stretch of our first year Louis's favourite chant was:

> *I'll turn my guineas to flowering trees,*
> *Flowering trees, flowering trees,*
> *I'll turn my guineas to flowering trees,*
> *And tell my sons what fame is.*

His first rooms in Merton were on the ground floor looking on to the Fellows' Garden. There was a green underwater light in them. He had a share in a gnomelike and gnomic manservant who won my heart by telling Louis that my father had called to see if we were in Louis's room and adding 'the finest figure of a man I ever saw'. (I sometimes wondered if there was something wrong with me because I did not seem to feel the same hostility to my parents that some of my friends expressed to theirs.) Louis was not a very early riser and his toilet tended to get mixed with his breakfast. He announced one day the great discovery that China tea was particularly good for shaving with.

At the end of the first summer term he came to stay in my parents' house while we waited to hear whether his father and stepmother would approve our going to Paris together. The suspense was ended by a telegram saying 'Prance to France'. I had first to go back to Oxford for Maths. Mods. I had spent too much of the year talking to Louis, or rather listening to him; nevertheless I was chagrined when a message reached the Hôtel de Blois, Rue Vavin, that I had got a second. Louis said it was of no consequence.

The Rue Vavin was a narrow street cutting across the corner between the boulevards Raspail and Montparnasse. On the nights around the 14th July, when the junction of the boulevards was occupied by people dancing with very quick steps to a number of small bands, all the traffic was diverted down it; and until five in the morning it was filled with an almost inextricable mass of hooting vehicles. This we found more fascinating than disturbing; we kept late hours anyway and on these nights were happy enough wandering among the crowds or watching the superb fireworks launched from the Seine bridges. One night, when Louis went off on his own and had an adventure with a lecherous old man, I sat on a bench entertained by the goods trains running on the tram lines till the watering-carts came out in the dawn. And on our last night, having spent our money and missed a train, we slept on a bench under the Eiffel Tower and were woken up by the police and taken off for investigation. When asked for papers Louis pulled a bunch of receipts and draft verses out of his pocket. We also managed to get left in the gardens of Versailles after closing time. We had got separated and when we met again Louis had had a great experience. All the lamps round a lake had suddenly come on and their reflections looked like organ pipes. As one of the main features of organ pipes is their close clustering this seemed to me a tenuous simile; but it had moved Louis profoundly and appears at the climax of the poem called 'Bound in Stupidity and Unbound' in his earliest published collection, *Blind Fireworks*. There he was 'Draggling home soggy with steaks and swipes/And resting on the cement by the gravel pit'. On this occasion we were rather hungry and in more formal surroundings.

Earlier that day he had said he did not want to live beyond the age of thirty.

Louis, who—although we were refused entry to the Opera as too ill-dressed; my fault perhaps—was something of a dandy, disliked carrying things in his pockets. I therefore had to act as carrier as well as courier. I cannot remember whether this principle applied when we made a three-day expedition out of Paris. Perhaps we both had rucksacks. Anyway after visiting Fontainebleau we set out at nightfall to walk through the forest in the direction of Chartres. The humped rocks on ridges by the road grew more sinister and the glow-worms in the bushes became more likely to be the burning cigarettes of apaches as Louis unfolded in great detail the whole history of Peer Gynt. Some time after midnight we lay down in a potato field and slept till about three when we woke in rain. As we stumbled on to the road and set off Louis propounded a carefully formulated question about the place of Léger in the post-impressionist scene. The rainy gloom vanished and we were safe in our Marlborough/Oxford polder—the beating seas barred out.

In Chartres we bought large floppy peasant straw hats. In the train to Paris Louis was sunk in composition.

Our wanderings round the smaller art-galleries of Paris were strung on the thread of a search for a suitable picture for Moore Crosthwaite who had given us a free hand to spend up to £15 on a contemporary work. After looking at several hundred Dufys and others we settled rather nervously on a small Gromaire, of whom we had not heard though he was already fairly well known. In the Louvre Louis spent a long time looking at Watteau's Pierrot.

A year later I stayed for a fortnight or so with the MacNeices in Carrickfergus. The archdeacon, though an impressive and awe-inspiring figure, had too much warmth and evident humanity to be really frightening. In a letter written later Louis said, however, that as a boy he had always been terrified of him. His stalwart frame bore a massive head with the long upper lip of the archetypal Irishman and a strong development of muscles beside the mouth, which became more marked in Louis also later on. Louis's step-mother, by contrast, had a sort of sharp-pointed vivacity, with bright darting eyes and quick movements; but her considerable deafness made communication difficult. Having refused to play backyard cricket I allowed Louis to teach me golf. We visited the country houses of some of Louis's relations, including a very lovely one under the Mourne Mountains. We visited his friend Richard Best of Christ Church at his home in Belfast. The archdeacon used his influence to get us taken round the Harland and Wolff ship-building works.

From Carrickfergus I went on to stay with Moore and Hamon, and do some work in the Dickies' beautiful, friendly house at Bray, south of Dublin. These Irish visits were in lieu of a projected Greek journey with Mariette's mother and stepfather. Moore and Hamon — as indeed all my Oxford friends—were doing Greats and had met Louis's future mother-in-law at her husband's lectures. I have a vivid memory of the luncheon party for her that Moore gave in his room. 'Vivid' is perhaps not the right word; I can recall no detail of the conversation. I only know that most of it was hers and that I had had no inkling up to that time that such a thing was possible; such torrential fire, such dazzling lights and shades, such breathtaking arabesques, such keen observation and analysis, such sublime disdain for pedestrian logic and consistency and the humdrum frame of things. I was never again quite so enthralled, though always fascinated. I became a little scared of giving unintended offence. On one such occasion she said I was like a rabbit; and Louis, to his everlasting glory, had the courage to say he thought I was more like a lion.

Mariette's father one gathered had been something in business, vaguely connected perhaps with the part of her mother's roots that were in Constantinople (as she still called it). Mariette at this period was very much in the background—retiring, raven-haired, large eyed, white skinned, rather fragile, with no seeming conversation or range of interests beyond clothes, dancing, cosmetics, scents, popular music and detective stories. She had a rather attractive husky 'little girl' voice when she did speak. I chiefly remember her at that stage on the tennis lawn in a wide floppy cerise hat.

It was in the autumn term after my visits in Ireland that Mariette began to pine, to lose sleep, to refuse food, to be visibly consumed with inner fires, to confide frequently—chiefly to Moore—her distraught condition, her oscillating hopes and fears, her total absorption in—an unknown object. Perhaps I was alone in being completely unaware of the identity of the object, though I did not think so. It was not until the following holidays when she summoned me to call on her at her grandmother's house in Bayswater that I learnt with complete astonishment that Louis was the object and that she had achieved it. Louis had been staying with us shortly before and perhaps to anyone less obtuse some of his more cryptic sayings would have given some inkling. They had become engaged on the last Tuesday of term after Louis had been totally abstracted throughout a lunch party in my room with my extraordinary Aunt Gertie—a confrontation that I had been much looking forward to—and had left abruptly after the meal without any attempt at excuse.

Some of the reasons for his abstraction, beyond the obvious ones, and for the cryptic nature of his utterances in the next week or two were given in a fifteen-page letter he wrote to me in the following autumn. Towards the end he says: 'Sorry if this is illegible; I have been up all night and it draws near to breakfast.' There is a PS., 'I don't mind you telling anyone anything in this', but scribbled in pencil on the folded back, 'Note – I am afraid the contents are rather grim.' Briefly, he had had difficulty in bringing himself to tell Mariette that he had a mongol brother; and just as he had screwed himself to the pitch she said she had a horror of lunatics; so he had had to write to her about it. This started an extraordinary and miserable chain of misunderstandings and cross-purposes depending on the question of whether there was anything hereditary in the condition of Louis's brother. The storm was just about blowing itself out when he was writing this letter.

The effect of Mariette's announcement to me, after the first astonishment, was to increase my respect and liking for her. This was partly because a genuine human being began to become apparent beneath the rather toy-like surface – as indeed had begun to happen during her earlier revelations of love-longing for an undefined object; and partly because it seemed logically inescapable that, if Louis's discernment and discrimination permitted the declaration of his affection, the loved person must be of great worth. Furthermore, that Mariette was so greatly enamoured of Louis in preference to all her dancing partners argued an estimable discernment and discrimination in herself.

So during the perturbations (see letters) that followed the breaking of the news to the parents and step-parents I was able without reservations to commend everyone to everyone else.

After this Louis became less accessible; Mariette was in his room or he was out with Mariette or we were all having tea with her mother. These teas were enjoyable, though still alarming – with unsuspected gaucheries waiting to be cauterised by Mrs. —, and the professor sitting palely silent or palely muttering to himself in French, occasionally addressing his wife as 'my dear man'.

In this Easter term of 1929 another event was the appearance of the first number of a magazine called *Sir Galahad* with whose engendering and further care Louis had a good deal to do. He had written to me in the summer between school and Oxford: 'Will you run a paper with me at Oxford to be called the Oxford Farrago? It would be a good show with a coloured cover. You could design that.' I did a design or two, but that was about as far as the *Farrago* got. *Sir Galahad*, which had a black and white cover, also designed by me – a stylised Sir G. ('stylised' was a favourite word) on a stylised horse with a sort of number plate 'HP 10'–ten horse-power because Heart Pure–got a bit further. I have copies of two numbers anyway.

Another suggestion in the same pre-Oxford letter came to earlier, though somewhat blighted, fruition. 'If you like I'll walk to your home with you at the end of next term. We will make lots of money for it's the great tongue I have.' We did set out at the end of the first term to walk the fifty miles or so to my home at North-wood. We arrived at the *Spread Eagle* in Thame in time for dinner. After dinner we spent a long time being shown by John Fothergill, who was then running the *Spread Eagle*, the pictures he had painted at the Slade. By the time we got away a thick mist had descended on the Aylesbury Vale. The road was very flat and, in the mist, inter-minably tedious. Striking matches to read signposts we reached Aylesbury in the small hours and allowed a suspicious policeman ('Been on the randy, have you?') to knock up the proprietor of an inn and get us beds. We caught a train in the morning. We made no money.

The first number of *Sir Galahad* included amongst others con-tributions by Stephen Spender, Harold Acton, Clere Parsons, Osbert Lancaster, Sonia Hambourg, Bernard Spencer and Louis (two signed and a third under the name of John Bogus Rosifer). It had a prologue by E. R. Copleston, who had also been at Marl-borough, as had Bernard Spencer. Contributors to the second number which appeared in May included some of the same people and Guy Morgan–of whom Louis I think saw a good deal though I scarcely knew him–Graham, Adrian, myself and Anthony Blunt. The list looks a bit symptomatic of a rallying of the old gang to save the foundering knight.

Anthony may seem an intruder in this Oxford venture. (He was one of the moving spirits behind a longer-lived Cambridge magazine called *The Venture*.) But our ties with him had held firm and there were some memorable expeditions to Cambridge and notable parties there. The Cambridge air seemed headier and the number greater per acre of intelligent and fully human beings, though this again may have been partly the effect of Anthony's flair for picking them out. Julian Bell, John Lehmann, George Rylands, Michael Redgrave and others seemed more three-dimensional, less odd and at the same time more exciting than most of what we could find among students or dons. (I regret that Wittgenstein, whom I would like to have met and who had rooms above Anthony's at Trinity, was one of his, not rare, *bêtes noires*).

Oxford : letters

15/10/26
(second day of
first term)

'Louis will now write a postscript and I will then continue. P.S. John is looking so nice and well and quite healthy in spite of the rain.

F.L.M.'

[I include this triviality partly because it is the first mention of Louis at the beginning of our Oxford life, partly because it is characteristic of one of his lines of clowning, cautious affection and chiefly, perhaps, because the sight of his bold black looping writing in the desert of my own excites me like treasure trove.]

25/10/26
'Louis MacNeice [at last got it right] is my mainstay. He is going to introduce me to the chief Oxford poet, whom he met at a champagne orgy, to which he was introduced by an ex-Marlburian dypsomaniac aesthete whom he did not really know. So you see I'm getting well into the worst company. You needn't think that Louis will get corrupted. He has more sense than one expects for all his delightful childishness. This evening he introduced me to the son of some plutocrats who know the Blunts and collect modern pictures. He has a marvellous straightforward way of getting to know people he wants to know. I suppose he may get too popular. His fame has already been spread before him so that he was practically met on the doorstep by representatives of the "Oxford Outlook" wanting contributions. He comes in every half hour or so and tells one how fed up he is with the world, especially after yesterday afternoon when he had to go to a sort of religious tea party, in drizzly rain, in the very centre of the worst sort of respectable ugly suburbs.'

29/10/26	'Louis has got a poem into the "Cherwell". I am jealous.'
16/11/26	'P.S. Louis abused me for ½ hr. yesterday and has given me up as a bad job.'
22/11/26	'As a matter of fact most of Oxford now know Louis. He is going to do literary criticisms for the "Cherwell". He has condescended to allow me to speak to him again.'
26/11/26	' . . . and Macneice [*sic*] is now interrupting and telling me of my shortcomings.

'I went out to tea yesterday with his people who are both much better than I had imagined. The father is very very Irish with a broad face and cheekbones and very simple and childlike. Mrs. M., although very deaf, is quite a wag and would keen very well, I feel. We had tea in the Shamrock tea-rooms with Erse welcomes and Yeats's poems round the walls, but no potato cakes although you can get stirabout for breakfast, whether with lumps gratis I know not. [v. *Crock of Gold*.]

'No one here has any interest in modern poetry or painting practically' [apropos of E. Sitwell's lecturing at Cambridge].

November '26 'On Saturday I was suddenly roped in to take Miss MacNeice to a dance, her partner having failed and Louis being unable to dance. Louis was coming too, but failed to turn up at my place, so I went round and at 7.30 he turned up in his ordinary clothes, we having arranged to meet his sister at St. Hugh's at 7.20. I then thought myself very clever to discover, by one or two minute signs, that he was drunk. He said he was ill and sent me off with a note to his sister, alone in the dark. It turned out that it was all a brilliant bit of acting on his part, to get off the dance. I have hardly forgiven him. His sister is very nice and was climbing mountains in the Dolomites about the time we were there. She had been doing a post mortem that morning in Oxford having risen at 4.20. She is at the Charing Cross Hospital. The dance was good, as she introduced me to respectable partners.'

[Took six people to Thame to see John Fothergill.] 'Louis and I walked over, the rest biking. I bicycled back and Louis did his wandering-genius-in-distress trick as successfully as usual.'

23/1/27 'Louis came over in a coal boat, 12 hours and a sea according to the Captain, would have made the devil sick . . . He has a clay pipe which he has already broken.'

'It is always disastrous to think too much—especially in this place which would fly into powder under the light of truth. The people in it seem to have got set in wrong moulds so that nothing short of an explosion will change them.'

'Succumbed to going to see Uncle Vanya with L.'

31/1/27 ' . . . am a busy man, talking for instance to Louis till twelve last night.'

'My brain is going faster. Going bad I mean. My memory is almost completely gone. I cannot keep up with Louis and in the effort miss everything else.'

'Louis and I are touring the West of Ireland at the beginning of the summer, if he isn't too tired of me.'

? [Having flu] 'Louis is very charming in the sick-room; he makes a great effort to be an ordinary mortal and succeeds in being an extraordinarily delightful one.'

21/2/27 [convalescing] 'I went to tea with Louis and furiously upheld science to him, having just seen the light myself . . .'

8/3/27 ' . . . yesterday morning I had to prepare to read a play in the evening with the queer gathering

that has formed round Louis and Schiff. We met
in Louis's room and ate potato cakes and read
"the Cenci" by the light of 21 candles and everything was great fun. Louis seems at last to have
found a pleasant man in Merton who came and
brought a skull which looked very well when I had
provided it with radishes for eyeballs. Crosthwaite, Dixon and Shepard also attended.' [Week-
end at Cambridge] 'I had tea with Blunt and Co.
and lunch the next day. His chief asset is an
extraordinary vitality; he is a perfect conductor
for the life-force.'

6/3/27   'I am going this afternoon with Louis to find out
about a scheme for 5 weeks' farming in Canada
in the summer. We have ordered a canoe for
next term.'

1/5/27   'Darling Louis then turned up and we went to
claim our canoe which we found neatly labelled
"Louis MacNeice Merton College; John Hilton
C.C.C." and lunched at the Cadena Café on
prawns on toast and ginger beer, Louis having
bought some tulips. We talked a lot, at least he
did but I can't remember it. He went back to a
collection on which he expects to have his
scholarship removed . . .'

'Louis says he "accepts the Universe" but
doesn't mean it.'

'Then I came back and went round to Louis
who was waiting to go out in the canoe. So we
went and launched out with joy and trepidation
and went down the Isis and up the Cherwell and
round all sorts of wandering branches and then
Louis got out to go to a similar examination poor
dear . . .'

'Later I walked round Magdalen with Louis.'

' . . . the next morning when we intended to go
down to hear the May morning singing from
Magdalen Tower.'

'In the morning . . . Louis not turning up as was to be feared . . .'

'I went round to Louis about 10 and found him still in dressing-gown. He read me several torrential compositions and eventually dressed and with two stale rolls and oranges we set out in our canoe up the river and wandered for hours . . . round all sorts of canals and dreadful places sometimes lifting it out of one into another and going under bridges flat on our backs. Once with much labour we hauled it up a bank to carry it through Osney Lock but half-way met the keeper who made us pay as though we had been through the lock itself. We came back through it and got back at tea-time. We had a bad tea at Fullers and came back.'

7/5/27 [Riverside picnic, F.L.M., Moore Crosthwaite, Graham Shepard, J.R.H.] 'Curried prawns, brandy and ginger ale, cucumber, lettuces, grapefruit, and radishes, oranges, Florence cake and Burgundy, cheese biscuits and butter and other cakes. [One of the canoes drifted away in a sinking condition. Louis swam and saved it; he could have taken the other canoe.] We drifted and paddled slowly back, getting in just before midnight. The purpose of the feast was to welcome in summer and very well it did it.'

14/5/27 ' . . . Louis and Shepard and I made a great voyage in the canoe by devious ways aiming for Bablock Hythe, but we did not get and had dinner in the Trout Inn at Godstow.'

17/5/27 'Would you perhaps bring "the A.B.C. of Atoms" (for Louis to read) . . .'

24/5/27 'We went in the canoe with Shepard a long way up the Cherwell to Islip but did not find Robert Graves's house. We had a fine supper of beer and bread and cheese in the pub. with all the village characters.'

'I never told you that a week or two ago I was persuaded by Louis to join in the production of "Troilus and Cressida", one of the longest of Shakespeare's plays, at the end of this term, not only taking on a fair part [blockish Ajax] but arranging most of the scenery and generally looking after Louis. Each person in turn pointed out to him that it was quite impossible and each found himself in a few minutes having promised to take a gigantic part. However Shepard . . . while discussing it at tea suddenly discovered that he had tacitly assumed that we were going to do it next term, which was such a shock to Louis that he gave it up. It was really a miserable business squashing his enthusiasm. We now talk about doing it next term, but the general spontaneous fire will have died a little. Shepard and I are to paint the back-cloths during the holidays. I trust it does not end with that.

'Everything is still very vague about the vacs. Louis says he wants me to take him to France, which might be a rather heavenly nightmare. I have given up Canada with sorrow, although I am secretary in my college for the movement.' [Holiday farm work presumably.]

'Then Anthony Blunt arrived and stayed as Louis's guest for two nights and then as mine. He further upset the universe. . . . We walked up the river last night and had dinner at the Trout and walked back in a marvellous evening. . . . On Thursday night our long promised "wake" as Louis calls it came off, more grand than the one at the beginning of the term. We had six people including Anthony and landed and ate in the same field.

'Louis has given up Ireland but wants to go to France he says, early in July. He is going with Anthony and his brother to Bavaria in September.'

2/7/27	'I wonder where Louis has got to and whether we shall ever see him again.'
Postmark Paris 9/7/27	'Everything has gone as it ought so far. We are both very sleepy.'
Postmark Paris 11/7/27	'We work very hard and well. Yesterday we have done the Louvre, Moulin Rouge, a terrible cabaret, a fair and all Paris several times and then spent the night wandering the streets separately. It is oh so hot.'
Postmark Paris 15/7/27	'The whole of Paris has been climbing up ladders and decorating itself for the 14th July and for three days' dances in the streets. We do a good deal in a rather haphazard way. Our hours are odd. Today we rose at 3 p.m. having come in quite reasonably at 2 a.m.
? 19/7/27	'. . . we are trying to leave tomorrow but as we have given no notice it may not be possible. We then intend to go to Fontainebleau and from there by walking and/or training to Chartres and back here. Time has ceased to have any fixed divisions. True we did get up soon after 8 this morning but that was unique as we were going to Versailles from where we have just returned. I have hardly digested it yet, but it rather frightened me. Louis thought that to own it would make one feel omnipotent, but I think it would make me miserable. He drew up lengthy plans for buying it and living there with a troop of poets and artists.

'. . . we go to the Louvre twice and see a lot of pictures and we go to fifteen exhibitions of modern artists and see a lot of things.'

| ? 20/7/27 | 'We are getting away as soon as possible as it is alright about the hotel people. Louis is a little slow. |

'. . . we climbed the tower of Notre Dame . . . we have drunk no absinthe nor anything very dangerous but iced coffee and chocolate.

'I must stop and try and get Louis away.'

'We have just got back to Paris after training to
Fontainebleau which is lovely, walking to
Etampes, sleeping the night in a cornfield on the
way and training to Chartres which is marvellous.
We are leaving here on Saturday getting home
Sunday. It took some persuasion to get L. to do
this. We are sitting in the Rotonde café spotting
famous artists.'

17/10/27 'Louis grows better every day. He has been
doing some work apparently. I have just been in
his room which is a splendid size and lit at the
moment of necessity by candles, the light having
broken.'

7/11/27 [Strindberg's *Easter*.] 'I . . . enjoyed the play
very much, though Louis said it was bad.'
    'On Thursday night five of us in Louis's room
read *The Jew of Malta* with some success.'

13/11/27 'I haven't seen much of Louis lately, which is a
good thing if it doesn't go too far. We are both
doing some work, I think.'

22/1/28 'Crosthwaite tells me Louis's sister is engaged.
He's an odd creature: he read me some of his
novel this evening.'

5/2/28 [To the cinema with Louis.] 'And now I am
going to tea with Louis, who is sitting in his
dressing-gown muttering at life.'

20/2/28 'It is interesting but disconcerting to combine
two persons who completely fail to understand
one another's outlook. It gets reflected in one's
friends, where it is more difficult to reconcile.
Thus, coming back from rowing yesterday with
two very charming men in the boat, we suddenly
met Louis appearing round a corner and one of
the rowers said (fairly justifiably I think; at least
an exclamation was justified, if not the particular
one, which has lost all meaning) 'My God!' and
was naturally rather unhappy when he found that
I knew Louis.

'Then again Anthony Blunt is coming over to stay in Oxford from Friday to Sunday and so I must combine two almost incompatible and very unharmonious pursuits.'

8/5/28 'Yesterday . . . Louis, Moore, Alistair Hamilton [Old Marlburian; member of the Anonymous Society] and I hired a 1928 Morris Saloon and visited Cambridge, Louis and I sharing the driving. We started off just after 9, Louis being brave enough to drive first . . . We lunched with Anthony & Co. . . . We all crowded in and went for a ride round and across the Cambridge country, coming back along a grassy Roman road where our springs remained fortunately whole. We had dinner all together and got off at 8, getting back intact in just over 3 hours.

'The day before . . . to town to see the Moscow actors . . . rushed up and joined Louis and Shepard in the theatre, had tea after and rushed back.'

13/5/28 'I have worked myself into enthusiasms for world peace and the millennium, which have evaporated, partly by their nature and partly at the thought of the just sneers of people like Louis at these "stupid utopianists". That was his comment on the Dean and his fellow speakers last Saturday.' [?]

28/5/28 'On Tuesday and Wednesday Louis read the main body of his novel to see what it sounded like. I can't attempt to criticize it because I can't escape from my knowledge of him and the originals of the chief characters in it. It is at least a very brilliant portrait of Anthony. It totters at times on the edge of the commonplace, I think successfully, but there are bad openings for unkind critics. The feeling that he really has a firm hand on the situation lends an excitement to these rashnesses like that of dangling with Barbaria over an abyss [?sic]. It left me in a state of rather inarticulate wonder. I hope to feel less overshadowed when I read the whole.

'I went to lunch with Moore to meet the amazing Mrs. — again. She is really very enchanting, the most wonderful talker I have ever heard, with eyes like a witch that change shape all the time and a very long rather Jewish nose. She is very frightening, terribly quick and penetrating and almost oriental, though she seems to be connected more with the Balkans. [Yesterday] . . . out in Louis's canoe with him and Moore and Moore's sister Lexy and a large lunch in a hamper. We went a long way up the little stream that goes parallel to the Isis for 5 miles, and all got very sunburnt.'

13/9/28   'The Rectory, Carrickfergus.

'Here is a sleepy line for you: written in bed, to Louis's murmuring in the background.

'Louis arrived at the quay just after I did and we left Moore's trunk in Belfast and got here for breakfast. Mr. N. [Nicholson, now Sir John N., to whom Louis's sister was shortly to be married] has left and the family is complete and alone and all very charming. The wedding is not till the 18th of next month. Presents and preparations are beginning.

'We have walked and talked and slept and read and been out in the car. The country is very delightful, by no means dull, though the town is not very attractive except for the castle and harbour where we have been after dinner.'

20/9/28   'Beech Hurst, Bray, Co. Wicklow.

'The MacNassa family were very delightful, especially Mrs. MacNeice, who turns out to be a stepmother, but defies all the traditions of that tribe. In spite of being very deaf she is a great joke especially when fighting or arguing with Louis or prancing after him prancing. Intervals

268

between wedding presents are getting shorter; so are tempers. The day before yesterday the cook was knocked over by a bus and broke her wrist. It will take until just after the wedding, probably, to mend. She was a very charming person who played reels on the concertina. We spent an evening in the kitchen listening to her and trying to play ourselves.

'We did a great deal, though not quite what I had expected to do: we did not see a bog, for instance, at all. We spent a wearing day clambering along the side of the neighbouring hill, the Knockagh, to find a favourite cave of Louis's. It was a dreadful precipitous place of brambles gorse nettles thistles and broken rocks, where you tobogganed and tore and broke and scratched yourself and got soaking into the bargain. We found the cave at last at the point we had started from, had lunch and built a vast fire of pine branches, which dried our socks (hung from a crack in the roof) but nearly killed us and brought down showers of stupefied bees and centipedes.

'We dined with a Belfast aunt, lately engaged in gun-running. We had tea with another aunt who lives in the most beautiful garden in Ulster with a famous poetess Miss Hine, writing as Elizabeth Shane, who is antipathetic towards Louis. They live underneath the Mourne Mountains by the sea.

'We also went to tennis with Richard Best, son of Lord Justice Best, of Belfast, whom I have met several times in Oxford.

'Yesterday we went over the biggest ship-works in the world. . . . Louis read me some more of the novel.

'Mrs. MacNeice threw Nietzsche downstairs this morning and the archdeacon said he was only fit to light candles with, but he is very broad, I should think, on the whole. He can put the weight further than Anthony or Louis and gave me several solemn warnings about the beautiful girls of Dublin.

'It is rather nice to get back to electric light. Oh I played Louis at golf yesterday until we lost two balls and was beating him on two strokes a hole.'

4/11/28

'On Wednesday we had a high tea, the very highest ever had, in Louis's room: Louis, Moore, Adrian Green-Armytage (Louis's college chum), Graham Shepard, Alistair Hamilton and a friend and Christopher Holme, a rather beautiful, clever and fairly sensible person. To give you some idea of the cultural circles in which I move, I should mention that at least four of the party were in the process of producing novels (not that the conversation ever rose above the level of the table). But the food was distinctly worth discussing, always displaying a pleasing heterogeneity due to the system of each guest bringing an Ερανος or contribution. So we began with a quart of winkles and smoked salmon and went on to chicken, ham, tongue and a great variety of polony and liver sausages in red and yellow. Oh but before I describe the food I should say that the room was lit by a great multitude of candles all round and on the heavily fruited round dark polished table, so that the Christmas party effect was very prominent and, since I had a cold, the smell of burning candles has been in my head ever since. The chicken was both fresh and bottled, the bread was ordinary, Irish soda, potato-cake and balm-brack but for astonishing variety the fruits were supreme: persimmons, passion-fruits and pineapple, mangoes, green figs, apples, nuts and chilis, tomatoes and bananas. The only excuse for the title high tea (we also

270

had fruit salad and cream, biscuits and honey-
combs) was that it began at 6, for we did not
even drink tea, but every other liquid in creation.

'There was a pretty little scene afterwards when
I sat on top of a chestnut tree in the moonlight
and played "Here we go round the mulberry
bush" on my tin whistle while the rest of the
party danced round the tree below.

'I have had flattering demands from Louis and
Adrian that I should share digs with them.'

12/11/28

'I hope this will be in time to stop your sending
the "Venture" as I meant to tell you, and I
thought I did, that I had been forced to subscribe.
Anything to help an old school friend. But it's
certainly a bit thin. Louis's two poems, he wrote
at Marlborough and didn't want put in, but they
insisted. . . . Louis is reviewing it in an Oxford
paper and not very enthusiastically. . . .

'While your minds are still preoccupied, I
hope, with this problem [my future] I can go on
to tell you how we all fell out of a car yesterday.
We fell through the roof: "a forest of legs" said
the woman. It was really most exhilarating, at any
rate for Louis and myself who were unscratched.
I was reading moral philosophy at the time, Louis
was driving and we wanted to get to Cambridge
in time for lunch. The road was greasy and
narrow and curving and sloping the wrong way
and a big Chrysler came the opposite way also too
fast and we touched the grass in avoiding it and
described the most delightful gyrations and
revolutions on all axes and ended on the grass
with the car on its side, nose to the road and
ourselves, as I say, shot neatly through the roof.
Adrian Green-Armytage cracked his collar-bone
half through, and Moore got a cut across the front
of his ankle which had to have 3 stitches in it.
("Sic transit gloria mundi" said Louis as we

271

emerged from shreds of roof and piles of glass.)
Fortunately it was the soft roof of a Morris
saloon which we had hired from the King's
Arms Garage here, which has now had 5 cars
smashed up in 10 days. "You undergraduates."
The two exasperating features of the incident
were (1) that Moore's spectacles were lying intact
on the grass, when just as he was going to pick
them up, he saw the irrevocable foot of Louis
remorselessly descending, looking for his hat; (2)
that when with the crowd of rustics we had pushed
the car to its feet, as we had forgotten to put on
the brake, it ran violently backwards down a steep
place into a ditch and was choked, nearly crush-
ing Louis and cutting his thumb in the process.

'In everything else we had incredible luck. We
were half a mile from one of the best R.A.C.
stations in the kingdom, to which Louis and I
went off in a friendly car. The broken ones were
taken into the cottage opposite, while we performed, where the most charming people looked
after them, giving them an excellent Sunday
dinner. Here Louis and I joined them after
telephoning to various people and fishing the
car out of the ditch with much difficulty and
rope-breaking. The engine still went, though
rather funnily as all the oil had run out etc., etc.
The licence disk still stuck up in front, though
all the wind-screen had gone, saying "Expiring
31st Dec. 1928" . . . the doctor, who was
fortunately near and nice, mended the other two,
with the delightful R.A.C. man as nurse.

'Then we took a very slow bus to Cambridge
and got there after 4 and Anthony was out and
Leonard Woolf had gone, whom we were going
to meet. [Back by train, dining at Greek restaurant in London whose proprietor's only English
was "Oh me darling".]

'My own chief memory of this entertainment (a little expensive perhaps) is one of sheer ecstasy in the process of rolling over, almost a glad contentment. I never had a suggestion of being hit by anything.

'The point about Leonard Woolf was that Anthony has apparently arranged that the Hogarth Press should publish Louis's poems, while Louis hadn't told him that he was trying Gollancz, who hasn't said anything yet.' [Moore Crosthwaite's sister Lexy was Gollancz's secretary at this time.]

2/12/28 '. . . there were also present . . . and Mariette who is pining away of unrequited love and on the verge of breakdown according to Moore. She managed to appear fairly cheerful. She is rather a dear, in spite of Father's opinions.

'If you're really so morbidly interested in the people who went to Marlborough and behave so amusingly, one is in this college, the Bursar's nephew, Spencer (Bernard). He had his whiskers forcibly removed the other day. The man Curtis prefers to be known as Capell. He has just flown over to Paris where he is holding an exhibition of his paintings. He had lessons from Juan Gris while still at Marlborough. The other interesting one is a man called Roditi (Edward) with various aliases such as "Pirouetti". On one night 3 parties of some 24 persons in all successively raided his rooms. The last was led by the honourable Stanley, vowed enemy of all aestheticism including Louis, who published the following triolet in the University News

> *God is complaining*
> *Of the honourable Stanley.*
> *It will not stop raining;*
> *God is complaining.*

273

He rows without training,
Because he's so manly,
God is complaining
Of the honourable Stanley.

By this time he could only cut off the electric
wires up to the ceiling and finish splintering the
doors and powdering the glass of windows and
pictures. Curtis or Capell was knocked down in
the Broad the other day by a hearty.'

28/1/29 'On Friday Louis read his paper "The Policeman" to the Pelican Club [a Corpus essay club].
I think the ones who thought it the best paper
they ever heard were more numerous than the
ones who thought it cheap, but he himself always
had doubts about it and I am not sure that it is
more than a tour de force, full of delight. "No
one knows what the soul is like who has not seen
a flower drunken, tousled flushed and swaying,
tugging and swearing at its stalk and trying to
break away and failing."'

4/2/29 'Coincidences go on happening. . . . On Saturday
morning a new Oxford paper appeared asking
what the police were going to do about Mr.
MacNeice seeing that he had read a paper on
them in Corpus; and on Saturday evening Mr.
MacNeice spent five hours in gaol. . . . [He got
drunk. He said, probably about this time, that he
sought through drinking what his father sought
through religion.]

'I have been spending my valuable time
designing a cover for a rotten new magazine a
man called Woolmer in Merton is starting. It is
to be called, somewhat ironically, Sir Galahad and
he is like this [drawing] only better.'

18/2/29 'I am going to tell you this story, only do not
publish it abroad, as the complications of people
who know and people who don't are bad enough

274

as it is. Only it seems a little helpful to air it, especially as at the minute things are running rather fast and may soon be beyond the comprehension of my pen. And indeed the complications are already more than can be grasped in an evening.

'Well

'All ears?

'Yes

'Yes

'Hush

'Yes

'Listen

'Louis is engaged to Mariette

'You'd guessed that of course.

'Well it was pretty clever of you; it was a big enough surprise to me. Never did I think he had noticed her and they have been engaged since the end of last term. I learnt first in a series of parables and allegories while walking round and round Hyde Park that day with Mariette. And of course I could not grasp it as a fact, as anything but a story, a dream.

'I rather cursed this world at first, because it seemed utterly silly.

'As Ben [my scout] said this morning, she didn't seem his style. But of course his perspicuity has far outstripped mine as usual and she is, I now believe, a very sensible and dear girl (in spite of lip-stick). But God knows what will happen.

'I can't go into all the ramifications of difficulty now. Mariette's grandfather won't leave her any money if she marries a Christian, but the real present and pressing difficulty is Louis's people. He wouldn't have told them even now if it hadn't been for his dons' writing to them about his escapade.[1] He loses all intelligence where his

[1] See letter of 4/2/29.

people are concerned: and indeed I am beginning to wonder whether they are as rational as I thought them. To forestall the official letter he sent off like a fool a brutally abrupt telegram which, after mentioning the letter, went on: "am engaged to be married". Then he wrote a pretty wild letter having torn up several wilder ones. At his suggestion, how wise I do not know, I sent an attempt at a reassuring telegram the next day. I also wrote a letter to his stepmother which went off yesterday, but I am afraid can have been no use. On Saturday he received a letter from his father. This morning he had letters from them both and I had one from his father in a terrible state ending "I am in a whirl and feel utterly, utterly crushed." They cannot stand the idea of a Jewess, they accuse Mariette's mother of setting traps (whereas she has been dead against it), they will never be happy again until it is broken off, they think that Louis probably ought to leave Oxford, they say that his poetry is rubbish.

'And this evening he has received a telegram saying that they are crossing tonight and he is to meet the train, bringing John. But the curse is that they can hardly have got my letter which would have helped enormously.

'So the stage is setting for a tip top storm. Picture the opposition of the Archdeacon, broad, magnificent, pontifical, Irish, backed by all the weight and majesty of the church and the darting, lightning, and witty Mrs. —. She's got all the cards really. "The idea of those country folk thinking their son such a great man in Oxford, that anyone should want him for their daughter."

'But before that we've got to meet these outraged parents. Think of trying to explain things to the deaf Mrs. MacNeice. The whole affair is too ludicrous for words. And not content with Mariette and his drunkenness, Louis seems to have chosen the moment, perhaps unavoidably, for revealing that he cannot really call himself a Christian. No more can I and I suppose they will want to know.

'One doesn't of course know that it would not be better for it to stop at once, but as far as I can see, which is a precious short way, one can only support the reasonableness of the engagement against both sides. Mariette at least (I talk as though I knew anything about anything) seems to me serious. But then her mother declares that it will not last. Neither is supposed to know their own mind, for opposite reasons, Louis because he has had nothing of the kind before and Mariette because of about six such affairs.

'She is a kind, sensible, bright creature, unless I am a fool. They are like a pair of kittens or birds, a little unreal and talking of course of love in a garret. (You should hear Mrs. — on garrets. If anyone can bring Louis to look at his feet, that lady will. You should hear her on his drunkenness, his conceit and all his little follies. Mariette too is an excellent influence getting him to go to bed in time, to smoke less, to brush his teeth and wear warmer clothes. Indeed I think it was the only and best thing that could have happened to him.)

'Well, I am prepared to assure the MacNeices that she is the only girl in the world for him. Heaven knows what is what.

'I had a lunch party today; the Coles [Mr. and Mrs. G. D. H.] and Graham Shepard. Graham is a very charming, wise, puckered creature. He is getting a little less faunlike; perhaps through hard work. The Coles are amazing and charming enough, but somehow a little dead-endish, in spite or because of their extraordinary mental ubiquity. . . .

'I leave you to make the best you can of digesting that tale.'

22/2/29 'Having spent 3 days trying to convey to each party concerned my conviction that everyone else was eminently reasonable and charming, it would be little wonder if I had some reaction and came in a weakened state to try to persuade you of the same thing. But I am sure enough and doubly sure because not only was everyone wonderfully reasonable at every point but they all even liked each other and came to the most concordant and harmonious conclusions.

'One of Louis's few words on the situation was an expression of gratitude as we left the station yesterday after seeing them off (they stayed two nights in the end) that on the whole the right people seemed to like the right people.

'I can never argue you into liking Louis I suppose. I can only hope that you might like him better now that he has grown up, than in the intermediate stage. But at least please do not prejudge the others because perhaps I have told you only their more trivial and eccentric characteristics.

'The fact that Mariette has been in love before, I should have thought, meant that she should know what she is talking about by now. The fact of n occurrences in the past does not prevent the $n+1$th from being the final one.

'The MacNeices, thank Heavens, had got my letter and calmed down completely (clever John). We met them at the station (we went to the Midland Station where they were not on the Liverpool train, and going to the G.W.R. to see if Elizabeth had come from London, found them coming away from a Birkenhead train) expecting them to look stricken to the ground, but they were almost full of beans, and we got into a taxi talking about the frost (after the Archdeacon had drawn me aside to explain that his letter had been too hasty) and took rooms at Oxenford Hall. They all lunched in my room, where Elizabeth and her husband afterwards appeared, when we all adjourned to Louis's room. After talking aimlessly for a bit, the first one of the few mentions of anything important was made when Louis suggested that he should bring Mariette to see his father and stepmother and his stepmother said it was perhaps a bit unfair when his father did not feel that he could give his consent. However it was so arranged.

'All the time Mrs. MacNeice was magnificent: her usual jocular birdlike self, prancing round the room, shaking her fist at Louis's pictures and covering them up with newspaper. The Archdeacon was thoughtful and silent except for a stupendous wink when Mrs. MacNeice was telling me how my telegram had arrived "vouch for Louis's nationality" instead of "rationality".

'The rest of us then went out, but going back to my room after a bit I found Louis and Mrs. M. there, having left the unfortunate Mariette face to face with the archdeacon. We went back and Mrs. M. took the place of the archd. as examiner. Then Mariette went home and the rest of us (I having been absorbed into the family) took tea at the Shamrock.

'Fortified by this breath of the old country the parents (?) sallied forth to battle. The opponents found themselves in perfect unison, agreeing that it was impertinent of Louis and, with a pleasing formality, that it should be called an understanding and not an engagement.

'We dined at the Oxenford Hall and talked about the food. I had breakfast with them the next day, and then Louis and his stepmother went to town to see the sister's flat. Yesterday we had a farewell lunch in Louis's room and all polished his table with furniture polish bought by Mrs. MacNeice and they went off by the 3.30. A train going out of a station leaves an impressive sensation of space.

'So now we must wait and see.

'Yesterday Ben had a son and Galahad was published.

'I am afraid I have got a lot of enjoyment out of this turmoil. If there is real unhappiness in the situation, I am afraid it is still to come.

'The contents of Galahad are not up to much. Wait till Louis is editor next term.'

4/3/29   'The drums and tramplings of three conquests are gone over us. "After–the shouting and the crying, prison and palace and reverberation–" the world goes steadily on its predestined courses. Voices from Hibernia say they enjoyed their visit to Oxford and the Archdeacon admires Mrs. —'s principles. Es giebts nichts zu sagen.

'Louis has some copies of his poems; to be published on the 18th; very handsome.'

28/4/29   'I have just finished Louis's novel in typescript, but am unable to give any useful criticism of it; trying, as always, to see him through it; except that it seems to demonstrate more of faith than of the morbid despair that his people fear they find in his work. It reproduces for me more vividly than I could have imagined possible the smells and cadences of Marlborough, but that is why I cannot criticize it. He is getting $7\frac{1}{2}$d per copy of his poems which is remarkably good.'

Postscript

It is disappointing not to be able to give more of an account of what we talked about or clear statements of Louis's views on important subjects—Religion, Politics, Sex, Education, Philosophy, Literature . . . I have skirted these topics rather as we skirted them at the time. Why did we skirt them? For a number of reasons, no doubt; partly personal and different for each; partly arising from our common reaction to the public climate. Perhaps too many things had been said with too much confidence. There was a need to start quietly with nearby things, for 'touching the skin of the lizard' as a contemporary writer said of the Sitwells' poetry. We set great store by experience, preferably coloured and palpable, if not tasty.

But experience had to be put into words and we were aware from our own efforts how precarious, provisional and tentative a process this must be; and, *a fortiori*, of how cautiously we were bound to give heed to the reported experiences of others—prophets, poets and purveyors of all kinds. Our polder, like an inverted Isle of Innisfree, was built on mud and wattles; and we trod cautiously, not because we were treading on Yeats's or anyone else's dreams, but because we knew that sensations and emotions as well as dreams and visions were not to be adequately described, though a skilled and honest craftsman could induce something of their labile substance to cling to the interstices of well-woven, pliant words.

Since any attempt at communicating the simplest sensation depended on this precarious wicker-work we were not positivists. 'Putting into words' the sight of water foaming from a weir, say, was just as impossible and absurd and needed something of the same order of grace as the similar process for, say, a vision of eternity. So if anyone wanted to devise a metaphysical framework and extrapolate from it, good luck to him; and better luck to him if he did it with some style and dash, panache and bravura. Wicker-work in foundations might be trodden firm, but might be rotting and no one the wiser; in coracles and fencing it could be overhauled more easily.

Louis in any case has incorporated enough of his views in his own writings. But if short answers are required on his apparent attitudes at this period they might be roughly as follows:

Religion. Questingly agnostic. His mind was of course well furnished with Christian images, concepts and lines of thought. We read with appetite *Varieties of Religious Experience*. Louis found a lot of nourishment in the Christian Fathers ('Soon I shall be producing a magnum opus on the Christian fathers who write a very amusing prose.'–Letter of about April 1932), and later divines ('I am very lazy but full of intentions e.g. to make an exhaustive study of 17th cent. English prose (e.g. Donne, Jeremy Taylor, Sir T. Browne, Milton etc.) and show how its cadences and imagery are a better union with God than any English prose before or since (except possibly Malory, in quite a different way, and of course mine); . . . to write (this I really mean as my next book) a Baedeker's Guide to Purgatory . . .'–Letter of summer 1928. ' . . . and Baedeker I have discovered in moving house and hope to go on with.'–Letter of summer or autumn 1930). I have mentoned his claiming at one moment to seek through alcohol what his father sought through religion; whether he thought he had found it is not clear. He was interested in shamanism; I think before he met Professor Dodds, the champion of shamanist influence on the Greeks. He sent me a card postmarked 23 December 1929, a reproduction of a Persian miniature with the title 'Alexander arrives at the temple of an idol in India', with the following verse:

> *With His face trodden down by the dons, dears,*
> *And His properties riddled with pens*
> *Let us sit down and butter our scones, dears,*
> *For the bottom is out of His ens;*
> *They have hauled down the fleet of His flags, dears,*
> *Which were safe while they stayed unfurled,*
> *Yet I hold Him tho' nothing but rags, dears,*
> *The best little x x x in the world.*

Politics. I have said how apolitical we were, perhaps wantonly so. Louis has recorded that we laughed over my copy of *The Mind and Face of Bolshevism* as we had laughed before over Kipling. I am not sure that I was greatly inclined to laugh at either, though sometimes amazed. Yeats is said to have regarded Louis as the most anti-left or unleft of that generation of poets; but at Oxford he was probably unanything. After leaving, I sent him a letter I thought he might like to publish in *Sir Galahad*. It was a rather frivolous anti-rearmament letter – a sort of period equivalent of a C.N.D. protest – aroused by antics of the Navy League who had sent a propaganda team to Oxford. The letter made Louis very angry – not, I imagined at the time, so much because it was anti-big-navy but because the topic was not one to be mentioned in nice society.

Sex. As far as I was concerned this only appeared in the most general way, in amorous poetry and occasional references by Louis to 'that not impossible She'. In his last term at school he cultivated a romantic attachment to a younger boy, which got as far as discussing with him his prospects on the rugger field. This – judging from a similar effort of my own – was a rather wilful proceeding designed not so much to be in a fashion as to achieve some of the enthusiasm and orientation which those in this fashion appeared to enjoy. I expect that his conversation with Graham ('Graham, you old capripede') had an earthier tinge; I have an impression that those two and perhaps Anthony had started at school in a small way a light-hearted cult of Pan, or Priapus perhaps – there was a reference to a 'fane' built in the woods, but I was not allowed to know more. Apart from such levities I doubt if Louis saw his future in any shape but faithful monogamy.

Education. I don't remember discussing 'the system'. We made what we could of it and grumbled at our pastors and masters. ('Half these dons are only stamp-lickers anyhow. If I am a don I shall launch all my letters into the void unstamped and God will have to pay the other end.' – Letter of autumn 1929?)

Philosophy. I am surprised at the space given in his autobiography to his philosophical thinking at Oxford. Much of it must have happened in the year after I left. I remember his reading with some interest Lange's *History of Materialism* and Vaihinger's *Philosophy of As If*, neither of which excited me much. We were on the other hand both exhilarated by T. E. Hulme's *Speculations*. But Louis's usual attitude was one of considerable impatience with this realm of grey abstraction. ('Lots of lovely particulars; I suggest keeping generalisations out of it. Leave that to the Chorus (see the Greek tragedians passim).' – Letter of 1930. 'Philosophy should be kept strictly on the mantelpiece. In my epic the young man is done in through having philosophy in his blood. Mixed up with ballet dancing.'–Letter of 1932?)

Literature. Enough said. ('Sorry for the delay but life's too short for tattle. That is if one "writes" at the same time. Always remember to keep clear of "writers". Apart from the inkpot everything is fine.'–Letter of 1930.)

Practical Psychology. Louis 'had a way with him'; but our means of assessing people were sparse: 'nice', 'nasty', 'intelligent', 'stupid', we said and sometimes added 'very', 'rather' or 'fairly' to these epithets. (A few years ago I took John Betjeman on a rapid tour of Istanbul. His only comments on the buildings were 'Gosh how lovely' or 'Gosh how awful'. Perhaps there is no more to be said.)

INDEX